CISTERCIAN FATHERS SERIES: NUMBER THIRTY-EIGHT

BALDWIN OF FORD

SPIRITUAL TRACTATES

CISTERCIAN FATHERS SERIES: NUMBER THIRTY-EIGHT

BALDWIN OF FORD

SPIRITUAL TRACTATES

VOLUME ONE

*Translated and annotated
with an introduction by*
DAVID N. BELL

Cistercian Publications, Inc.
KALAMAZOO, MICHIGAN
1986

© Copyright, Cistercian Publications, Inc. 1986

Baldwin of Ford, monk of Ford Abbey 1169 / 70 – 1175, abbot of Ford, 1175–1180, bishop of Worcester, 1180–84, archbishop of Canterbury 1184–1190.

This translation is based on the Latin text contained in Robert Thomas (ed.), *Baudouin de Ford, Traites; Pain de Cîteaux* 35–40 (Chimay, Belgium 1973–75), and compared with the text contained in J.-P. Migne, *Patrologiae cursus completus: series latina*, 204.

Library of Congress Cataloguing-in-Publication Data

Baldwin, Archbishop of Canterbury, ca. 1120–1190.
    Baldwin of Ford, spiritual tractates.

    (Cistercian Fathers series; no. 38, 41)
    "This translation is based on the Latin text contained in Robert Thomas (ed.), Baudouin de Ford, Traités; Pain de cîteaux 35–40 (Chimay, Belgium) 1973–75"—T.p. verso.
    Bibliography: p. 37
    Includes indexes.
    1. Catholic Church—Sermons.   2. Sermons, Latin.
I. Bell, David N., 1943–   .   II. Baldwin, Archbishop of Canterbury, ca. 1120–1190.   Traités.   III. Title.
IV. Series.
BX1756.B334B35   1986   252'.02   85–22363

ISBN 0-87907-438-8

TO
MAURICE MULLETT

Of right and wrong he taught
Truths as refin'd as ever Athens heard;
And (strange to tell!) he practis'd what he preach'd.

John Armstrong,
The Art of Preserving Health

TABLE OF CONTENTS

INTRODUCTION

BALDWIN OF EXETER, Baldwin of Ford, Baldwin of Worcester, and Baldwin of Canterbury: the distinguished ecclesiastical career of this complicated cleric reflects the different worlds in which, with varying degrees of success and acclamation, he lived and moved and had his being. He was a teacher, canonist, monk, abbot, papal legate, bishop, archbishop, and a candidate for the College of Cardinals. He was deeply learned, unquestionably ascetic, godly and gullible, and, according to Gerald of Wales, a better monk than abbot, a better abbot than bishop, a better bishop than archbishop.[1] His considerable writings as abbot of Ford reveal a man with a thorough, accurate, and perspicacious grasp of the nature and purpose of the spiritual life; his unfortunate activities as primate of England show us a bishop whose judgement neither of situations nor of persons could safely be trusted. All human beings are by nature complex, but Baldwin, perhaps, was more complex than most.

We know little of his early years. Gervase of Canterbury tells us that he was born at Exeter of humble stock,[2] but this comment on his parents' station may well reflect less the truth than the attitude of the Canterbury monks who (as we shall see) had good reason to dislike Baldwin and may well have calumniated him. As Christopher Holdsworth has pointed out, there is clear evidence from another source that Baldwin's mother could read Latin—a rare phenomenon among women of the time—and if this were so, it would indicate an aristocratic and educated background for Baldwin rather than a lowly one.[3]

Gervase, however, goes on to say that Baldwin was learned in both sacred and secular subjects,[4] and it is probable that his studies were begun, if not completed, at the cathedral school of Exeter. If, as seems eminently likely, the learned and influential Robert Pullen taught theology there before moving to Oxford in 1133, it is possible that Baldwin studied under him.[5] It is also possible, but by no means certain, that in the course of time he himself rose to become master of the school.[6] He did not, however, stay in England, for a letter of John of Salisbury reveals that Baldwin was in Italy in 1150 when he was presented to Pope Eugenius III at Ferentino.[7] The most likely reason for his being in Italy was to pursue his legal studies at one or other of the Italian universities, and it is possible (though this is pure speculation) that he studied at Bologna in the 1140's under the future Alexander III. The latter, as we shall see, knew him well, had a high opinion of his legal expertise, and in later years often appointed him papal judge-delegate. Already by 1150 he was known for his learning, for he was appointed as tutor to Gratian, a nephew of Innocent II. How long this relationship continued and how long Baldwin stayed in Europe we do not know, but he was certainly back at Exeter by 1159/60, for he is included in a list of clerks to the bishop of Exeter, Robert Warelwast, who died in 1160[8]. Robert's successor, Bartholomew, a friend of Baldwin and an eminent canonist in his own right, was also sufficiently impressed with him to appoint him archdeacon of Totnes shortly after his consecration in 1161[9].

Now the next year, 1162, was a year of great importance in the ecclesiastical history of England, for of far greater significance than Baldwin's elevation to the archdeaconry of Totnes was Thomas Becket's elevation to the archbishopric of Canterbury; and over the next eight years the great conflict of king and archbishop was gradually to embroil the whole of Europe and lead the archbishop to a martyr's death on the stones of Canterbury Cathedral. Baldwin's sympathies were unquestionably with Becket,[10] and there can surely be no doubt that the virulence of the controversy played a significant part in his decision to resign from his position of archdeacon and enter the monastic life in 1169 or 1170.[11] Baldwin's austere and ascetic tendencies (which were, in any case, not altogether suited to archidiaconal office) led him to choose the cistercian abbey of Ford, a daughter-house of Waverley, the first cistercian abbey to be established in England. In

1136, an abbot and twelve monks had moved from Waverley to Brightley in Devon, where they founded a house on land given to them by Richard fitzBaldwin de Brionis. This site, however, proved unsuitable, and the monks had left and were on their way back to Waverley when they met Richard's sister and heiress, Adelicia, who offered them the site at Ford. This they accepted, and the abbey at Ford (then in an enclave of Devon, but now included in the boundaries of Dorset) was founded in 1141, some thirty years before Baldwin arrived there.[12]

It was during his decade in the abbey that Baldwin produced nearly all of his extant spiritual writing: all but three of the *Tractates* translated in these present volumes, the lengthy *De sacramento altaris*,[13] the *De commendatione fidei*,[14] and the two sermons (*De sancta cruce* and *De obedienta*) which are being prepared for publication by Br. Bernard-J. Samain of the Abbaye d'Orval, and which we shall discuss in more detail a little later.[15] These works reveal a man thoroughly and happily at home in cistercian spirituality, an acute theologian well aware of contemporary currents and events, and one of the last true representatives of the rich patristic–monastic tradition which was so soon to give way to the often arid scholasticism of the thirteenth century. By 1175 Baldwin had risen to become abbot of Ford (his claustral prior, we might note, was John, whose important sermons on the Song of Songs have already been translated in this present series[16]), and three years later we find one of the cardinals of Alexander III recommending him for the red hat, and informing the pope that his learning, integrity, and religion were known throughout the whole cistercian order.[17] It seems, in fact, that Baldwin's relationship with the papacy for the entire period from 1170 to the early 1180s was fairly close. Apart from his abbatial duties and his spiritual writing, he was much involved with the development of decretal legislation in England and, as Charles Duggan has pointed out, of the four figures who played a major role in this matter (Baldwin, his friend and colleague Bartholomew of Exeter, Roger of Worcester, and Richard of Canterbury) Baldwin's was "the clearest and most decisive personality".[18] As we mentioned a little earlier, he was often commissioned as papal judge-delegate by Alexander, and both as abbot of Ford and bishop of Worcester (the see to which he was appointed in 1180) he was deeply concerned with the definition and codification of papal jurisdictional authority in England.[19]

His four years as bishop of Worcester were not especially eventful. He seems to have gone about his pastoral duties with care and diligence, and the only occurrence of any note which comes from these years is the dramatic story of how he saved one Gilbert of Plumpton from the gallows. This Gilbert, it seems, was unjustly accused of rape and condemned to be hanged, and despite the opposition of a large crowd, he had been taken to the gallows and actually hoisted aloft before the bishop of Worcester appeared on the scene. His Lordship, threatening the executioners with excommunication, demanded that they cease their business, both because it was a Sunday and because it was the feast of St Mary Magdalen. Accordingly, the rope was loosened and the knight lowered to the ground. His enemies could well wait until the next day and re-hang him on Monday. Overnight, however, the king intervened. He was aware of the injustice of the proceedings and therefore commanded that Gilbert should remain alive, but imprisoned, until he should decide what was to be done with him. And although his imprisonment was fairly lengthy (it lasted until the king's death some five years later), it was to Bishop Baldwin that Gilbert owed his salvation.[20] These remarkable events occurred towards the end of Baldwin's sojourn in Worcester, and they bring to end the happier part of his life, for in 1184 he was consecrated archbishop of Canterbury, and the story of his remaining years is, on the whole, gloomy and depressing.

'What can I say of Baldwin?', asks Gervase of Canterbury. 'My intention and my promise was to say favourable things about kings and archbishops, and to tell my readers in some way of the good things done in the church of Canterbury. But when I look at what Baldwin did, I am forced against my will to speak not of the good, but of the many evils'.[21] Herbert of Bosham, too, saw Baldwin's archiepiscopate in a dismal light,[22] and Gerald of Wales accuses him of being too lax, too lenient, and too easily led. Admittedly, Gerald says it more delicately than that, but that is what he means.[23]

His election to the primacy was itself contested. The monks of Christ Church, a disputatious body who had long claimed the sole right to elect the primate, objected to Baldwin as they always objected to the bishops' choice, and put forward three candidates of their own: Odo, the abbot of Battle, an able, charming, and saintly man; Peter de Leia, the Cluniac bishop of St David's; and Theobald, abbot of Cluny. The king was forced to intervene, and with some difficulty persuaded the contumacious monks to accept the bishop of Worcester. Baldwin himself had said that he would accept the primacy only if the prior and the monks agreed,[24] and after the compromise had been effected, he accordingly took office and expressed his hope, his first and highest desire, that he and the monks would be 'one in the Lord'.[25] His hope was not to be fulfilled. Indeed, it is doubtful if ever it could have been. Baldwin was a Cistercian and a canonist: learned, ascetic, and cosmopolitan. Christ Church was a powerful, luxurious, and jealous community, intent on preserving its own privileges, its own powers, and its own way of life—a way of life which by this time was monastic in name alone. 'The independence of the convent', says Hunt, 'was grievous to Baldwin as archbishop, and its luxury disgusted him as a Cistercian,[26] and from the very beginning his relationship with the monks was doomed.

Clashes took place almost immediately. Certain offerings and revenues which were traditionally the perquisites of the monastery were seized by Baldwin, and the monks were deprived of the control of certain properties.[27] But these problems were as nothing compared to the furor that erupted as a result of the archbishop's plans to establish at Hackington (about half a mile from Canterbury) a collegiate church for secular priests, complete with prebendal stalls for the king and all the bishops.[28] The monks of Christ Church were (predictably) horrified. Apart from the fact that the college was to be endowed partly from Christ Church property, they saw in it a direct threat to their own prestige, and the beginning of a gradual take-over by which they would be deprived of their right to elect the primate. In this, we might add, they were probably correct, for the bishops, as also the king, had long been dissatisfied with the prevailing practice, and there is no doubt that they would have relished a reduction in the electoral powers of the Christ Church convent. Be that as it may, the monks resisted the plans of the archbishop and appealed to Rome, and the affair became more and more violent and its ramifications more and more wide-spread. A succession of inconsequential pontiffs – Urban III, Gregory VIII, Clement III – supported the monks, while Henry II supported Baldwin; and at one stage the situation became so bad that for more than eighteen months during 1188 and 1189 the monks were actually imprisoned within the conventual buildings, and for most of this period no liturgy was celebrated in the cathedral. It is not surprising that rumours were spread abroad that the archbishop was either mad or dead.[29]

After Henry's death in 1189, Baldwin attempted to effect a reconciliation, but when he failed to do so, turned instead to threats and violence, and tried to force the convent into submission. As part of his plan he appointed as prior Roger Norreys, an ungodly move which is surely comprehensible only in terms of out-and-out *realpolitik*.[30] Norreys had been treasurer of Christ Church, but there was nothing monastic about either his character or his conduct. He was intelligent, crafty, self-seeking, calculating, and tyrannical, and although we have no knowledge of his appreciation of music, he certainly liked wine and women. He may well have been a splendid raconteur and an entertaining dinner-guest, but he was utterly unsuitable for any ecclesiastical or monastic office. The monks were reduced to desperation, and had no option but to throw themselves on the mercy of the new king, Richard I. The king, after some preliminary negotiations, visited Canterbury in November 1189 and managed to effect a compromise which vindicated Baldwin and which, if not wholly satisfactory to the convent, at least rid them of their two greatest worries: Hackington and Norreys. On the one hand, it was acknowledged that the archbishop had the power to build himself a church wherever he pleased; on the other, the archbishop agreed to demolish the buildings at Hackington and construct his college elsewhere. On the one hand, it was acknowledged that the archbishop had the right to institute his own prior; on the other, the archbishop agreed to relieve Roger Norreys of his office.[31] The monks, as we have said, were far from happy about this final settlement, but had no choice but to accept it. The archbishop, for his part, kept his side of the bargain: he sent Norreys to Evesham, where he continued in his immorality, tyranny, and mismanagement unabated, and announced his intention of transferring his collegiate foundation from Hackington to Lambeth. Little was done in the matter, however, for Baldwin left England on crusade in March of the next year, and died in the Holy Land eight months later.

It seems that the crusade was something fairly close to his heart, for he had taken the cross at Geddington in 1188, and later that year preached the crusade in Wales, a country which he had visited a year earlier as papal legate. In so doing, he killed two birds with one stone, for not only did he attract large numbers of Welshmen to the cross, but as a 'token of investiture' (*investiturae signum*), he combined with his preaching the celebration of mass in all the cathedral churches of Wales.[32] His pilgrimage, in other words, was also a means of asserting his metropolitan authority in Wales and of demonstrating to the Welsh bishops that the see of Canterbury was truly supreme. The fact that certain of the Welsh bishops remained unpersuaded is not part of this story. In the course of this pilgrimage the archbishop also showed that his austerity and asceticism concealed a dry sense of humour, for while he and his party were on their way to Bangor they had occasion to pass through a steep and rocky valley, and by the time they had negotiated it, they were all panting and out of breath. It was at this juncture that the archbishop called for someone to whistle a tune. He himself could do it, he said, but no-one seems to have taken up his challenge. And all this, says Gerald of Wales (who was with him at the time), was 'a pleasantry highly laudable in a person of his approved gravity'.[33]

Shortly after the archbishop's return to England, Henry II died, and Baldwin, as was his duty, presided over the coronation of his successor. It is here that we come across another episode which reveals a different and darker aspect of the archbishop's character: that intolerance, anger, and less than Christian charity which also appears in some of the letters of the Hackington controversy. The coronation of

Richard 1 was a solemn and splendid affair, but only male Christians were permitted to attend. Women and Jews were banned from the proceedings 'because of the magic arts which they are wont to practise at royal coronations'.[34] Despite this ban, on the day of the coronation, a Jewish deputation bearing rich gifts presented itself at Westminster Hall, and a few of the Jews, most unwisely, slipped inside to see what was going on. They were immediately and violently driven out, and the event precipitated a riot. Several Jews were beaten and some were killed, and one, Benedict of York, escaped with his life only by being baptised in the nearby church of the Innocents by William, a priest who happened to come from his own city. The next day Benedict was ordered to appear before the king, and there renounced his recent baptism by identifying himself to the monarch not as William (the name with which he had been baptised) but as Benedict of York, "one of your Jews". The king then turned to Baldwin and asked him what should be done with the man, and Baldwin, 'less prudently than was fitting, and in a spirit of anger', said: 'If he will not be God's man, let him be the devil's!' His advice was followed, and Benedict remained a Jew, and died at Northampton shortly afterwards. Even then his troubles were not over, for the Jews refused him burial because he was a Christian and the Christians refused him burial because he was a Jew, and I have no idea what became of his body. Roger of Hoveden admits freely that Baldwin was wrong in this. He says that Baldwin should have answered: 'We demand a christian trial for him, since he became a Christian and now contradicts it', but as we have seen, this is not what the archbishop said, and there can be no doubt that this regrettable episode casts a further shadow upon Baldwin's reputation.[35]

After the coronation of Richard, Baldwin had little more than a year to live. In November 1189 the Hackington affair was resolved, and in December of that year Richard left for the crusade. In March 1190 Baldwin, together with Hubert Walter, bishop of Salisbury, 'who were the only English bishops to fulfil their vows, followed the king to Sicily, and arrived before him in the land of Judah'.[36] Baldwin's role in the crusade was an active one, both ecclesiastically and militarily:

on the one hand he deputised for the Patriarch, Heraclius, who was ill, and on the other he provided a company of two hundred knights (*milites*) and three hundred followers (*satellites*) to fight under the banner of St Thomas of Canterbury. He himself was one of those in charge of the christian camp, and it was he who blessed the army and gave it absolution as it set forth to fight the infidel.[37] By this time, however, he was an old man, and the conditions and climate of Palestine were less than kind to old men. The unchristian conduct of the crusading army further afflicted him, and having contracted a fever, he died during the siege of Acre on the 19th or 20th November, 1190.[38] This is how a contemporary chronicler describes the events:

> When the archbishop of Canterbury saw what he had earlier heard—that the army was wholly dissolute, and given to drinking, whoring, and gambling—his spirit, which was unable to endure such excesses, was afflicted with a weariness for life. And because a disease which is general is difficult to cure, on a day when the worst reports of this sort were coming more frequently to his ears, and knowing that though man has the care of things, God is over all, he sighed and burst out in these words: 'Lord God, now there is need to reprove and correct with holy grace, that if it please your mercy, I should be taken away from the turmoil of this present life; I have tarried long enough in this army!' It was as if the Lord had heard him, for not fifteen days had passed since these words than he began to feel somewhat cold and stiff, and giving way to a burning fever, he happily fell asleep in the Lord a few days later.[39]

The archbishop was buried where he died, and his will, leaving all his wealth for the relief of the Holy Land, was executed by his friend and fellow-bishop, Hubert of Salisbury.[40] His vestments—a tunicle, dalmatic, and chasuble, all rich with gold, and two mantles—were left at Canterbury.[41] News of his death reached England the following March (Gervase does not tell us of the glee with which this must have been greeted by the Christ Church convent), and in 1193 Baldwin's executor and co-crusader, Hubert Walter, was elected his successor as the next archbishop of Canterbury.

BALDWIN'S TRACTATES

The Tractates account for just about half of Baldwin's published work, and the process by which they have arrived at their present form is somewhat complicated. There is no doubt that they were originally delivered at various times as sermons, but then, on two separate occasions, they were edited and in some instances amalgamated to form more literary productions. Most of the titles and sub-titles which appear throughout the Tractates would presumably have been added as part of this process. Now John Pits, writing in 1619, lists among the works of Baldwin a volume of thirty-three sermons but makes no mention of the Tractates, and Bertrand Tissier repeats this information in his *Bibliotheca Patrum Cisterciensium* published some forty years later.[42] No surviving manuscript, however, contains thirty-three sermons, and we may therefore ask what became of them and what was their relationship to the treatises which are here our concern. There seems little doubt that Pits' original manuscript has vanished, but in 1911–12, P. Guébin presented a persuasive case that part of it—perhaps two-thirds or even three-quarters—is to be found copied in a manuscript of the late twelfth or early thirteenth century which may originally have come from Bec and which is now in the collection of the Bibliothèque Nationale.[43] We may refer to this as Manuscript A, and a casual glance at its contents reveals immediately that the 'sermons' are in fact the 'tractates', even though they are not referred to as such and even though they appear in a quite different order from that in which they occur in this present translation.

What authority, then, do we have for this present arrangement? The answer is to be found in a second manuscript—Manuscript B—which originally formed part of the excellent library at Clairvaux and is now to be found at Troyes.[44] Manuscript B, I suspect, is a little later in date than Manuscript A, and it differs from the latter both in its content and in its arrangement. As far as content is concerned, it contains both more and less than Manuscript A. Two sermons which appear in the latter—an exegesis of 1 Samuel 15: 22, 'Obedience is better than sacrifices' (*De obedientia*), and an encomium on the Holy Cross (*De sancta cruce*)[45]—are not to be found in Manuscript B; but four sermons which do appear in B (Tractates IX/IV, X/II, XIII, and XIV) are absent from A. On the other hand, it seems likely that Manuscript A was never completed, and if Guébin was correct, it might well have gone on to include not only these sermons, but also certain others which are now irretrievably lost. The arrangement of the Tractates in Manuscript B is also quite different and reveals much more substantial editing than appears in Manuscript A. A certain amount of adjustment had already been made in the latter. Tractate XV, for example, almost certainly originated as a series of three separate sermons, each of about the same length, but in both Manuscripts A and B it is presented as one single treatise.[46] Yet although Manuscript A is at least one stage removed from the original sermons, Manuscript B is still further distant and represents the second major stage in editing. In Manuscript A, Tractates I/I, I/II, IX/I, IX/II, IX/III, and X/I still appear as separate sermons, whereas in Manuscript B they have been amalgamated to form Tractates I, IX, and X. Furthermore, we have already mentioned that two treatises included in Manuscript A make no appearance at all in Manuscript B, and of those which do appear only in the latter, I strongly suspect that two (IX/IV and X/II), which have either a very abrupt beginning or a very abrupt ending, are far from complete. The reasons for these amalgamations, omissions, and additions are still not wholly clear to me.

Why, then, should we decide to use this second and more severely edited manuscript as the basis for our translation? The answer is simple: it was this manuscript which was used by Tissier for his edition of the Tractates published in the *Bibliotheca Patrum Cisterciensium*, and it was this edition, in turn, which was reproduced in 1855 in the Migne Patrology. Like much in Migne, therefore, it is this arrangement of the Tractates which has become standard. Moreover, it was this same manuscript which was used by Fr Robert Thomas as the basis for his edition of the Latin text of the Tractates[47] — an edition, which while not strictly critical, is nevertheless much more accurate than that of the redoubtable Migne — and it was from this edition of Fr Thomas that the English version of the Tractates here presented was translated. We must also remember that Manuscript B is a good and accurate manuscript, and that the major differences between itself and Manuscript A relate not to the text, but to the arrangement of the materials therein contained.

In conclusion, therefore, what we have here are not Baldwin's sermons as they were originally delivered, but an incomplete thirteenth-century edited version of these sermons. How incomplete is difficult to say, but if we include the two sermons / tractates which appear only in Manuscript A, and treat Tractates i, ix, and x as eight separate treatises, we arrive at a total of twenty-three sermons. If we prefer to think of Tractate xv as comprising not one but three sermons, then the total comes to twenty-five. In other words, out of the volume of thirty-three sermons reported by Pits, it is quite possible that up to ten have been lost, and there seems now little chance of recovering them. They may very well still be extant — the number of anonymous twelfth-century sermons still in manuscript is legion — but the question of identification is entirely another matter.

The great majority of the treatises — all but three, in fact (Tractates i, ii, and xii) — clearly derive from a monastic milieu. The other three date from Baldwin's later years as either bishop of Worcester or archbishop of Canterbury (I think probably the latter). Taken together they cover a very wide range of subjects and represent our main source for the elucidation of Baldwin's spiritual teaching. We find discussions of the meaning and symbolism of the eucharist, the purpose and importance of the incarnation, the nature of the Trinity, the place of Mary and her role in the process of redemption, the relationship of church and state, the responsibilities of the priestly life and ecclesiastical office, the nature of the soul and the process of its reformation, faith and reason, doubt and certainty, sin and contrition, abstinence and renunciation, humility and discipline, asceticism and mortification, the meaning of martyrdom, concupiscence and its control, the nature of true poverty, the theology of community and the common life, the idea and ideal of the monastic profession, and, of course, a great deal of material on those matters which lie at the very heart of the Cistercian way: charity and obedience, and the love of God and our neighbour. But throughout all this material, the author, as John Morson has pointed out, 'is constantly preoccupied with the stages towards union with God, from a rudimentary self-knowledge to that wisdom or charity which is a forerunner of the face-to-face vision'.[48] Baldwin, in other words, was truly a *spirituel* and did have a spiritual teaching—a teaching which was grounded in the ideas and ideals of Cîteaux, but which nevertheless bore the characteristic marks of his own ascetic and austere temperament.[49] The pivotal points of his thought are no different from those of the other great Cistercians; indeed, no different from those of twelfth-century monasticism as a whole. We have retained God's image, our potential for deification, but have lost his likeness; sin and self-will separate us from God. How, then, shall we restore this likeness and actualize our potential? There are two aspects to the answer, one which looks inwards and the other outwards. On the one hand we need the discipline, obedience, abstinence, and renunciation by which self-will and self-love are controlled, and on the other we need the love of God and of our neighbour. The two aspects are not, of course, separate: we cannot truly love God and yet reject his will; and his will, enshrined in his commandments, leaves us in no doubt as to what we should do.

> The charity of God and obedience are bound each to each with an unbreakable bond and in no way separated from each other. The Lord shows us that there cannot be charity without obedience when he says: 'If anyone loves me, he will keep my word' (Jn 14: 23): that is to say, he will observe my commandments, and in observing them, he will obey me. And he also shows us that there cannot be obedience without charity when he says: 'Whoever does not love me does not keep my words' (Jn 14: 24). If, then,

he who loves obeys, and he who does not love does not obey, it follows that just as there cannot be charity without obedience, neither can there be obedience without charity.[50]

Everything, therefore, centres on the love of God: to love God is to love your neighbour; to love God is to deny yourself; to love God is to keep his commandments; to love God is to imitate Christ; to love God is to die; and to die is to gain eternal life. The *via monastica* is neither more nor less than the *imitatio Christi*. This is Baldwin's teaching, just as it was the teaching of Bernard, Aelred, William of St Thierry, or any other of the cistercian writers; yet the fact that these abbots were one and all representatives of a great tradition did not prevent them from adding to this tradition their own elaborations and enrichments. William of St Thierry, for instance, offers us an awe-inspiring trinitarian mysticism, and Aelred of Rievaulx presents us with a vitally important theology of friendship. And Baldwin, whilst not the equal of these great figures, is no simple retailer of second-hand cistercian spirituality. In his fifteenth Tractate, for example, we find a theological analysis of the origins and nature of the common life which, as I have attempted to demonstrate elsewhere, presents us with a real and positive contribution to our understanding of this important subject,[51] and although his third Tractate is so deeply and so obviously indebted to Bernard, what he says he says in his own way and with his own emphases. His thought and his writings inevitably reflect his temperament, and it is for this reason that I have referred elsewhere to his spirituality as an ascetic spirituality.[52] This is not to deny the central importance of charity—for Baldwin, as we have seen, asceticism is a necessary concomitant of charity—but simply to indicate that when two different artists paint the same subject, their paintings will not be identical. We do not find in Baldwin the warm humanity of an Aelred of Rievaulx or the startling charisma of a Bernard. Why should we? Baldwin is Baldwin, and unlike some of the other abbots of his order, his life and personality may be difficult to understand, but they are far from shadowy. Together with his many faults he is very much his own man, and those who wish to know him and his teaching better will find in the Tractates a rich and profitable store of information. We may see in them a little library of medieval monastic thought, and they well repay intelligent browsing.

BALDWIN'S SOURCES

No-one ever denied that Baldwin was learned. He was well and widely read, and as I have indicated elsewhere, thoroughly abreast of the theological developments and controversies of his times.[53] His learning, however, was that of a canonist, not that of a speculative theologian. Law and precedents were of first importance to him, and he had no time for the rational investigation of areas into which reason had no business to go. 'We ought not to enquire into what God has not wished to reveal',[54] he says, and what God has wished to reveal is to be found in the Scripture and in the writings of the 'orthodox Fathers'.[55] His faith is 'founded unshakeably on the words of God himself',[56] and if faith and reason conflict (as they often do), then the latter must give way to the former. 'The eye of human reason is often offended by the pious devotion of faith, but when it offends, it is cast out. It is better for you to enter life having one eye of sound faith, than to be cast into hell-fire with two eyes, one of faith and one of human reason'.[57] Faith is rooted in divine authority, and its beginning and its foundation is Truth itself.[58] For Baldwin, the defences of the faith reduce to the authority of Holy Scripture,[59] and the purpose of reason is two-fold: to make a rational decision between good and evil, and to understand as clearly as possible the meaning and significance of what God has revealed.[60] The Scriptures are central to his thought, his faith, and his style. His fundamental attitude, Leclercq has said, is a profound respect for the sacred text, and nothing alien should be mingled with it. He uses Scripture to interpret Scripture, and he sees the writings of the Fathers only as commentaries on this divine revelation.[61]

Baldwin's knowledge of the Bible, like that of most of his contemporaries, was encyclopedic. There are very few books which are not quoted at least once in his writing, though as we might expect, some appear much more frequently than others. In the Tractates, the *De sacramento altaris*, and the *De commendatione fidei*, there are more than three thousand direct quotations from Scripture, and a huge multitude of echoes, allusions, and reminiscences. The only biblical books from which I have been unable to find a quotation are Ruth, 1 Chronicles, 1 Esdras, Judith, Obadiah, Nahum, Haggai, Philemon, 2 and 3 John, and Jude, and it will not have escaped the reader that most of these books are notable for their brevity. Nor could I guarantee that some echo of their text is not to be found hidden away in Baldwin's work. As I mentioned, however, some parts of Scripture are cited much more frequently than others, and this is particularly true of the Psalms. They comprise more than fifty percent of the total number of Old Testament quotations and more than a quarter of the whole, and there is no doubt that these high proportions are a simple reflection of the place they occupied in the liturgy. They were engrained in the thought and speech of any monk or priest of Baldwin's day, and with a little manipulation could be used to illustrate virtually anything. And if we include with Psalms the four Gospels, we find that we have accounted for more than half the total number of biblical quotations in all Baldwin's spiritual writings.

In many cases, these quotations are not in accordance with the Vulgate text. Out of eighty-three direct quotations in Tractate IV, for example, one-third have been in some way amended, and these emendations, together with the many which appear elsewhere, may be classified into four main groups: (1) those in which there are minor additions (such as *enim* in [3] below) or omissions (such as in Hosea 2:19, *Et sponsabo te in justitia*, which omits *mihi* after *te*[62]); (2) those in which we find inversion or transposition of words or phrases (e.g. Song of Songs 1: 3, *Trahe me post te: in odorem unguentorum tuorum curremus*, for *Trahe me, post te curremus in odorem unguentorum tuorum*[63]); (3) those in which we have a conflation of two or more verses (e.g. *In custodiendis illis retributio multa. Justitiae enim Domini rectae, laetificantes corda*, which is a conflation of verses 12 and 9 of Psalm 18 [19] together with an additional *enim*[64]); and (4) those in which words have been changed. This last group may be further divided into two: (4.a) minor changes, such as *enim* for *autem, sive . . . sive* for *et . . . et*, a singular instead of a plural, or a different tense; and (4.b) major changes, in which the version given is completely different from that of the Vulgate. Two examples will suffice: in the Vulgate, Isaiah 66: 10 reads *Laetamini cum Jerusalem, et exsultate in ea, omnes qui diligitis eam*, but in Tractate IV, Baldwin renders this as *Laetare, Jerusalem, et diem factum agite omnes, qui diligitis eam.*[65] Again, the Vulgate version of Isaiah 7:9 reads *Si non credideritis, non permanebitis*, but in Tractate VI (and elsewhere), Baldwin gives this as *Nisi credideritis, non intelligetis.*[66]

What are the reasons for these changes, major and minor? Most of the minor variants can be explained simply by lapses of memory or a trifling adjustment so as to fit the context better, but the major variations are more interesting, and there are two main explanations which account for them. The first is that the passage concerned may have been drawn from the liturgy rather than directly from the bible, for there are a considerable number of cases in which the scriptural text as it appears in the liturgy represents a different tradition from that which appears in the Vulgate. The reasons for this are not our concern here, but the variant form of Isaiah 66: 10 quoted above is to be accounted for in this way. The second explanation is that the variant text represents not the Vulgate, but the Old Latin, and since we may rest assured that Baldwin did not have access to Old Latin manuscripts, the sources for these variants are undoubtedly the Church Fathers. This in itself is useful, for if we can trace the probable source from which the Old Latin version is taken, it gives us a profitable glimpse into our author's patristic authorities. The reading of Isaiah 7: 9 which we cited above is just such an Old Latin variant, and Baldwin may well have found it in Augustine's *De Trinitate* (see Tr. VI–4). Other possible sources for such Old Latin variants are Jerome (especially Jerome!), Ambrose, Gregory the Great, and even the *Rule of St Benedict* (see Trs. I–12, II–18, VI–4, VI–18, VI–42, VIII–5, VIII–9, IX/II–4, and IX/III–9).

It is not often that Baldwin names his patristic authorities. In the whole of the Tractates, for example, only Augustine is mentioned, and he only three times (see Trs. I–34, IV–29, and VII–9). But in his other works we find him referring by name to Ambrose, Gregory the Great, Hilary, Jerome, Origen, and pseudo-Dionysius, as well as the bishop of Hippo.[67] None of these names comes to us as any great surprise, save perhaps that of pseudo-Dionysius. Baldwin's quotation, 'The being of all is the Divinity which is beyond being',[68] appears to derive from John Scot Eriugena's translation of the *Celestial Hierarchy*[69], and we know that at least three works of pseudo-Dionysius — the *Celestial Hierarchy*, the *Ecclesiastical Hierarchy*, and the *Mystical Theology* — were all to be found in the library at Ford.[70] It is typical of Baldwin's approach, however, that his explanation of this phrase and the context in which it appears are alike augustinian, and there is no trace in Baldwin of that fascination with dionysian thought which we find in the work of his fellow Cistercians, Isaac of Stella or Garnier of Rochefort.

Augustine, without question, was Baldwin's master. Apart from naming him more often than any other writer, Baldwin penned a multitude of passages which either are founded on Augustine's thought, or in which we hear an echo of his teaching.[71] It is true that his approach to Augustine was not uncritical,[72] but there is no doubt that he held him in the highest veneration, and the fact that his name appears only three times in the Tractates is no reflection of his overwhelming importance. In any case, as we stated above, Baldwin rarely names his sources, and the determination of those he does not name is not always easy. The main reason for this is that Baldwin was not a plagiarist. He read the "orthodox Fathers", pondered and meditated upon them, and gradually assimilated them into his own thought and his own theology, but when he wrote, he wrote as Baldwin of Ford, and not as Augustine or Jerome. Sometimes we catch a glimpse of one or other of the Fathers — Benedict, for example (see Trs. vi–42, vi–43, xii–10, xv–25, xvi–15), or a couple of quotations from Gregory the Great (see Trs. x/1–16 and xv–28), or an echo of Hilary (see Tr. x/1–3), or the influence of Leo the Great (see Tr. xiii–2), or a snatch of Maximus of Turin or Venantius Fortunatus[73] — but more often we find ourselves in a spiritual and theological atmosphere which certainly has its roots in the patristic tradition, but in which individual voices can only rarely be distinguished.

Of his contemporaries, Baldwin names none at all, neither in the Tractates nor elsewhere, and it is difficult to get a clear picture of the extent to which he was acquainted with their works. Some of them certainly influenced him. Bernard, for instance, clearly had a profound effect on his conception of charity, and there is no difficulty in seeing his impact on the archbishop's third Tractate.[74] Similarly, I do not think there is any doubt that in his teaching on the common life and the nature of community, he was indebted to Aelred of Rievaulx, and I have attempted to demonstrate this indebtedness elsewhere.[75] His Mariology seems to echo Anselm of Canterbury, for I strongly suspect that the curious terms used in the seventh Tractate to describe the Mother of God — *superspeciosa, supergratiosa, supergloriosa* — derive from one of the *Orationes* of Baldwin's archiepiscopal predecessor (see Tr. vii–16). John of Fécamp may also have influenced him, for J. C. Didier has drawn our attention to a number of expressions which certainly seem inspired by passages in John's work.[76]

The influence of the Victorines is more difficult to determine. They were certainly represented in the library at Ford,[77] but I cannot recall any direct and incontrovertible evidence for Victorine influence. There is an expression in Tractate viii which could possibly have come from Richard of St Victor (see Tr. viii–15), but since it was a well-known saying at the time and could have come from any number of other places, it can hardly be considered as any real proof. It is true that I suspect that in one or two passages we may see the shadow of Hugh of St Victor, but the similarities are too general to permit any categorical statement. The situation with regard to the Cistercian William of St Thierry is in some ways similar. In a number of places, Robert Thomas has directed our attention to passages in William's work which seem to parallel Baldwin's ideas (see Trs. iii–4, ix/1–9, ix/1–23, ix/2–11, and xiii–10), and it would be both interesting and important if we could demonstrate that William was indeed one of his sources. His *De contemplando Deo* and *De natura et dignitate amoris* were both available at Ford,[78] but the parallels adduced by Fr Thomas are too general and too indefinite to warrant any definite conclusion.

Among the pagan writers, we find in the Tractates quotations from Cicero, Ovid, Virgil, and Lucan, though none of them is cited by

name.[79] Nor should we be surprised to find them, for the embellish-
ing of one's works with classical quotations was a standard practice of
the period. In its dispute with Baldwin, for example, the convent of
Christ Church quoted Ovid, Lucan, Juvenal, and Horace in its letters
of appeal and declarations of woe.[80] No attention was paid to the
context from which the quotation was drawn (many, in any case,
would have been taken from *florilegia*), and no difficulty was experienced in adorning writing which might be very spiritual (such as
Baldwin's sixteenth Tractate) with Ovidian passages taken from a
very secular work. What is notable—or perhaps what is typical—of
Baldwin is not that he should quote these pagan poets, but that he
should quote them so infrequently. He makes no public display of his
undoubted learning, and has no interest in impressing his readers
with his comprehensive knowledge of the classics. For Baldwin, it is
the faith, rooted in the bed-rock of God's revelation, which is important, and there is no doubt that he would have agreed wholly with
Tertullian that Athens and Jerusalem have very little in common:

> What has Athens to do with Jerusalem? What has the
> Academy to do with the Church? What have heretics to
> do with Christians? Our instruction is from the Porch of
> Solomon, and it was he himself who taught that the Lord
> should be sought in simplicity of heart (Ws 1:1). Away
> with those who would produce a Stoic and Platonic and
> dialectic Christianity! We have no need for curiosity after
> Christ Jesus, nor for investigations after the Gospel. We
> believe; and we want nothing beyond what we believe![81]

It is this spirit which is reincarnated in the teaching of the abbot
of Ford.

Such, then, are some of Baldwin's sources, but what of Baldwin
himself as a source? To what extent were his own spiritual writings
used and read by his contemporaries? Copies of his works seem to
have been fairly widely distributed—there were manuscripts at
Alcobaça, Bec, Byland, Canterbury, Clairvaux, Durham (though this
is not certain), Fountains Abbey, Glastonbury, Gloucester, Holme

St Benets, Jervaulx, La Trappe, Longpont, Louvain, Margam, Oxford (Balliol College and Lincoln College), Ramsey, Reading, Revesby, Rievaulx, Saint-Sépulcre at Cambrai, Saint-Victor of Paris, Waltham, and possibly Windsor[82] — but how much these manuscripts were actually utilised is a different matter. Peter of Blois was certainly acquainted with Baldwin's treatise on the common life (Tractate xv),[83] and in the thirteenth and fourteenth centuries, substantial extracts from the archbishop's works were included in lengthy *catenae biblicae* which formed part of the library at Clairvaux.[84] Extensive extracts are also included in an early thirteenth-century *catena* of twelfth-century writers which enjoyed considerable popularity and which was printed a number of times in the sixteenth century.[85] Apart from these, however, I know of no other cases which demonstrate unequivocally the influence of our author. The appearance of certain passages from the very end of the *De sacramento altaris* in two commentaries on St Paul discovered by Arthur Landgraf in 1928 and 1935 are no evidence of this influence.[86] As Landgraf himself suggested, they come from an appendix to the *De sacramento altaris* which was not from Baldwin's pen, but which was subjoined to his treatise at a later date by a later editor. Although it appears as part of the work in Tissier and the Migne Patrology, it is rightly omitted in the text edited by John Morson and published in 1963.[87]

On the other hand, there is some evidence that interest in Baldwin's work survived at least into the 1500's. Two manuscripts were copied in the fifteenth century,[88] and in 1521, one of the first books ever printed at Cambridge contained the first two Tractates, that on the eucharist and that on the corrupt way of life of the clergy and people.[89] After this, however, the archbishop sinks into oblivion, and appears only twice in the course of the next three and a half centuries: once in the pages of Tissier's *Bibliotheca Patrum Cisterciensium* published in 1622, and once when this edition was reprinted in the Migne Patrology of 1855. But the times change and we change with them, and as is clear from such series as this present one, there has recently been a notable revival of interest in the spiritual writings of the twelfth century. New editions and new translations of Baldwin have appeared,[90] and he is only one among many obscure men who, in recent years, have been raised from their tombs in the later volumes of the Migne Patrology to a new and better life. The place which Baldwin should occupy in this goodly fellowship remains to be seen, but it is the hope of the translator that this English version of his Tractates will make the writings of this complex man a little more accessible, and assist those more qualified or more christian than I to make an accurate assessment of his worth.

NOTES

Abbreviations

B. of F./B. de F. Baldwin of Ford / Baudouin de Ford.
CF Cistercian Fathers Series, published by CP.
CP Cistercian Publications, Kalamazoo, Michigan.
CS Cistercian Studies Series, published by CP.
PC *Pain de Cîteaux*, now published by La Documentation Cistercienne, Rochefort.
PL *Patrologiae Cursus Completus, Series Latina*, ed. J. P. Migne, Paris.
RS Rolls Series, published by H.M.S.O., London.
SCh *Sources chrétiennes*, published by Les Éditions du Cerf, Paris.
Tr. Tractate.

1. See Giraldus Cambrensis, *Itinerarium Kambriae* II, XIV (ed. J. Dimock; RS 21/6 [1868] 149) and *Vita Sancti Remigii* XXIX (Ed. J. Dimock; RS 21/7 [1877] 71).

2. See Gervase of Canterbury, *Historical Works* (ed. W. Stubbs; RS 73 [1879–80]) 2: 400: 'In Exonia ex infimo genere natus, litteris saecularibus et sacris eruditus est, et in omni honestate conversatus est'.

3. See C. J. Holdsworth, *Another Stage . . . A Different World: Ideas and People Around Exeter in the Twelfth-Century* (Exeter, 1979) 12.

4. See n. 2 above.

5. See R. L. Poole, 'The Early Lives of Robert Pullen and Nicholas Breakspear', in A. G. Little and F. M. Powicke, edd., *Essays in Medieval History Presented to T. F. Tout* (1925; rpt. New York, 1967) 62–63; K. Edwards, *The English Secular Cathedrals in the Middle Ages* (Manchester, 1967²) 186–187.

6. Gerald of Wales calls him *scholarum magister egregius* (*Speculum Ecclesiae* II, XXV, ed. J. S. Brewer; RS 21/4 [1873] 81), but we cannot always believe Gerald. In R. Hakluyt's *The Principal Navigations, Voiages and Discoveries of the English Nation* (London, 1589) 1: 14, we are also told that Baldwin *scholarum rector primum erat*, but Hakluyt's source is probably Gerald.

7. See Poole, 69 citing John of Salisbury, *Letter* 292.

8. See Poole, 63.

9. For Bartholomew and his relationship with Baldwin, see A. Morey, *Bartholomew of Exeter: Bishop and Canonist* (Cambridge, 1937), especially 105–109. The precise date of Baldwin's appointment is uncertain: Morey suggests 1161 (see Morey, 105), but it may have been early in 1162.

10. See B. Smalley, *The Becket Conflict and the Schools: A Study of Intellectuals in Politics* (Totowa, N.J., 1973) 217–220. Smalley cites certain letters of John of Salisbury which make it clear that the latter regarded Baldwin as a strong supporter of Becket (see 217 n. 5).

11. The date has been established by Morey, 121.

12. For a brief account of the history of the abbey and a comprehensive bibliography, see M. A. Dimier's article 'Ford ou Forde' in the *Dictionnaire d'histoire et de géographie ecclésiastiques* (Paris, 1971) 17: 1020–1022.

13. PL 204: 641–774 reproduces the edition of Bertrand Tissier published in 1662 in the fifth volume of his *Bibliotheca Patrum Cisterciensium*. A critical edition of the text by John Morson was published in 1963: *Baudouin de Ford, Le sacrement de l'autel*, ed. J. Morson/tr. E. de Solms (SCh 93–94; Paris, 1963). In the dedicatory letter, Baldwin refers to himself as *frater B., Fordensis monasterii servus* (PL 204: 641A; SCh 93: 70), so the work was produced sometime between 1170 and 1180. Leclercq's dating—between 1161 and 1180—is incorrect (see his introduction to Morson's critical edition, SCh 93: 9–10).

14. PL 204: 571–640 again reproduces Tissier's edition, but the present writer has a critical edition in preparation. The work was written probably between 1171 and 1178 (the arguments are presented in D. N. Bell, 'The Preface to the *De Commendatione Fidei* of Baldwin of Ford', forthcoming in *Cîteaux*.

15. These sermons were the subject of P. Guébin's brief but important article, 'Deux sermons inédits de Baldwin, archevêque de Canterbury 1184–1190', in *Journal of Theological Studies* O.S. 13 (1911–12) 571–574. Guébin provides summaries of the sermons, but no editions of the text.

16. See John of Ford, tr. W. M. Becket, *Sermons on the Final Verses of the Song of Songs* (CF 29, 39, 43–47; [1977–1984]). Seven volumes. For John's appointment as prior, see Hilary Costello's introduction to volume 1 of the translation (CF 29), 4.

17. See Morey, 106, n. 4 for the Latin text of the letter. See also P. Glorieux, 'Candidats pour la pourpre en 1178' in *Mélanges de science religieuse* 11 (1954) 17–19.

18. C. Duggan, *Twelfth-Century Decretal Collections and Their Importance in English History* (London, 1963) 119.

19. See generally *ibid.* 110–115, 149–151. For an excellent discussion of what a papal judge-delegate was and the sort of things he had to do, see Morey, chapter IV.

20. This is the story as recounted in the *Chronica* of Roger of Hoveden (see *Chronica Magistri Rogeri de Hovedene*, ed. W. Stubbs; RS 51/2 [1869] 286). There is an English translation in *The Annals of Roger de Hoveden*, tr. H. T. Riley (London, 1853) 2: 32–33.

21. Gervase, 2: 400.

22. See Smalley, 216, who cites as evidence Herbert's *Liber Melorum* III (PL 190: 1403A–1404A) and the dedicatory letter of his *Vita Sancti Thomae* (PL 190: 1073A–1074A).

23. See his comments in his *Itinerarium Kambriae* II, XIV (RS 21/6: 149) and *Vita Sancti Remigii* XXIX (RS 21/7: 71). For other assessments of Baldwin's character, see my 'The Ascetic Spirituality of B. of F.' in *Cîteaux* 31 (1980) 227–228.

24. See Gervase 1: 324: 'As you know', said Baldwin, 'my brothers the bishops of England elected me against my will; but I say now what I said then: that I will not and I ought not undertake the government of the church of Canterbury, except through the prior and the convent'.

25. See *ibid.* 2: 401: 'Hoc est primum, fratres, et summum in desideriis meis, ut unum simus in Domino . . . .'.

26. See W. Hunt's article 'Baldwin' in the *Dictionary of National Biography* 1: 952. Gerald of Wales bears eloquent witness to the luxury, laxity, and gluttony of Christ Church, and even if his account is somewhat exaggerated, it is clear that the Canterbury monks were guilty of very serious lapses from the monastic ideal (see Giraldus, *De Rebus a se Gestis* II, v [ed. J. S. Brewer; RS 21/1 (1861) 51–52] and *Speculum Ecclesiae* II, iii–vi [RS 21/4: 38–46]. There are plenty of similar accounts in the contemporary literature).

27. See D. Knowles, *The Monastic Order in England* (Cambridge, 1950) 318–319, who cites the relevant authorities.

28. For a detailed history of the Hackington controversy, see W. Stubbs' introduction to his edition of *Chronicles and Memorials of the Reign of Richard I: II, Epistolae Cantuarienses* (RS 38/2 [1865]). A day by day calendar of the events will be found therein, cxxi–clxvii. For a briefer account and a consideration of the motives of the various parties, see Knowles, 317–322.

29. See Gervase, 1: 423. The date is April 1188.

30. Cf. Stubbs, *Epistolae Cantuarienses* lxxv: 'It is hardly conceivable that Baldwin ever intended to maintain Roger Norreys in the position of prior. . . . The archbishop probably thought that such an appointment would compel the monks to submit, and that done, the obnoxious prior might be provided for elsewhere'. Further on the career and character of Roger Norreys, see Knowles, 331–343.

31. For a description of these dramatic events, which took place in the gloom and fog of a late November afternoon, see Gervase, 1: 475–481.

32. See Giraldus, *Itinerarium Kambriae* ii, 1 (RS 21/6: 104–105).

33. See *ibid.* ii, vi (RS 21/6: 124–125), quoted in the translation of Sir Richard Colt Hoare (see T. Wright (ed.), *The Historical Works of Giraldus Cambrensis* [London, 1894/442).

34. Roger of Wendover, *Flores Historiarum* (ed. H. G. Hewlett; RS 84/1 [1886]) 166. See C. Roth, *A History of the Jews in England* (Oxford, 1964³) 19, n. 1.

35. My account of the incident follows Roger of Hoveden, 3: 12–13 (see Riley's English translation, 2: 119–120). For other accounts in contemporary sources, see Roth, 20, n. 1. Roth also provides a more detailed description of this unfortunate episode.

36. Richard of Devizes, ed. J. T. Appleby, *The Chronicle of Richard of Devizes of the Time of King Richard the First* (London, 1963) 15.

37. See the *Itinerarium Regis Ricardi* lxi (ed. W. Stubbs; RS 38/1 [1864] 115–116).

38. For a brief discussion of the date of Baldwin's death, see my 'B. of F. and Twelfth-Century Theology' in E. R. Elder, ed., *Noble Piety and Reformed Monasticism: Studies in Medieval Cistercian History VII* (CS 65 [1981]) 144 n. 13.

39. *Itinerarium Regis Ricardi* lxv (RS 38/1: 123–124).

40. See Roger of Wendover, 1: 189.

41. See Gervase, 2: 406.

42. See J. Pits, *Relationum Historicarum de Rebus Anglicis* (Paris, 1619) 259–260, and B. Tissier, *Bibliotheca Patrum Cisterciensium* (Bonnefontaine, 1662) 5: 1 (Tissier's list is reproduced in PL 204: 401–404). The same list also appears in C. de Visch, *Bibliotheca Scriptorum Sacri Ordinis Cisterciensis* (Douai, 1649) 27–28.

43. For Guébin's article, see n. 15 above. The manuscript in question is Bibl. Nat. lat. 2601. My discussion of these manuscripts, their dates, and their relationships has

been deliberately simplified in this introduction, and for a more detailed account the reader must be referred to my 'The *Corpus* of the Works of B. of F.' in *Cîteaux* 35 (1984) 221.

44. This is Troyes 876. There are other manuscripts which also arrange the Tractates in this order, but for details the reader must once again be referred to my 'The *Corpus* of the Works of B. of F.'.

45. See n. 15 above.

46. See Tr. xv–1. Cf. also Beryl Smalley's views on the structure of the second Tractate (see Tr. 11–12).

47. R. Thomas (ed. / tr.), *B. de F., Traités*, PC 35–40 (Chimay, 1973–75), six volumes. This supercedes the Tissier / Migne text in PL 204: 403–572, but since the latter version is probably more readily accessible, I have indicated *in loc.* all the major areas in which revision or correction of the Migne text is necessary.

48. J. Morson, 'B. of F.: A Contemplative', in *Coll. O. C. R.* 27 (1965) 160.

49. For a more complete account of Baldwin's spirituality and of its relationship to that of his contemporaries, see my "Ascetic Spirituality of B. of F." *passim.*

50. See Tr. III PL 204: 426A–B (PC 35: 152; CF 29:92).

51. See my "Heaven on Earth: Celestial and Cenobitic Unity in the Thought of B. of F." in E. R. Elder, ed., *Heaven on Earth. Studies in Medieval Cistercian History IX* CS 68 (1983) 1–21.

52. See my article cited in n. 23 above.

53. See my 'B. of F. and Twelfth-Century Theology', *passim.*

54. *De commendatione fidei* PL 204: 607A.

55. See Baldwin's unequivocal statement in *De sacramento altaris* PL 204: 653B–C (SCh 93: 116) translated in Tr. VI–5 below. For his use of the term 'orthodox Fathers', see my 'B. of F. and Twelfth-Century Theology', 147, n. 67.

56. See *De sacramento altaris* PL 204: 679B (SCh 93: 208) and elsewhere.

57. Tr. I PL 204: 407D (PC 35: 46; CF 38:50).

58. See *ibid.* 408A–B (PC 35: 48; CF 38:51).

59. See *De commendatione fidei* PL 204: 621A translated in my 'B. of F. and Twelfth-Century Theology' 140 n. 60.

60. See generally *ibid.* 139–141, especially 140 n. 56.

61. See Leclercq's introduction to Morson's edition of the *De sacramento altaris*, Sch 93: 25–26.

62. Tr. IV PL 204: 439B (PC 36: 68; CF 38:121).

63. *Ibid.* 439C (PC 36: 70; CF 38:122).

64. *Ibid.* 435A (PC 36: 46; CF 38:113).

65. *Ibid.* 432D (PC 36: 34; CF 38:108).

66. Tr. VI PL 204: 452C (PC 37: 26; CF 38:154). These variants are not always to be found in the Migne Patrology; in some cases (in many cases in the *De sacramento altaris*), Baldwin's version has been tacitly corrected to conform to the *textus receptus.*

67. For a list of all these citations, see my 'B. of F. and Twelfth-Century Theology', 147–148 nn. 69–75. According to Gervase of Canterbury, 1: 476, the archbishop also appealed specifically to the *Rule of St Benedict* in his dispute with the monks of Christ Church. It would have been odd had he not done so.

68. See *De sacramento altaris*; PL 204:720B; SCh 94:374: 'Esse omnium est super esse divinitas'.

69. See PL 122:1046C.

70. Our evidence for this comes from the *Registrum Librorum Anglie*, 'a location list of selected books available in the cathedrals and monasteries of England and southern Scotland, compiled by Franciscans probably at Oxford in the second half of the 13th century' (R. H. and M. A. Rouse, 'The *Registrum Anglie*: the Franciscan 'union catalogue' of British libraries', in A. C. de la Mare and B. C. Barker-Benfield, *Manuscripts at Oxford: An Exhibition in Memory of R. W. Hunt* [Oxford 1980] 55). Professor Rouse is at present engaged in preparing an edition of the *Registrum*, and I am most grateful to him for his kindness in providing me with a list of the books from Ford.

71. See M. Pellegrino, 'Reminiscenze bibliche, liturgiche e agostiniane nel *De sacramento altaris* di Baldovino di Ford', in *Revenue des études augustiniennes* 10 (1964) 39–44, and the indexes of names both in Morson's edition of the *De sacramento altaris* and in this present translation, s.v. Augustin / Augustine.

72. Cf. *De sacramento altaris* PL 204: 732C–D; SCh 94: 424–426, in which Baldwin disagrees with Augustine on the matter of the exegesis of Ex 12: 5.

73. For the identification of Maximus, we are indebted to Henri de Lubac (see his *Exégèse médiévale, les quatre sens de l'Écriture* [Paris, 1959–64] 1: 343); for Venantius Fortunatus, see *De sacramento altaris* 671C (SCh 93: 180) where we find the phrase *hoc opus nostrae salutis* from the hymn *Pange, lingua, gloriosi proelium certaminis*. Baldwin would have been familiar with this hymn through the Easter liturgy. In my earlier note on Baldwin's sources (see my 'B. of F. and Twelfth-Century Theology' 141) I also suggested that we might see traces of the influence of Cassiodorus (see SCh 93: 130, n. 3), Isidore of Seville (see Tr. 11–3), and Bede in Baldwin's writings. On further reading and reflection, I think that the evidence is too weak to permit the certain identification of these writers. The *Registrum* records their works at Ford and Baldwin would surely have known them, but I have not yet proved it to my own satisfaction.

74. See Tr. 111–6, 15, 16. See further the index of names in this present translation, s.v. Bernard of Clairvaux, and in Morson's edition of the *De sacramento altaris*, s.v. Bernard, Saint. The *Registrum* (MS Oxford, Bodleian Library, Tanner 165, ff. 115–116) records eleven works at Ford by or attributed to Bernard. Of these, eight are genuine and three pseudonymous.

75. See my 'Heaven on Earth' *passim*. I suggested there that the most important direct sources for Baldwin's theology of the *vita communis* were Augustine, Aelred, Bernard, and Benedict.

76. See J. C. Didier, 'Le *De sacramento altaris* de B. de F.', in *Cahiers de civilisation médiévale* 8 (1965) 59–60 n. 4. The passages cited by Didier are to be found in John's prayer *Summe sacerdos*, and any priest who celebrated Mass would have been familiar with it. It is still to be found in the Missal, though attributed there to Ambrose of Milan. On the other hand, the works of John of Fécamp were very widely read, and it is quite possible that Baldwin knew more of his writing than just this single prayer.

77. The *Registrum* (ff. 119ᵛ–120ᵛ) records eight works at Ford by or attributed to Hugh of St Victor (five of these are genuinely his), and eleven works by Richard of St Victor, all of which appear to be genuine.

78. See the *Registrum*, f. 115ᵛ, where we find, attributed to Bernard of Clairvaux, a *De amore Dei*. This is a standard designation in medieval catalogues (and also in many manuscripts) for the *De contemplando Deo* and *De natura et dignitate amoris* of William of St Thierry.

79. For Cicero, see Tr. VI–7; for Ovid, Virgil, and Lucan, see Trs. VIII–10, IX/II–30, 32, XIV–2, XV–42, XVI–8, and my 'B. of F. and Twelfth-Century Theology' 148, nn. 82–84.

80. See Stubbs, *Epistolae Cantuarienses* 60, 69, 96, 151, 193 (Ovid); 32 (Lucan); 68 (Juvenal); 116, 157, 309 (Horace).

81. Tertullian, *De Praescriptione Haereticorum* VII PL 2: 20B–21A. We may compare Baldwin, *De Commendatione Fidei* PL 204: 591A, in which our author makes it clear that he has no time for Plato and worldly wisdom ('B. of F. and Twelfth-Century Theology' 142).

82. See my 'The *Corpus* of the Works of B. of F.' for the identification and locations of these manuscripts. I will not be in the least surprised if this list needs to be extended as a result of further researches.

83. See A. Landgraf, 'The Commentary on St Paul of the Codex Paris Arsenal, lat. 534 and Baldwin of Canterbury', in *Catholic Biblical Quarterly* 10 (1948) 61–62. In my earlier study ('B. of F. and Twelfth-Century Theology' 141), for reasons which now escape me, I suggested that Peter was one of Baldwin's sources rather than *vice-versa*. That suggestion was incorrect.

84. See Leclercq's introduction to Morson's edition of the *De sacramento altaris*, SCh 93: 46 n. 1, referring to Leclercq's 'Les écrits de Geoffroy d'Auxerre' in *Revue Bénédictine* 62 (1952) 289 (= J. Leclercq, *Recueil d'études sur saint Bernard et ses écrits* [Rome, 1962] 1: 42–43). The manuscripts in question are Troyes 1423 and 1696.

85. See T. M. Käppeli, "Eine aus frühscholastischen Werken exzerpierte Bibelkatene", in *Divus Thomas* Ser. 3 Vol. 9 (1931) 309–319.

86. For the commentary discovered in 1928, see A. Landgraf, 'Familienbildung bei Paulinenkommentaren des 12. Jahrhunderts' in *Biblica* 13 (1932) 169–193, and the same author's 'Untersuchungen zu den Paulinenkommentaren des 12. Jahrhunderts', in RTAM 8 (1936) 254; for the commentary discovered in 1935, see his article cited in n. 83 above, 55–62. Leclercq incorrectly accepts these passages as evidence of Baldwin's influence (see SCh 93: 46 n. 1).

87. See the discussion in SCh 93: 23 n. 1 (Leclercq) and 59–60 (Morson). Landgraf's doubts are expressed in his 'The Commentary on St Paul . . .' 59.

88. Cambridge, *Corpus Christi* 331 and the fine manuscript in Brussels, Bibl. Royale 5277, dated 1453. Both contain the *De sacramento altaris*. Further discussion of these manuscripts will be found in my 'The *Corpus* of the Works of B. of F.'.

89. *Reverendissimi in Christo patris, ac domini, dñi Balduini, Cantuariensis archiepiscopi, de venerabili, ac divinissimo altaris sacramento, sermo devotissimus, sacraeque scripturae floribus undiquaque respersus* (Cambridge, 1521). The volume was printed by John Siberch.

90. For the Tractates, see n. 47 above; for the *De sacramento altaris*, see n. 13 above, and B. of F., *Sacramento del Altar*, ed. Monasterio Ntra. Sra. de los Angeles (Azul, Argentina, 1978).

BIBLIOGRAPHY

A. *Editions and Translations of Baldwin's Works*

1. Collected Works (*Tractatus Diversi, De Commendatione Fidei, De Sacramento Altaris*)

   B. Tissier, *Bibliotheca Patrum Cisterciensium* (Bonnefontaine, 1662), volume 5.

   J. P. Migne (ed.), *Patrologiae Cursus Completus, Series Latina* (Paris, 1855), volume 204.

2. *Tractatus Diversi*

   Reverendissimi in Christo patris, ac domini, dñi Balduini, Cantuariensis archiepiscopi, de venerabili, ac divinissimo altaris sacramento, sermo devotissimus, sacraeque scripturae floribus undiquaque respersus (Cambridge, 1521). Latin text of Trs. I and II.

   Baudouin de Ford, Traités, ed. / tr. R. Thomas (PC 35–40; Chimay, 1973–1975), six volumes. Latin text and French translation of Trs. I to XVI.

   C. Waddell, 'The Treatise *On the Common Life* by Baldwin, Archbishop of Canterbury and Quondam Abbot of Ford', in *Liturgy O.C.S.O.* II (1977) 19–65. English translation (together with a useful introduction) of Tr. XV.

3. *De sacramento altaris*

   Baudouin de Ford, Le sacrement de l'autel, ed. J. Morson / tr. E. de Solms, introduction by J. Leclercq (SCh 93–94; Paris, 1963), two volumes with continuous pagination. Latin text and French translation.

   Baldwin of Ford, Sacramento del Altar, ed. Monasterio Ntra. Sra. de los Angeles (Padres Cistercienses; Azul, Argentina, 1978). Spanish translation. There is a review-article of this work by R. Summers in *Cistercian Studies* 15 (1980) 295–300.

4. *Letters*

   W. Stubbs (ed.), *Chronicles and Memorials of the Reign of Richard I. Volume II: Epistolae Cantuarienses–The Letters of the Prior and Convent of Christ Church, Canterbury from A.D. 1187 to A.D. 1199.* (RS 38/2; London, 1865). Latin text of nine letters (Nos. 8, 22, 32, 84, 111, 140, 191, 338, 345).

   PL 202: 1533. Latin text of one letter.

B. *Dictionary Articles*

   By J. M. Canivez, in *Dictionnaire d'histoire et de géographie ecclésiastiques* 6: 1415–1416.

   By J. M. Canivez, in *Dictionnaire de spiritualité* 1: 1285–1286.

   By C. Duggan, in *New Catholic Encyclopedia* 2: 28.

   By W. Hunt, in *Dictionary of National Biography* 1: 952–954.

   By J. Morson, in *Dictionnaire des auteurs cisterciens* 90–91.

C. *Early Works to 1900*

For references to the works of Cave, Ceillier, de Visch, Fabricius, Henriques, Manrique, and Oudin, see the article by Canivez in the *Dictionnaire d'histoire et de géographie ecclésiastiques* cited in Section B above.

D. *Works Devoted Entirely to Baldwin*

Bell, D. N. 'The Ascetic Spirituality of Baldwin of Ford', in *Cîteaux* 31 (1980) 227–250

———. 'Baldwin of Ford and Twelfth-Century Theology', in E. R. Elder, ed., *Noble Piety and Reformed Monasticism*. Studies in Medieval Cistercian History VII, CS 65 (Kalamazoo, 1981) 136–148.

———. 'Heaven on Earth: Celestial and Cenobitic Unity in the Thought of Baldwin of Ford', in E. R. Elder, ed., *Heaven on Earth*. Studies in Medieval Cistercian History IX, CS 68 (Kalamazoo, 1983) 1–21.

———. 'The *Corpus* of the Works of Baldwin of Ford', in *Cîteaux* 35 (1984) 215–234.

———. 'Baldwin of Ford and the Sacrament of the Altar', forthcoming in Studies in Medieval Cistercian History XI.

———. 'The Preface to the *De Commendatione Fidei* of Baldwin of Ford', forthcoming in *Cîteaux*.

J. C. Didier, 'Le *De Sacramento Altaris* de Baudouin de Ford', in *Cahiers de civilisation médiévale* 8 (1965) 59–66.

———. 'Baudouin de Ford et la dévotion au Sacré Coeur de Jésus', in *Cîteaux* 26 (1975) 222–225.

P. Guébin, 'Deux sermons inédits de Baldwin, archevêque de Canterbury 1184–1190', in *Journal of Theological Studies* O.S. 13 (1911–12) 571–574.

C. Hallet, 'La communion des personnes d'après une oeuvre de Baudouin de Ford', in *Revue d'ascétique et de mystique* 42 (1966) 405–422.

———. 'Notes sur le vocabulaire du *De Vita Coenobitica* de Baudouin de Ford', in *Analecta Cisterciensia* 22 (1966) 272–278.

A. Landgraf, 'The Commentary on St Paul of the Codex Paris Arsenal, lat. 534 and Baldwin of Canterbury', in *Catholic Biblical Quarterly* 10 (1948) 55–62.

J. Morson, 'Baldwin of Ford: A Contemplative', in *Collectanea O.C.R.* 27 (1965) 160–164.

M. Pellegrino, 'Reminiscenze bibliche, liturgiche e agostiniane nel *De Sacramento Altaris* di Baldovino di Ford', in *Revue des études augustiniennes* 10 (1964) 39–44.

E. *Works With Important Sections Devoted to Baldwin*

Extremely valuable material may be found in the following two doctoral dissertations, neither of which has been published:

C. J. Holdsworth, *Learning and Literature of English Cistercians 1167–1214, with Special Reference to John of Ford* (Cambridge University, typescript, 1960).

B. E. A. Jones, *The Acta of Archbishops Richard and Baldwin: 1174–1190* (London University, typescript, 1964).

Lesser amounts of material may be found in the following works:

C. Duggan, *Twelfth-Century Decretal Collections and Their Importance in English History* (London, 1963) 110–115.

R. Foreville, *L'Église et la royauté en Angleterre sous Henri II Plantagenet* (Paris, 1943) 533–554.

C. J. Holdsworth, 'John of Ford and English Cistercian Writing, 1167–1214', in *Transactions of the Royal Historical Society*, Series v 11 (1961) 117–136.

D. Knowles, *The Monastic Order in England: A History of Its Development from the Times of St Dunstan to the Fourth Lateran Council, 943–1216* (Cambridge, 1950) 316–322.

A. Morey, *Bartholomew of Exeter: Bishop and Canonist. A Study in the Twelfth Century* (Cambridge, 1937) 105–109, 120–121.

B. Smalley, *The Becket Conflict and the Schools: A Study of Intellectuals in Politics* (Totowa, N.J., 1973) 216–220.

ABBREVIATIONS

B.	Baldwin
CF	De commendatione fidei
DLF	A. Blaise, *Dictionnaire Latin-Français des Auteurs Chrétiens* (Turnhout, 1954).
hom.	homoioteleuton
lit.	literally
M.T.	Massoretic Text
n.	note
O.L.	Old Latin
RB	*Regula S. Benedicti*
RSV	Revised Standard Version
SA	De sacramento altaris
SBO	*Sancti Bernardi Opera*, edd. J. Leclercq—H. M. Rochais—C. H. Talbot (Rome, 1957-)
SC	Sources chrétiennes (Paris: Cerf)
Tr.	Tractate

Psalms have been cited according to Septuagint-Vulgate enumeration; Hebrew enumeration appears in brackets

CITATION OF BALDWIN'S WORKS

Tractates: cited by volume and page number of Fr Robert Thomas's edition of the text: R. Thomas (ed./trans.), *Baudouin de Ford, Traités, Pain de Cîteaux* 35–40 (Chimay, 1973–75).

De sacramento altaris: cited by column number of PL 204 and (in parenthesis) by page number of Fr John Morson's edition of the text: J. Morson (ed.)/E. de Solms (trans.), *Baudouin de Ford, Le sacrement de l'autel*, SCh 93–94 [continuous pagination] (Paris, 1963).

De commendatione fidei: cited by column number of PL 204.

BALDWIN OF FORD
SPIRITUAL TRACTATES

TRACTATE I
ON THE MOST HOLY SACRAMENT
OF THE EUCHARIST[1]

O N ACCOUNT OF ITS WORTH and reverence, the sacrament of the body and blood of the Lord is worthy to be handled worthily by those who are worthy, to be prepared worthily, to be received worthily, and to be distributed worthily. Great and inestimable is the worth of this sacrament, and who is there able [to conceive] it? Its greatness surpasses the limits of our understanding and exceeds the bounds of our capacity. Great indeed is the price of the world,[2] a price without price, a priceless price, which cannot be assessed or appraised. 'Great is the sacrament of godliness, says the Apostle, which was manifested in the flesh, was justified in the spirit, appeared to angels, was preached to the Gentiles, believed in the world and taken up in glory.'*

1 Tm 3:16

This sacrament is the sacrifice of truth. Nothing in it is false, nothing in it is feigned, nothing counterfeit, nothing faked by magical manipulations. There is only true sincerity and sincere truth: truth in that which is evident; truth in that which is hidden. That which is evident is the true and visible form of bread.[3] Before the consecration, we have here the true substance of bread, but in the consecration, it is transubstantiated[4] and changed by virtue of the power of the words into the true flesh of Christ. After the consecration, the whole of Christ,

Ps 17:12[18:11]

Is 45:15

Dt 32:4

Ps 32[33]4

who made darkness his hiding-place,* is hidden under the visible form. To him the prophet said, 'Truly you are the hidden God, the king of Israel, the Saviour.'

Christ was hidden from the beginning in the bosom of the Father; afterwards, he was hidden in the form of a servant which he assumed; and now he is hidden in the sacrament which he instituted. Faith finds him hidden in the bosom of the Father; no less does faith find him hidden in man; and it is faith which finds him hidden in the sacrament. The great power of faith possesses the great grace of intimacy with God. Wherever it finds him, it can approach him, and with a certain familiar and audacious intimacy, it rushes into his sanctuary and his bed-chamber. It gives no thought to being hindered by the guardians of the entrance or the door-keepers or the chamberlains: it enters carefree and unites itself confidently but reverently to the mysteries of God's intentions.

And is it surprising that God entrusts his intentions to the faith of his faithful? Do kings and princes of the people not impart the mystery of their intentions to their faithful [subjects]? God is faithful and without any iniquity,* and his faithful friends, who preserve their faith for him and serve him in faith, are [also] without iniquity. All his works are done in faith,* and without faith it is impossible to please him.[5]

God tests his faithful and his elect so as to find them worthy of him. He tests their faith, and he tests their hope, and he tests their love. But at the moment we are discussing faith, which is tested by God in many ways and is put to the proof most of all in this sacrament.

With an eternal intention, God determined to save the world by the death of his only-begotten Son and to send into the World its Saviour and its salvation; nor [did he intend to send] any other salvation apart from the Saviour himself.

That which he determined he also promised, and he revealed his intention to his faithful. [With this] the faith of the saints rested content; they believed it, and they awaited the fulfilment of his promise. But God delayed his Christ. Why he delayed him is known to him alone and is his secret, but in the meantime he was exercising the faith of the just. To test their faith, God wished to overshadow that which he had promised in a number of ways and to prefigure it with various symbolic objects and sacrifices. All the old rites of legal sacrifice, instituted by the law and approved by the prophets, were done as a reminder of the promise and as a mystical symbol of its future fulfilment. Thus, through the continual round of sacrifices it would be impossible to forget the object of this wonderful promise, whose future [realization] would be yet more wonderful and to which the law and the prophets bear witness.

In these signs of things yet to come, faith was being continually exercised in the service and honor of God, so that the fervor of its devotion would not grow cool from languishing in idleness and the hope of its expectation would not be lost as a result of forgetfulness. And if any of the faithful asked himself what these things meant for him, his reverence and devotion always regarded as certain that which remained hidden in the conviction of faith.

This was the way of things until the shadows withdrew and their place was taken by truth. He who was to come is come; the holy one of Israel is

come! He was made man, was seen upon earth, and
conversed with men.* He made known to the world
the ways of life,* and when he had accomplished
the divine plan⁶ for which he came, he ascended into
heaven where now he is, seated on the right hand of
God. [But] before he ascended into heaven, he com-
forted his disciples and the other faithful who would
follow them that they might not lose hope or despair of his help when his bodily presence had been
taken from their eyes: 'Behold', he said, 'I am with
you, even to the end of the world.'*

Our Jesus, therefore, is with us. Why should I not
call him 'ours' since he was given⁷ to us? 'For unto us
the Son is given.⁸ He who says, 'As for me, I will rejoice in the Lord, and I will exult in God my Jesus,'⁹
claims for himself a certain right to this Jesus. This
Jesus of ours, with whom God has given us all things,*
cannot bear to be absent from us. He loves us so much
that he who is the Wisdom of the Father says, 'My
delight is to be with the sons of men.'* He was with
us in the flesh before he died for us; he was with us
in [his] death, insofar as his bodily presence was not
yet lifted from the earth; [he was with us] after
death, when he appeared to his disciples and gave
them many proofs [of his resurrection];* and he is
with us even now, even to the end of the world,*
until [the day that] we shall be with him, for we
shall be always with the Lord.* See how greatly
Jesus loves us!¹⁰

Neither death nor life can separate him from us in
the charity with which he loves us. For that reason,
neither death nor life should separate us from his
charity.* Whom should we love if not [Jesus]? Or
rather whom should we love in the way that he [is
loved]? For apart from all else, if we are not ungrate-

Bar 3:38
Ps 15[16]:11

Mt 28:20

Rm 8:32

Pr 8:31

Ac 1:3
Mt 28:20

1 Th 4:17

Cf. Rm 8:38–39

ful and mean, it should be enough that he loves us.
To someone who loves is owed above all an exchange of love. He who loves wants to be loved,
and this is indeed right and proper. But if someone
wants to be loved and does not want to love, it
would be very strange if he judged himself and ac-
quitted himself of being unjust. It is a true judgement that he who does not love the one that loves
him is himself unworthy to be loved, and truly, he
who does not love Jesus puts himself in great danger,
worthy of the Apostle's execration and curse: 'If anyone does not love our Lord Jesus Christ, let him be
anathema, Maranatha!'* [But] contrary to this is the   1 Co 16:22
same [Apostle's] prayer: 'Grace be with all them that
love our Lord Jesus Christ in incorruption.'[11]*   Eph 6:24

Jesus loved us first indeed, and lest we not love him,
he is with us even to the end of the world. 'The Lord
of hosts is with us, the God of Jacob, our protector.'*   Ps 45:8[46:7]
From the time that the God of Jacob, the wrestler
who supplanted [his brother], was made our protector and assumed our flesh, the Lord of Hosts is
with us. He himself says of the just, 'I am with him in
tribulation',* and to him the just man says, 'Though   Ps 90[91]:15
I should walk in the midst of the shadow of death, I
will fear no evils, for you are with me'.* Emmanuel is   Ps 22[23]:4
with us against those who oppress us and who rejoice
at the evils which befall us. He is with us in our moment of need, aiding and protecting us, favoring us
with every [possible] help and consolation.

This is also the way it was with the just men of
days gone by, but now, through the mystery of the
Incarnation, [he is] with us by his fellowship in our
common nature. But even this extremity of love,
when he is with us in such a way, is not enough for
Jesus. He clasps us with a tighter embrace and unites

[himself to us] in a wonderful way through the sacrament of communion, so that he might be in us and we in him, as he says, 'Anyone who eats my flesh and drinks my blood remains in me, and I in him'*. But the Christ who remains in us also lives in us, as the Apostle says, 'It is no longer I who live, but Christ who lives in me'.* If Christ lives in us, the Spirit of God also dwells in us,* and according to the same apostle, 'Anyone who does not have the spirit of Christ does not belong to him. But if Christ is in us, the body indeed is dead because of sin, but the spirit is alive because of righteousness. And if the Spirit of him that raised Jesus Christ from the dead dwells in you, he that raised Jesus Christ from the dead will give life to your mortal bodies also through his Spirit dwelling in you.'* And the Lord himself says, 'Anyone who eats my flesh and drinks my blood has eternal life.'*

In this sacrament, therefore, our life is hidden with Christ in God.* Here is hidden eternal life, and that true salvation which was promised to those of old and given to us, [salvation] which will be revealed to us when God comes to be glorified in his saints and to be made wonderful in all who have believed.* The Lord has done great things for us,* for what he promised to those of old he has already in large part shown to us. In this sacrament he has shown us the truth of that intention [he had from] of old, of which the Prophet says: 'Lord, let your intention of old be true'.[12] This is the truth of God's promises, the truth of the signs, the truth of the sacrifices, the truth of the shadows and prefigurements. In short, it is the Truth himself, Christ, who says, 'I am the Truth',* the truth which Pilate failed to recognize when he said, 'What is truth?', and went outside.* Let him remain outside who has gone outside, and

Jn 6:57

Ga 2:20
Rm 8:11

Rm 8:9–11
Jn 6:57

Col 3:3

2 Th 1:10
Ps 125[126]:3

Jn 14:16
Jn 18:38

if he who is faithless departs, let him depart!* But as   1 Co 7:15
for us, lest we remain outside and be counted
among the faithless, let us enter into the sanctuary
of God; let us be led by faith and enter into the
powers of the Lord.* In the faith of this sacrament   Ps 70[71]:16
let us consider the powers of God,[13] for whom
nothing is impossible,* whose word is all-powerful   Lk 1:37
and always true, and who can always do what he
wills when he wills.[14]

As a testimony to this faith, it is enough for us
that Christ, who is the power of God and the
wisdom of God,* said to his disciples, 'Take this,   1 Co 1:24
this is my body'.* If our human wisdom murmurs   Mt 26:26
[against this] in our heart, let the pious devotion[15] of
faith restrain its murmurs. Let us show honor to the
words of God in the humility of faith; let us offer all
[our] reverence to so venerable a sacrament and so
excellent a grace with cleanness of hands* and purity   2K 22:25, Jb 22:30
of life.

When the time came for him to pass from this
world to the Father, Jesus, in his great kindness and
generosity,[16] left us this pledge of his love, and in his
desire to test the faith and charity of his own, he
made this sacrament a sort of arena in which those he
chose to test might be exercised. First and foremost,
it is divine faith and human reason which struggle
together. This they do that one might gouge out the
other's eye, and there is no end to the combat until
one of them is blinded. Human reason has its eye,
and so does faith, but the eye of reason is dim and
often cannot see things which are visible and placed
near to it. The eye of faith, however, is keen and
with it are clearly seen the invisible things of God.*   Rm 1:20

Faced with the power of this sacrament, the mind
is dulled, the eye of reason darkened, and every

sense of the body blunted. Our hands, which are so inquisitive and so diligent in touching things, put forth all their skill, but all they can find are normal characteristics of ordinary bread. When we taste it and examine it carefully with our eyes, its flavor, color, appearance,[17] form, and other qualities [again] suggest to our thoughts that it is bread and not flesh. When our reason is consulted, it replies that these fleshly thoughts have persuaded it and the bodily senses have convinced it. The eye of human reason cannot comprehend the invisible things of God unless it be anointed with the eye-salve of grace and enlightened with the true light, of which it is written, 'The commandment of the Lord is full of light, enlightening the eyes.* If your eye offends you', says the Lord, 'pluck it out and cast it from you',* and it is not inappropriate to regard this as [referring to] the eye of human reason. It is often offended by the pious devotion of faith, but when it offends it is cast out. It is better for you to enter life having one eye of sound faith than to be cast into hell-fire with two eyes—one of faith and the other of human reason.* And whoever is led by human wisdom, accepting only those parts of faith which appear to be in accord with human reasonings, is just like a man with two eyes.

Our faith, however, has a greater testimony than that [which comes] from human reason. It is based on divine authority, which is the supreme reason, incomparably surpassing every human reason. What human reason suggests to the heart should not be more convincing to it than what [is suggested] by the Spirit of God. It is he who suggests all truth and secretly conveys it to us by a hidden inspiration. He uncovers the ear of the heart and speaks in

Ps 18:9[19:8]
Mt 18:9

Cf. Mt 18:9

a gentle whisper of the simplicity of pious devotion
and of the mystery of faith, and his conversation is
with the simple.* 'And he that is of God hears the
words of God.'* It was not flesh and blood, not the
wisdom of the flesh nor the bodily senses[18] that revealed to Peter the mystery of faith, but the heavenly
Father who is in heaven.*

Our faith, then, is based on truth and has its beginning and its foundation[19] in the God of truth
himself, to whom is said, 'The beginning of your
words is truth'.* God does not deceive, for he is
supreme Truth; nor is he deceived, who is supreme
Wisdom; nor is he weakened who is supreme
Power. All that he says or proclaims will be done.
For him, to do something is as easy as saying that it
be so. As he has determined, so shall it be,* and all
his intentions shall stand.* If he has decreed it, who
can deny it? Our faith, therefore, should be based
on certainty: it does not wander about in conjec-
tures, it does not waver as if [dealing] with something doubtful, nor does it hesitate as if [concerned
with] something uncertain. It does not falter, does
not vacillate, does not fluctuate, but stands upon a
steadfast rock, on a foundation which none can
change,[20] [the foundation] which is Christ Jesus.

If faith is the knowledge of salvation, why should
we not believe that it possesses certainty? 'I know', says
Job, 'that my redeemer lives'.* 'I know', says Martha,
'that whatever you will ask of God, God will give it to
you'.* And speaking of her brother, she says, 'I know
that he will rise again in the resurrection on the last
day'.* 'I know', says the apostle, 'whom I have believed, and I am certain'.* And speaking of Abraham,
the same [apostle] says, 'He did not hesitate through
mistrust, but was strengthened in faith, giving glory to

Pr 3:32
Jn 8:47

Mt 16:17

Ps 118[119]:160

Is 14:24
Is 46:10

Jb 19:25

Jn 11:22

Jn 11:24
Rm 4:21–22

God, knowing that whatever God promised he is also able to perform'.*

Rm 4:21–22

Is the conviction of faith therefore without certainty? Only someone who does not believe or whose belief is lukewarm will say this. Faith is based on supreme authority, truth, and certainty, and therefore by authority it excludes anything counterfeit, by truth it excludes error, and by certainty it excludes doubt. But whoever doubts irreverently is close to [being] one of the faithless.[21]

Thus, we see that it was from doubt that the sin of faithlessness and the crime of apostasy took their origin in mankind. When the Tempter approached the woman, he began with a question loaded with doubt: 'Why has God commanded you not to eat', etc.[22]* This question, like the hissing [of a snake], disturbed the woman's soul, and she became proud and puffed up,[23] swollen with the venom of the serpent. So she hesitated, and soon her heart inclined to doubt, and she said, 'Perhaps it was so that we might not die'.* The doubt she conceived in her mind she expressed in a doubtful word, and the word which God spoke she recalled in doubt, and a sort of trial was conducted in the woman's heart. The woman's proud reason sat in the seat of pestilence* as the judge in the tribunal, and the word which God spoke is led into the centre [of the court] as the defendant. The accuser approaches and charges the defendant with being a liar and says: 'You shall never die'.* It is just as if he had said: 'This word, this threat of God which threatens you with death, is false!'

Now the woman was not yet so fully persuaded by doubt as to fall, but she was wavering like a leaning wall and a tottering fence* and still did not

Gn 3:1

Gn 3:3

Ps 1:1

Gn 3:4

Ps 61:4[62:3]

know whether to believe God's threat or the devil's suggestion. Meanwhile she considered the tree in question, and saw that it was good to eat and fair to the eyes and beautiful to behold.* Its alluring appearance made it wholly effective as a witness on behalf of the accuser; no sign of death appeared in it, so she could not deduce from this that what the accuser said was false or what God said was not. Added to this was [the fact] that the woman naturally loved life, which the serpent was promising, and, equally, had no love for death, which God was threatening. And having experienced life but never having experienced death, she preferred to follow that to which love and experience were drawing her. And so, conquered at last, she stretched forth her hand to iniquity.* So she was seduced, first [being brought] to doubt and [then] being led from doubt to unfaithfulness until she believed that what God had proclaimed was false. Beginning with desire and ending with consent, she was so convinced that she presumed [to do] what God had forbidden.24

All the while, proud reason was sitting in the tribunal, and delivered the woman from the fear of death. It did not justify God in his words but by a proud judgement convicted him of being a liar. Thus the woman transferred to the glory of the Tempter that honor of faith which should have been shown to the words of God, believing the former and not believing God. By the side of proud reason sat proud will, which renounced the honor of obedience to God and, through disobedience, subjected itself willingly to the Tempter. In the woman, therefore, reason was corrupted by pride, for she doubted whether God's word could be trusted.25 But it is wicked to doubt the words of God and impious not to accede to his instructions.

Gn 3:6

Ps 54:21[55:20]

Created in the image and likeness of God in the judgement of his reason and the freedom of his will, man should naturally and justly conform to God in these things and be subject to him, so that he might always be willing to submit to him from whom he derived his being. He should so humble his reason before him as to believe all his words and so [humble] his will as to obey all his precepts. It is the pious devotion of faith which humbles reason in man and obedience [which humbles] his will. The pride of human reason which rejects pious devotion and knows not how to humble itself to faith is a culpable blindness of the heart and hateful to God, since it refuses to believe that which is beyond its understanding.

When the Lord gave light to the man born blind, the Pharisees, who did not believe, were made more blind, and their eyes were darkened that they might not see.* The Lord directed his explanation of this new and great miracle against them[26] and said: 'I came into this world for judgement, that those who do not see may see, and those who see may become blind.'* [In other words] that those who do not see because of pride may see by the grace of humility, and those that see through pride may not see by the removal of grace. But after saying this, he adds, 'If you were blind, you would not have sin; but because you say, "We see," your sin remains'.*

Not to see great things in oneself and to be devoutly ignorant of things we are not permitted to know is a good blindness. In [the realm of] heavenly mysteries and divine sacraments, therefore, every impious doubt should be banished far from our heart, and all inquisitive questionings should be restrained, so that faith, which possesses the conviction of truth, should also possess a devout ignorance.

Rm 11:10,
Ps 68[69]:24

Jn 9:39

Jn 9:41

The wisdom of God is incomprehensible and cannot be confined within the narrow limits of human reason.

In this sacrament, therefore, the whole of human reason should be humbled under the pious devotion of faith. Such a thing was right and proper, for the course of our restoration required that the image of God, which had been deformed by the pride of reason, should be reformed through the humility of reason in this sacrament of our redemption. Thus, by humbling the whole of his reason to God, man may believe of this sacrament that which the Lord ordained to be believed, when he said: *This is my body*.* Mt 26:26

Let us believe this firmly, let us believe it without any doubt, let us confess it faithfully. If it appears impossible according to human reason or unbelievable according to human wisdom, let it remain ever true and certain in the conviction of faith because of our reverence for the divine word. Let man have faith in[27] God rather than himself. Let him have faith in God lest God should not have faith in him. Let him trust his spirit to God so that his spirit be faithful to God.* Let him trust his reason to God Cf. Ps 77:8[78:7] and deny himself, and as he hears from God so let him judge, following him who says, 'As I hear, so I judge'.* Jn 5:30

In himself, Christ presented us with a twofold example from which we can profit: in his humility of judgement and his humility of will. Of his humility of judgement it is written, 'As I hear, so I judge',* *Ibid.* and through the Prophet he says, 'His judgement was taken away in humility'.* Of his humility of Is 53:8 in Ac 8:33 will he says, 'I came not to do my own will, but the will of him that sent me'.* Jn 6:38

Neither the being of Christ nor his works derive from himself,[28] but from the Father, as he himself

Jn 5:30

says, 'I cannot of myself do anything'.* As the Son's
being is from the Father, so it is from the Father
that he possesses judgement and the will to work,
although in these things he is the equal of the
Father. Man, therefore, who does not derive his being from himself but who was made by God, should
learn from this to judge nothing from himself, but
from God, to will nothing from himself, and to perform no works from himself, especially with regard
to those works which engender salvation, or in
which he works with God to bring it about.[29]

This sacrifice which we are now discussing is not
only a sacrament which sanctifies us, but it contains
in itself an example which we should imitate. It is a
sacrament through the mystery of faith and an
example of the way we should live. As a sacrament
[it brings about] the humbling of our will, and the
sacrament benefits those who imitate the example.
Those who do not imitate the example, the sacrament does not benefit.

The way we should live, however, is not only set
forth in this sacrifice, but was already pointed out in
an earlier prefigurement of this sacrifice. In the law
of Moses, one is commanded to offer up each year
on the tenth day of the seventh month a victim
whose flesh is burned outside the camp and whose
blood is carried into the sanctuary.* As the Apostle

Lv 23:27, 16:27

says, 'The bodies of those animals whose blood is
brought into the sanctuary are burned outside the

Heb 13:11

camp'.* The day on which the animal in question is
offered up is called the Day of Atonement, and in
referring to this day the Scripture adds, 'Every soul
that does not mortify itself on this day shall perish

Lv 23:29

from among his people'.*[30]

In what way is a day of mortification a day of

atonement? Is it that mortification is atonement? We should ask instead in what way mortification is *not* atonement, if every soul that does not mortify itself on this day shall perish. It is certainly better to mortify oneself on this day than to perish from among [God's] people. 'The bodies of those animals whose blood is brought into the sanctuary are burned outside the camp.'* The souls of those who are not willing to mortify themselves here below with discipline[31] cannot be accepted into heaven, but when a soul is received into heaven, it is then that the blood is brought into the sanctuary. In holy Scripture, the soul is often symbolized by blood, and Scripture itself makes no secret of the reason for this symbolism, saying, 'The soul of all flesh is in the blood'.* Thus, the Lord symbolizes the soul by blood when he says to that watchman of the house of Israel who fails to inform the sinner of his sin, 'I will require his blood from your hand'.*

Heb 13:11

Lv 17:11

Ezk 3:18

No one is exempt from the necessity of christian discipline; no one is excused. No condition, no sex, no age, no rank, no dignity, no power. Every soul that does not mortify itself on that day will perish. This agrees with what is written in the psalm: 'Embrace discipline, lest at any time the Lord be angry, and you perish from the just way'.* Whoever does not embrace discipline will certainly perish. Thus, the Apostle says, 'If you are without discipline, then you are bastards'.* You are not of Christ, but of the devil, who is an adulterer and no [true] husband.

Ps 2:12

Heb 12:8

Through discipline we share the sufferings of Christ, just as through mercy we share those of our neighbour. It is always kind to show that compassion[32] which stems from mercy, though we cannot always bestow it because of our own personal indigence.

Sometimes, therefore, it exists only in our will, but anyone who has not the wherewithal for these works of mercy is excused them. The shared sufferings, the compassion, of discipline, however, should not be measured by mere will but should be borne for Christ in the actual and real experience of mortification by those who profess the name Christian.

Jm 3:2

For since we all offend in many ways,* no one is exempt from sin, and no one, therefore, can be free from punishment. Everyone who stumbles because of sin deserves punishment. But anyone who deserves punishment and does not undergo it is like a man who turns to deceit by reneging a debt. Then, just as in civil judgements, when those expert in law have determined that damages be doubled in cases where debts are reneged, so it is in divine judgements, except that those sentenced by God are not sentenced to twice the amount [of the debt], but to the punishment of eternal death, [hidden] from the

Is 2:10

face of God and the glory of his majesty.* And to disregard penitence is a sort of reneging on the debt of punishment. Because of penitence, God disregards

Ws 11:24

the sins of man,* but man disregards penitence! From this latter sort of disregard is born dissension, and in due course eternal enmity comes into being under the cloak of hidden hatred and continues indefinitely.

We are the debtors of Christ who has taken upon himself all that we owe and has paid [it] for us, as he himself says, 'I paid the debt which I did not con-

Ps 68:5[69:4]

tract'.* But he demands from us the like of that which he paid for us, and who is able to avoid it?[33] A vast amount of suffering was owed to God for the liberation of the human race, and as blessed Augustine says, we ought each of us to contribute to this amount until there are no more contributions to be made and God is paid [in full]; owners of fields or estates normally render to the state or the treasury a certain fixed payment, each according to the amount he possesses; in the same way we should render to a sort of state [treasury] the tax of suffering which we owe, each of us [giving] more or less in accordance with our resources and in conformity with our age, dignity, and rank.[34] What is more just than that man should suffer for Christ when Christ suffered for him? Hence the Apostle says, 'In my flesh I complete what is lacking in the sufferings of Christ.* Therefore we are debtors, but not to the flesh to live according to the flesh. For if you live according to the flesh, you will die'.*

Col 1:24

Rm 8:13

Notice how this sentence of death is aimed at those who live according to the flesh. But it is not yet implemented, since it is still possible to avoid it by penitence and discipline. But when it is implemented, there is no appeal which will be able to hold it back, nor can we evade it or elude it by any artifice[35] or subterfuge.

Because Christ suffered for us, if we live a life of voluptuous luxury and make every provision for the desires of the flesh,* we should then not only be afraid, but ashamed. Is it not shameful, is it not ridiculous, if the Lord—and such a Lord—hangs upon the cross, hangs there for his servant, and the wicked servant, who is the one that deserves to be wounded, carries on in luxury? Is it not infamous, is it not scandalous, if Christ, hanging on the cross, says, 'I thirst',* and our hearts are weighed down each day with intoxication and drunkenness?* As the popular saying goes: In this game, the sides aren't equal! The passion of Christ is certainly not a game, or anything like a game. But we reckon our life to be

Rm 13:14

Jn 19:28
Lk 21:34

like a game, something arrayed and arranged for our amusement.

We still dwell in the world, as on a battlefield where Christ our Lord has been killed. Anyone who leaves this field without a wound or a swelling or a bruise can reckon on no repute. 'By his bruises we are healed.'* The Lord has been killed for us on the field of battle, and if we escape unharmed, our bodies healthy and whole, are we not judged guilty of treason to Christ and guilty of his death? Those who brought about his death were also guilty of his death, and so, too, those who agreed to it, and also their accomplices who crucified him. But in a certain way, anyone who in himself annuls the power of the death of Christ by his wicked life is guilty of his death. For although he does not take away the fact that Christ died, he nevertheless acts in such a way that for him Christ died in vain. For him the death of Christ does not effect salvation, and for such a person, who refuses to carry his own cross and thereby destroys himself, the cross of the Saviour is of no advantage. If the cross of Christ, which we are charged to carry, stands opposed to sensual pleasure, and sensual pleasure [stands opposed] to the cross, how can those who love sensual pleasure avoid being judged as persecutors of the cross? Of these, the Apostle says: 'They are enemies of the cross of Christ. Their end is destruction, their God is their stomach, and they glory in their shame, their minds being set on earthly things.'*

These, as we have said, are guilty of the death of Christ, not as those who actually brought it about, or their supporters or accomplices, but as those who scorn his death, who annul in themselves the sacrament of his dispensation and invalidate the intention

Is 53:5

Ph 3:18–19

of the Most High. They make themselves unworthy
of heavenly blessing and ineffable grace, and carrying on in voluptuous luxury, they jeer at the mystery of the cross. They trample underfoot the Son
of God and say[36] that the blood of the testament,
by which they were sanctified, is unclean, and they
offer insults to the Spirit of Grace.*   Heb 10:29
according to the flesh is an affront to God, a reproach to the cross, and an overwhelming insult to
the whole Trinity. It is an affront to the Father, for
the Son is trampled underfoot; it is an affront to the
Son, for his blood, as it were, is made unclean; it is
an affront to the Spirit, for grace is scorned.[37]

   You priests of the Lord, beware of the sensual
pleasures of the flesh and the vain way of life of the
world. Honor your ministry, you who shine as lights
in the world.* Pursue righteousness, embrace disci-   Ph 2:15
pline.* You were bought with a great price, so glo-   Ps 2:12[11]
rify and bear God in your body.* carrying [with you]   1 Co 6:20
the mortification of Jesus.* Show yourselves in all   2 Co 4:10
things as ministers of God.* Bear in your body the   2 Co 6:4
marks of Jesus,* and that which brands you as a   Ga 6:17
member of his army. [Live] in abstinence and con-
tinence, in chastity and sobriety, in patience and
humility, and in all purity and holiness,* so that all   Cf. 1 Tm 2:15
who see you may know to whom you belong, and
that the word of the prophet may be fulfilled in you:
'You shall be called the priests of the Lord, the ministers of our God'.* And again, 'All that see them shall   Is 61:6
know that these are the seed which the Lord has
blessed'.*

   'Priests of the Lord, bless the Lord!'* Bless him who   Is 61:9
has blessed us with every spiritual blessing in the   Dn 3:84
heavens,* him who has blessed the house of Aaron.†   Eph 1:3
Let God be sanctified in you so that in you he may   †Ps 113[115]:12

Heb 7:26   appear as he truly is: holy, unstained, and undefiled.*
Do not let your conduct lead others to blaspheme
his name, nor let your ministry be censured on your
2 Co 6:3   account.* In the midst of a wicked and perverse
Ph 2:15   people,* let your way of life be such that those who
see you say, 'Truly these are the priests of the Lord;
truly these are the ministers of our God; truly these are
the disciples of Jesus Christ, successors of the apostles;
Is 61:9   truly these are the seed which the Lord has blessed.'*

Give heed to the dignity of the sacrament,[38] for its
preparation and distribution have been committed
to you. Because your hands have been given you to
conduct such a venerable sacrifice, be sure they are
clean from all the filth of unclean gifts,[39] lest you be
counted among those in whose hands are iniquities,
Ps 25[26]:10   whose right hand is filled with gifts.* Draw near the
altar with your hands washed; approach with him
who says, 'I will wash my hands among the innocent
Ps 25[26]:6   and go about your altar, O Lord'.* Keep your mouth
Ps 33:9[34:8]   clean to taste the sweetness of the Lord,* to receive
the Eucharist, the living bread which came down
Jn 6:33   from heaven.*

The mouth of a priest should not be polluted
with perjury, or with false testimony, or with lying,
or with obscenities or idle chatter, or by speaking
scurrilously of something which should not be sullied by such words, or by spreading scandal and
slander about one's enemies. In the mouth of a priest
should be the offering of thanks and the voice of
1 Tm 2:1   praise, prayers, supplications, and appeals.* From
him should come no evil word, but only that word
which is good, which shows to those who hear it
the grace of edification, and which becomes that
spoken by the Lord: 'I will bridle you with my
Is 48:9   praise, lest you perish'.* Bridled by this praise,

therefore, [the Psalmist] says, 'I will bless the Lord
at all times; his praise will ever be in my mouth'.*   Ps 33:2[34:1]
The mouth is bridled with the praise of God lest it be
opened wide with filth and disgrace through unbri-
dled license of speech. The mouth which must touch
the sacred banquet should not be foul and impure.

Beloved brethren, let us hold most firmly and believe beyond doubt that the authority of God himself and of the holy Fathers directs us to believe in
this sacred communion. In this sacrament is contained the power of our restoration and the price of
our redemption. To exercise our faith, the truth is
hidden, and the conduct and chastisement⁴⁰ of
Christ is displayed as an example for our own lives.
For this reason, when the Lord instituted this sacrifice and entrusted it to his disciples, he said: 'Do this
in memory of me'.* Do that which I do; offer that   Lk 22:19
which I offer; live in the way that I teach you. Take
from this a model for living and for dying, [a model]
which I entrust to you by my own example.

The effect of this sacrament on us is that Christ
lives in us and we in him. Its effect in us is that just
as Christ died for us, so, too, we die for Christ. All
who die in Christ or for Christ, who fall asleep in
pious devotion, have great grace laid upon them.*   2 M 12:45
For them is promised and reserved the glory of resurrection, the restoration and salvation which is
[obtained by] the worthy reception of this sacrament, by whose power God will reform our lowly
body to be like his glorious body.* What do we   Ph 3:21
have worthy to repay the Lord for so much grace bestowed upon us? How can we requite him for so much
honor? It is futile to ask if he loves us, who, as a sign of
his inestimable love, offers us in himself the bread of
eternal life and the cup of everlasting salvation.⁴¹

It is only right, therefore, that as far as our human weakness allows, we should receive worthily and reverently so excellent a gift of God, so exceptional

Dt 32:10, Ps 16[17]:8 a favor, and guard it as the apple of our eye;* more, in fact, than as the apple of our eye: as our life, as our salvation,⁴² as the hope and reality of our resurrection and glory.

However much we have sinned hitherto through neglecting reverence for so great a sacrament, let us atone for it in the future by being more exacting and exerting greater care, and let us make up for the faults of earlier days and of the life we once led by a more honorable resolution and a better intention, making the most of the time, because the days are

Eph 5:16 evil.*

1. Title in PL 204:403–404. This first tractate seems to have been formed from what were originally two separate sermons – the one ending and the other beginning at n.37 – and in certain manuscripts this is how they are presented. The two parts are separated by what appears now as Tractate XII (for details, see P. Guébin, 'Deux sermons inédits de Baldwin, archêveque de Canterbury 1184–1190', in *Journal of Theological Studies* O.S. 13 [1911–12] 571–574). I suspect that in the process of editing, part of both sermons has been lost, but it is impossible to say just how much. Both discourses, however, were obviously concerned with the same topic – the nature, distribution, and reception of the eucharist – and for this reason, I have retained the form of one single tractate in my translation. The second sermon is clearly that of a bishop or archbishop addressing his priests, and while I suspect that this is probably true of the first sermon as well, the internal evidence is not quite as conclusive. For further material on Baldwin's understanding of the nature and importance of the eucharist, see my 'Baldwin of Ford and the Sacrament of the Altar', due to be published soon by Cistercian Publications.

2. Baldwin has in mind 1 Co 6:20 and other similar pauline ideas. The conception of the eucharist as a re-enactment of the sacrifice of calvary dates from the early patristic period.

3. PL 204: 403B suggests that we add here, 'that which is hidden is the true body and blood of Christ', but there appears to be no manuscript justification for this.

4. Baldwin also used this term in his *De sacramento altaris*, and included there a defence of its usage (see PL 204: 662C–D [SC 1481]). For a full account of its development, see DThC 5: 1287–1293. By the latter part of the twelfth century, the term was in widespread use.

5. As Thomas observes (35/30–31, n. 1), the word *fides* means both 'faithfulness / fidelity' (as in Ps 32[33]:4) and 'faith / belief' (as in Heb 11:6). We may compare the ideas in this paragraph with Baldwin's comments in Tr. IX.1, n. 13.

6. *Dispensatio* is here the Latin equivalent of the Greek *oikonomia*, 'economy', i.e. God's plan and design for the world. See Eph 3:9.

7. PL 405C omits *datus*.

8. Baldwin's exegesis demands 'the Son' rather than 'a son' in this quotation of Is 9:6.

9. Hab 3:18 according to the Vulgate. 'Jesus' is here being used in its etymological sense of 'saviour'. The O.L. rendering was much clearer: 'gaudebo super Deo salutari [or salvatore] meo' (see Jerome, *Commentaria in Abacuc* II [in Hab 3:18]: PL 25: 1335C–D).

10. *Ecce quantum nos amat Jesus.* Thomas (35/37, n. 1) compares Bernard, SC 17.7; PL 183: 858C; (SBO 1:102): 'Quomodo me amas, Deus meus, amor meus! Quomodo me amas . . .'. The idea is certainly similar, but we cannot say more than that.

11. *In incorruptione* renders the Greek *en aphtharsia* and should be translated (as in the RSV) by some such phrase as 'with undying love'. It is eminently possible, however, that Baldwin understood it to mean something like 'without corrupt thoughts'.

12. Thomas (35/43, n. 1) admits ignorance as to the source of this text. It is, in fact, the O.L. version of Is 25:1 which Baldwin may well have found in Jerome's

Commentariorum in Isaiam Prophetam VIII (in Is 25:1); PL 24: 289A: 'consilium antiquum verum fiat'.

13. The passage from 'being led by faith' to 'the powers of God' has been omitted in PL 407A by homoioteleuton.

14. *Cui semper subest, cum voluerit, posse.*

15. In nearly all cases, I have rendered *pietas* by 'pious devotion', although it is not a satisfactory term. *Pietas* indicates an inner attitude and consequent conduct which involves duty, devotion, affection, gratitude, loyalty, and love. It is therefore our dutiful conduct with regard to God and the things which are God's which, because it arises from a heart truly turned to God in love, devotion, and gratitude, is both natural and a joy to perform.

16. *Benignissimus Jesus.*

17. *Superscriptio.* The term here would seem to mean 'appearance' or 'distinguishing characteristics', even though the dictionaries do not give this meaning.

18. *Sensus animalis*, i.e. the physiological, as distinct from the spiritual, senses. *Animalis* is the Latin equivalent of the Greek *psychikos* (see DLF, s.v. *animalis*).

19. PL 408A omits *et fundamentum*.

20. Thomas (35/48) has *mutare*; PL 408B has *revocare*, 'which no-one can take away'.

21. For a similar argument that faith is also true knowledge (*scientia*), see Baldwin's CF, 584A–C.

22. The 'etc.' is in the text.

23. The verb is *tumescere*, 'to swell with venom or excitement or pride'. Hence my 'proud and puffed up'.

24. For a similar account of the unfortunate events in Eden, see CF, 626B–D.

25. PL 409C has *de fide sermonis Dei dubitavit*; Thomas (35/54) omits *Dei. Fides* here means 'fidelity' or 'trustworthiness' (see n. 5 above).

26. *At Dominus novitatem miraculi tanti contra eos interpretans* . . . PL 409D substitutes *intentans* for *interpretans*.

27. The verb is *credere*. This would normally be rendered as 'believe', but it also means 'have faith or trust in' (as in Ps 77:8, which is echoed here).

28. Lit. 'Christ is not from himself and does not effect things from himself'. The same construction occurs elsewhere.

29. *Nil a se velle, nil a se operari, in iis maxime quae ad salutem operantur, vel cooperantur.* On the significance of *operari*, see Tr. v, n. 5.

30. PL 410D is quite different here, and substitutes for this last sentence: 'The day of mortification is the day of atonement from sin'.

31. *Disciplina.* This is an important term for Baldwin and it comprises a number of meanings. Blaise (DLF, s.v.) gives six such, of which two are of particular importance: (a) *disciplina* as the regular discipline of the monastic / ascetic life; and (b) *disciplina* as correction or penitential chastisement. It is this second meaning which B. has in mind here. See also n. 40 below.

32. Etymologically, compassion means "suffering with someone, shared suffering", and not just feeling sorry for him.

33. *Quis poterit ei extorquere?* PL 411D has *ea* for *ei*.

34. Baldwin's source here is Augustine, *Enarratio in Psalmo* 61.4; PL 36: 731.

35. Thomas (35/68) has *nulla arte*; PL 412B reads *occulta arte*.

36. PL 413A, influenced by the Vulgate, has *ducunt*. Baldwin however, wrote *dicunt* (see 35/72, n. 1).

37. See n. 1 above.

38. For *sacramenti*, PL 413C has *sacerdotii*. Thomas (35/76) gives *sacramenti* in the latin text (which is correct), but translates as if it were *sacerdotii*.

39. Baldwin may have been thinking of priests who charged fees for the sacraments. This was quite contrary to canon law, but was certainly done on occasion. In the thirteenth century, for example, the clergy at Bristol were charging two pence for each baptism (see J. R. H. Moorman, *Church Life in England in the Thirteenth Century* [Cambridge, 1955] 128, n. 6).

40. Once again, the word is *disciplina*, but here it involves Christ's disciplined and ascetic life as well as the sufferings he willingly accepted. Hence my 'conduct and chastisement'.

41. A formula from the liturgy.

42. PL 414D omits *sicut salutem nostram*.

TRACTATE II
ON THE CORRUPT WAY OF LIFE
OF THE CLERGY AND PEOPLE[1]

S EE HOW DANGEROUS are these times in
which we live, and how corrupt and abom-
inable the sons of men have become in all
their endeavors!* The earth is full of iniquity, and
just as all flesh had corrupted its way* in the days of
Noah, so too [it is] at this present time. In those
days, before the waters of the flood came over the
earth, they were preceded by a spiritual flood in the
dissipated manners of mankind and in human immorality was prefigured the manner of that just retribution which was to come. Torrents of iniquity
have overflowed,* and those who are in the flood of
many waters have not come near God.* Thus, the
depths have overwhelmed them, and they have
sunk into the deep as a stone.*

While the abyss of sins called upon the abyss of
God's judgements* and its clamor entered the ears†
of the Lord God of Hosts, the fountains of the great
deep were broken and the flood-gates of heaven
were opened,* and the Lord blotted out flesh from
the face of the earth. [Then] he placed in the clouds
the bow of his covenant,* so that mankind might
no more fear the waters of the flood. But this does
not mean there is nothing left to fear: for when God
bent his bow and made it ready,* he gave a sign to
those who feared him so that they might flee from
before his bow.* In the recollection of that judgement which is past is rooted the dread of that which

Ps 13[14]:1
Gn 6:12

Ps 17:5[18:4]
Ps 31[32]:6

Ex 15:5

Ps 41:8[42:7]
†Ps 17:7[18:6]

Gn 7:11

Gn 9:13

Ps 7:13[12]

Ps 59:6[60:4]

is to come, and with the bow which God placed in the clouds there appears, in all its many colors, the terrible sign of judgement by water and fire. From judgement by water we are pardoned; but terrible is the expectation of judgement and the rage of fire which shall consume his adversaries.*

Heb 10:27

See how it is that even now human conduct reveals in advance the manner of the judgement to come. The fire of cupidity and lust and malice has been kindled in the midst of the people and everywhere ravages² all who dwell on earth, as if the flaming destruction of the world had even now drawn nigh. When it arrives, the punishment will be modelled on the sin, and what the nature of the sin now is, so will be the nature of the punishment. [Thus], since the life of the wicked is [one] of fire, fire will be their punishment. [But] since the life of the just is also fire, fire will be their glory. For now the just burn with the fire of divine love, the fire which the Lord came to spread on the earth, but which he also wishes to see kindled.*

Lk 12:49

There is now a fire in Sion, but there will be a furnace of fire in Jerusalem.* The just shall indeed burn in the future, but they will burn like the Seraphim.³ They will blaze like the sun in the sight of the Lord* and will shine in the brightness of the saints.* Such shall be the glory of those who, like bright and flaming lamps, burn within with [the fire of] charity and outwardly shine as an example to others.

Is 31:9

Mt 13:43
Ps 109[110]:3

The wicked too shall burn in the future, but in a different way. Of them, the Prophet said to the Lord, 'You shall make them as an oven of fire in the time of your anger'.* Even now they burn, those of whom it is said, 'They are all adulterers; their hearts

Ps 20:10[19:9]

Hos 7:4

Ps 57:9[58:8]

are like an oven'.* And the Psalmist says of the
wicked: 'Fire has fallen upon them, and they shall
not see the sun'.* The fire with which they burn
gives no illumination, but only darkness, so much
that it prevents them from seeing the sun. Thus, in
the last days, moaning within themselves in anguish
of spirit, they shall say, 'The light of justice has not
shone upon us, and the sun has not risen upon us'.[4]

The signs which shall precede the day of judgement will also be modelled on our present conduct,
and the things which will come to pass in reality[5]
may now be seen in us spiritually. It is written that
'the sun shall be turned into darkness and the moon
into blood before the great and terrible day of the
Lord shall come.'[6]* What the sun and moon are in
the sky [corresponds] in the church of God to the
order of prelates[7] and the life of those who are subject to them, and also to ecclesiastical authority and
secular power. The moon is inferior to the sun and
shines not of itself but from the sun. So too the life
of those in their charge[8] is inferior to the life of the
prelates by whom they should be enkindled and enlightened. For to the latter it is said: 'You are the
light of the world'.*

Jl 2:31

Mt 5:14

Mt 15:14

Jl 2:31

Mt 24:12
Rev 14:20

But in those prelates who are ignorant and in
error, who are blind and leaders of the blind,* the
sun is changed into darkness; and therefore in the
life of those subject to them the moon is changed into blood[9]*—into the blood, that is, of corruption
and cruelty. See how the charity of many grows
cold and iniquity abounds!* 'The blood has risen
from the pool as far as the bridles of the horses',* as
far as the guides and leaders[10] of the people,
and there is blood and more blood, murder upon
murder.[11]

The laity do not find in us that which they should imitate; they find that which they would rather persecute. They persecute us with lies; they persecute us with injury, invective, and taunts. And they even persecute us with swords.

Not long ago the fury of our persecutors wounded us in the head.[12] They have persecuted to the death that man of the Lord Christ, most blessed Thomas, our bishop, for his noble defence of the freedom of the Church. And if we can believe what has been spread abroad as the reason for this deed, something which troubles the conscience of many, it was our undisciplined life which spawned so great an evil and kindled so great a hatred. A certain man did not regard us as ministers of Christ and dispensers of the mysteries of God;* but he shall bear the judgement of God, whoever that man may be.[13]

1 Co 4:1

Perhaps we appeared unworthy of those ancient privileges which, for the peace and freedom of the clergy, were granted us by the favor of the roman pontiffs and the noble kings of old. We were indeed unworthy! If only it were otherwise! But according to our merits we were totally unworthy! Yet in any priest at all, the priestly ministry is always holy and the priestly sacrament honorable.[14]

There comes to our mind now that time when Doeg the Idumean slew with the sword eighty-five priests vested with the ephod.* Remember those days of old and [remember] too the blood of Zachariah, the son of Barachiah, who was slain between the temple and the altar.[15]* In our times, too, there are many notable cases of sacrilegious cruelty, but when compared with this single deed, the enormity of a host of crimes is set at nought. God knows what things the enemy has done wickedly in the

1 S 22:18

Mt 23:35

sanctuary!* All the wickedness of our times—even
though there is now so much of it—has been ab-
solved by this one single act. One single act—but in
that one act there is [contained] a multitude of crimes!
For carefully cultivated wickedness, cunningly con-
triving at its own ruin, intended that there be nothing
lacking from perfect villainy, and brought the whole
business of wickedness to its consummation in an
extremity of malice.

But if we consider it a likely view that it was our
disordered and undisciplined way of life which was
responsible for such an evil deed, what can we do
but call upon the Lord our God until he have mercy
upon us?* He is compassionate and full of mercy.†
What is more beneficial and what more honorable
than to recall our life to order and discipline and to
show ourselves in all things as ministers of God,* so
that those who persecute us and speak against us as
evildoers may see our good way of life* and themselves be led by our example to penitence?

If the light itself is darkness, how great will the
darkness be?* If we still walk in the works of darkness, we, who were appointed in the Church of God
that our life might enlighten others by our good
works, then is it surprising if those who are subject
to us, unknowing and ignorant, [also] walk blindly
in darkness and, by our example, become yet more
blind?

Will their blood not be required from our hands?*
And that most blessed martyr who, for us, laid
down his life, will he not lay a charge against us?
Will the voice of his blood not cry out against us
from the earth,* and will we not all be found guilty
before the judgement seat of a severe judge? Did he
not die for our faults? And was it not through our

Ps 73[74]:3

Ps 122[123]:2
†Ps 102[103]:8

2 Co 6:4

1 P 2:12

Mt 6:23

Gn 9:5

Gn 4:10

faults that he died? For if they did not provide the [actual] cause of his death, they were responsible for its happening. If we continue in sin—as may well be the case—he will no longer be [our] advocate for justice, no longer an intercessor for our pardon, but an accuser and witness for our punishment. In the evils which we suffer by the just judgement of God, we have no right to rage at anyone save ourselves. We have deserved worse and are not yet suffering what we really deserve.

We are justly to blame—and it redounds to our peril—that the secular power has arrogated ecclesiastical jurisdiction;[16] that it is not governed by ecclesiastical authority; that it neither uses nor trusts to the council of the Church but resists it; that the sword of Peter is blunted and the keys of Peter are not reckoned with; that the sacraments of the Church are scorned; that the holy and terrible name of God—with no thought of perjury—is taken in vain; that the respect due to inviolable churches is not given and the honor due to ecclesiastics not shown; and that the venerable name of holy religion is brought to scorn. All these things, and many more like them, are laid at our door and blamed on our sins. Our conduct and our iniquities have brought them upon us. But God has the power whenever he will to free the bride whom he loves[17] from the hands of those who persecute her. He is a little angered,* for it is we who have encouraged wickedness. The [secular] power seems to be striving to subject the Church to itself lest it be itself subject, but what does Scripture say? 'The multitude of nations', it says, 'fighting against Ariel shall be as the dream of a vision by night.'*

Today there are things happening on earth which are both bewildering and extraordinary. Contrary

2 M 7:33

Is 29:7

to [the natural] order of things, the moon is exalted over the sun and does not remain in her place. But what does Scripture say? 'The sun has been raised, and the moon has remained in her order.'[18] May the sun [indeed] be raised and recalled to its own place; may the priestly life return to what it should be, ordered and disciplined. Then the moon, too, will remain in her order. Then the life of those subject to us will be ordered and disciplined, content within its bounds.

What is more fitting for those who have entered [holy] Orders[19] to live an ordered life? What an abuse it would be, both factually and verbally, if those who are spoken of as being in Orders were found to be in disorder. When the prophet says the moon remained in its ordered place, he implies that the moon, which is inferior to the sun, does indeed have an order. But if order and discipline are demanded in the life of those in their charge, how much more so in the life of the prelates? The latter, clearly, should do everything in an ordered manner and, by their judgements, order the conduct of others. They are the throne of God on which God sits and hands down his judgements, that throne of which the Father, speaking of the Son, says: 'His throne is like the sun in my sight'.* And there is added, 'and as the moon, perfect for ever'.

Ps 88:38[89:35]

By this order, God will bring to perfection the glory of the just. For the prelates and those who have led perfect lives[20] the throne of God will be like the sun, far more glorious than the moon and far superior [to it]. And for those in their charge and those who are now less than perfect, the moon will [also] be for ever perfect, but perfect within its own order. May God lead us to this glory, each of us in his own order, he who is above all things for every blessed.
Amen.*

Rm 9:5

1. Title as in PL 415–416. For a discussion of the nature of this tractate and its date, see n. 12 below.

2. *Depopulator* in Thomas' text (35/90) is a typographical error for *depopulatur*.

3. Seraphim, etymologically, means "the burning ones". Cf. Isidore, *Liber Etymologiarum* VII, v, 24; PL 82: 273D–274A.

4. Ws 5, 6 in the Vulgate reads *sol intelligentiae*, but Baldwin omits the second word.

5. *Visibiliter.*

6. Jl 2, 31 in the Vulgate reads *horribilis*; Baldwin substitutes *terribilis*.

7. *Ordo rectorum. Rector*, in medieval usage, was a word of wide meaning, but it normally referred to a bishop.

8. *Vita subditorum.* Lit. 'the life of those who are subject to them'.

9. Baldwin changes the future *convertetur* of Jl 2:31 to the present *convertitur*.

10. Once again, *rectores*, which I have rendered as 'guides and leaders'.

11. *Sanguis sanguinem tetigit* is a quotation from Ho 4, 2. I have given both a literal and (following the RSV) a meaningful translation.

12. Baldwin is referring to Thomas Becket, and his *in capite* may perhaps be understood in three ways: (i) the body of the Church has been wounded in its head; (ii) the head of the Church has been wounded; (iii) the head of the Church has been wounded in the head, for it was well known that when Thomas was martyred, William Tracy's first blow cut into the crown of his head, and Richard Brito completed the murder by slicing off the top of his skull. Baldwin says this occurred 'not long ago' (*nuper*), but it is difficult to say precisely how long before he wrote. Becket was killed at the very *end of* 1170, and at that time Baldwin was a monk at Ford. This sermon, however, is unquestionably addressed to clerics (perhaps bishops and / or suffragan bishops—see n. 7 above), not to monks, and the person delivering it is unquestionably a high ecclesiastic. In other words, Baldwin is either Bishop of Worcester (as Thomas thinks [34/85]) or Archbishop of Canterbury (which is the opinion of Beryl Smalley; see *The Becket Conflict and the Schools* [Totowa, N.J., 1973] 219 — and also that of the present writer): since he was elevated to the former see in 1180 and to the latter in 1184, the events he narrates must have taken place at least a decade earlier. It is possible, of course, that we have here a later sermon incorporating earlier material (see Smalley, 219, n. 11), although this is not my own view. Baldwin also touches on Becket's martyrdom (without mentioning him by name) in his earlier *De sacramento altaris*, written while he was still at Ford (see Smalley, 218–219 for a brief discussion).

13. Baldwin is referring (cautiously!) to Henry II, who was still very much alive. He died in 1189, one year before Baldwin.

14. See also Tr. XII, n. 9.

15. A very apt biblical reference (Mt 23: 35), since Becket's murder did indeed take place close to an altar: he was martyred in Canterbury Cathedral, just by the massive pillar between the Chapel of St Benedict and the Lady Chapel. Ps 73[74]:3, which Baldwin quotes a little further on, also echoes this, as does his complaint that no respect is shown to inviolable (*sacrosanctus*) churches, nor any honor to ecclesiastics.

16. As far as Becket was concerned, this was what Henry was trying to do in 1164 at Clarendon.

17. *Quam sibi zelat.* We could also render it as 'whom he guards jealously for himself'.

18. This text does not occur in the Vulgate, but Thomas' suggestion (35/102–3, n. 1) that it is from an O.L. version of Joshua is incorrect. It is indeed O.L., but it is Habakkuk, not Joshua. Baldwin may well have found it in Jerome's *Commentaria in Abacuc* II (in Hab 3:11); PL 25:1323C.

19. Baldwin is playing on the word *ordinatus*, 'ordained / in orders'.

20. Lit. 'the prelates and the perfect'. *Perfectus*, in medieval usage, can refer not only to one who has achieved perfection, but to one who is devoting himself wholly to its achievement. Thus, when the later writer Uthred of Boldon, on the authority of pseudo-Dionysius, refers to monks as *ordo perfectorum*, he is describing them in relative rather than absolute terms. For Uthred, see W. A. Pantin, 'Two Treatises of Uthred of Boldon on the Monastic Life', in R. W. Hunt *et al.*, *Studies in Medieval History Presented to F. M. Powicke* (Oxford, 1948) 363–385.

TRACTATE III
ON THE LOVE OF GOD[1]

You shall love the Lord your God with all your heart, and with all your soul, and with all your strength, and with all your mind. *

Mt 22:37

W E MAY BE DISTURBED — and it would not be unjust to say that we should be disturbed — when we consider the purpose of this accumulation of words, this earnest injunction which is so loving, so accurate, so exact, so extensive, and yet one single commandment. It is one single commandment, not several, and of it is written: 'This is the first and greatest commandment'. *

Mt 22:38

Although it says 'You shall love the Lord your God with all your heart', then, as if this were not enough, there is added 'and with all your soul', and then, as if what has been said still does not suffice, there is added 'and with all your strength'; and finally, as though all these words were not enough, there is added 'and with all your mind'.

What is the intention of all this? Was it idly and to no purpose that these things were so carefully written down? Anyone who believes this believes wrongly! If no leaf falls from the tree save by the decision of the Father, how much more is the word of God — and most especially this word, the first and greatest among the words of his commandments —

Mt 5:18

spoken by the decision of God, so that not a jot or a tittle should be taken away?*

We should therefore make a real effort to inquire into this, and investigate with the greatest care what it is that God willed to be commanded and written so carefully. No quest is more profitable, nor any discovery more useful, provided that those who seek and find do what is commanded.

It would seem that it is because of the hardness of our hearts that God took such care to insist on this commandment, and by commanding it [repeatedly], as it were, to drill it into us really deeply. It is like driving a nail into hard wood: normally, the hardness of the wood prevents the whole nail from going in all at once, and we therefore drive it in with blow after blow until the whole [nail] has gone in and we consider it driven home. This injunction is a sort of nail which must be driven into our hearts; for if, as Solomon said, the words of the wise are like goads and like nails deeply fixed,* how much more is the word of God a goad and a nail, when it is living and effective, and more penetrating than any two-edged sword?* Thus, because God wanted to pierce our hearts through and through, and penetrate them completely with this nail of his divine word and divine love, he says: 'You shall love the Lord your God with all your heart'; and driving it in further, he adds, 'and with all your soul'; and to make it enter yet more deeply he adds, 'and with all your strength'; and to make it reach all the way to the utmost depths, he adds finally, 'and with all your mind'. Such a commandment exceeds all measure, for he wants us to exceed all measure in putting it into practice.*

Qo 12:11

Heb 4:12

Ps 118[119]:4

But we may also see that there is another possible explanation for the [four-fold] division of this one commandment: because the love of the world occupies our whole heart and fills up all its chambers, the love of the world must be cast out from our whole heart. Only then shall the Prince of this world be cast out* and the love of God enter in to claim for itself all our heart. Only then shall God be known in all the most secret places of our heart and all the ends of the earth remember the Lord and turn to him.* Only so shall God possess all our heart and the heart [possess] God, so that we can say with the Prophet, 'God of my heart, and God, my portion for ever'!*

Jn 12:31

Ps 21:28[22:27]

Ps 72[73]:26

THAT IN THIS PRESENT LIFE
GOD IS NOT LOVED PERFECTLY

Because of the condition of this present life, God is only known imperfectly and in part,* and in just the same way, he is loved only imperfectly and incompletely. If we compare our knowledge of God in this present life—however great it may be—with that full and complete knowledge of God when God will be seen in his glory,* when he will show us his face and we shall be saved,* it is like [comparing] the morning light entering a house through the narrowest of cracks with the sun in its midday splendor, shining in its full strength.* The same is true of the sort of love for God we can have in this present life. It is like a tiny spark of fire beside that great flame of love with which the just shall blaze in Jerusalem among the ranks of the Seraphim.[2] There is now a fire in Sion, but there will be a furnace of fire in Jerusalem.*

1 Co 13:9

Ps 101:17[102:16]
Ps 79:4[80:3]

Rev 1:16

Is 31:9

In the meantime, you should love God with your whole heart in accordance with the measure of your imperfection. But how can this be with your *whole* heart? How is this possible when your whole heart

Jb 17:11

Ps 39:13[40:12]

2 S 7:27

is not yet wholly yours, but is torn apart by strangers? This is why a certain man, amidst other lamentations, complained that 'My thoughts are dispersed; my heart is tormented'.* And another said: 'My iniquities overwhelmed me, and I could not see. They are more than the hairs of my head, and my heart has forsaken me.'* Forsaken by their heart, they are forsaken, as if they were without a heart.

Meanwhile, we do not have a whole heart with which to love God. Neither do we have a heart with which to adore him,³ so that [through this adoration] our heart might be restored to loving him. David, therefore, says in one place: 'Your servant has found his heart that he might pray to you with this prayer'.*

Speaking for myself, I do not find my heart when I come to pray. Where, then, is it? Or rather, where is it not?⁴ When I look for where it is, I can find no place where it is not! It dashes away and flies back; it sallies forth, scampers about, and hurries back again. When it returns it does not stay; when restrained, it is not detained; and when I try to grasp it, it slithers out from my hands as if it were greased!

O man, if you should feel this in your heart—and because you are a man you certainly feel it to some degree—you have in yourself your own proof that you do not yet love God perfectly with your whole heart. I mean according to that measure of perfection in which he wants you to love him.

Yet if you love God in truth and offer your heart to God as much as you possibly can, then in giving it to God you make it your own. Or, more accurately, he to whom you give it makes it not your own, and unless he makes it not your own,⁵ it cannot be your own! Thus, the more of your heart you give to him, the more he makes it your own.

If you could unwaveringly direct to him all your thoughts, all your affections, and all your intentions, and hold and maintain them unswervingly, even burning within yourself, in all your marrow, with the fire of love, then indeed you might be able to love God more perfectly with all your heart. But because our human weakness does not permit this, then if you cannot love as much as you should, as much as you are obliged to love, love as much as you can, as much as is in your power, as much as you are capable.[6] [In so doing], you begin to love God here below with your whole heart—so far as it is now your own—so that in the end you may love him with your whole heart[7] more perfectly, when [your heart], which is not yet wholly yours, is more perfectly your own.

You should not wish to imitate an unjust debtor who, if he does not have enough to repay his debt completely, refuses to pay as much as he has, as if he were no more guilty in paying nothing at all than in paying only in part. God is a kind-hearted creditor and pours out his mercy on anyone who pays as much as he can so he may be able [to pay] more.

THAT GOD SHOULD BE LOVED WITH ALL OUR HEART IN HIS BLESSINGS[8]

The four divisions of this commandment introduce to us the four main feelings[9] of love or its four forms. But although we speak of these feelings as a specific group of four, they actually contain in themselves innumerable different forms and divisions of feeling. God should be loved in his blessings with all our heart, loved in his promises with all our soul, loved in his judgements with all our power, and loved in his commandments with all our mind. By these four things—that is, blessings, promises, judgements, and commandments—the four feelings of divine love are formed in us by the inspiration of God. Just as in our present life God is known in his creatures in a mirror and a riddle,* until he be known more fully in himself, as he is, so too God is loved in this present life in his blessings and the other things we have mentioned above, until he be loved more fully and perfectly as if in himself.

1 Co 13:12

Among the blessings of God, some are the blessings of creation, others of restoration, and others of day-to-day consolation. The blessings of creation are that we were created in the image and likeness of God, that in him we live and move and have our being and are his offspring,* and that by his gift we have a soul and body and all the senses of soul and body in their full number and completeness. Whatever good things we possess as a result of our creation, these we receive by God's generosity, and all these good things of ours are nothing but gifts of God.

Ac 17:28

The blessings of restoration are the sacrament[10] of the incarnation, the mystery of the passion of Christ, and all the sacraments which Christ took upon himself for us or which he instituted for us to receive. Such are the sacrament of the body and blood of Christ, the sacrament of baptism, and all the other sacraments of the Church by which the merciful God has bestowed grace and power for the remission of sinners and the salvation of believers.

The blessings of everyday consolation are those which the Father of mercies and the God of all consolation, who consoles us in all our tribulation,* accords us in his mercy day by day. Our Father knows all that we need, we, I say, his unjust servants

2 Co 1:3-4

who, by his condescension, are yet his children.
From our Father himself we receive [the power] to
desire, to ask, and to hope.[11] From him we can look
for relief from all our sufferings, support in all our
needs, and the remedy for all our infirmities. Who
else shall we look to for all these things, if not him?
'Where does my help come from?' asks the prophet.
'My help is from the Lord, who made heaven and
earth.'*

See how the Lord has done great things for us!*
He overwhelms us with the multitude of his blessings
and by his blessings strives to wrest from us our love.
Surely God should be loved with our whole heart
because of these great and manifold blessings! It is
only right and proper and just that we should give
[our heart] to him if he himself thinks fit to ask for
it. And he *has* thought it fit! 'Give me your heart',*
he says to man! He who asks you to give him your
heart wants to be loved from the heart. God wants
our whole heart for himself, that it may draw back
from the love of the world and wordly things and
turn to him, that in him, before all else, it may take
its pleasure, and whatever is displeasing to [God]
may be wholly displeasing [to it]. But what is displeasing to God is wickedness and vanity, for he
loathes wickedness and despises vanity. This is why
the prophet says, 'You detest all those who commit
wickedness',* and again, 'You detest all who care
about useless vanities'.*

The love of God, then, begins from a jointly-held
hatred and contempt. But it is God's will that that
which he hates or despises should be equally hated
and despised by us. As long as we love that which
God hates, we are not at peace with God; but if we

Ps 120:2[121:1–2]
Ps 125[126]:3

Pr 23:26

Ps 5:7[5]
Ps 30:7[31:6]

find ourselves in accord with God in hating evil, then we love God from the heart.[12] We love God from the heart if we remember both the good which we have received from God and the evil which we have committed against God, if we return thanks for the good and do penance for the evil, and if we are reconciled to God by returning from discord to concord.[13] This is the first degree of love: the conversion of the heart from evil to good, from vanity to verity, from the things which displease God to the things which please him.

The prophet, therefore, wishing to disparage the things which God hates, says, 'Incline my heart to your testimonies and not to covetousness'.* And the Apostle shows how his heart has turned to God through his contempt for vanity by saying, 'Whatever gain I had, I counted loss for the sake of Christ. Indeed, I count everything as loss for the excellent knowledge of Jesus Christ our Lord. For him I have suffered the loss of all things, and I count them as dung, that I may gain Christ.'*

When we read 'You shall love the Lord your God with all your heart', the word 'heart' can indicate this first feeling of divine love. And rightly so. Through this we begin to enter into accord with God and to give our heart to God.[14] He showed us the grace of his blessings, but he also makes demands on us, lest we repay his grace with injury and sin against him who is our benefactor. If we detest with our whole heart the evil which he hates, then, in accordance with our imperfection, we love God with our whole heart. This is why the prophet says: 'You who love the Lord, hate evil!'*

Ps 118[119]:36

Ph 3:7–8

Ps 96[97]:10

THAT GOD SHOULD BE LOVED WITH ALL OUR SOUL IN HIS PROMISES

God should be loved with all our soul in his promises, for he has [already] given us great things and has promised us yet greater. He has promised us rest from labor, freedom from servitude, security from fear, alleviation from suffering, resurrection from the dead—and in the resurrection, fullness of joy, a supreme and unfailing joy. Finally, he has promised us himself, as he promised to our fathers, that he would give himself to us.*

Lk 1:73

Great and inestimable, therefore, are the promises of God, and for these and in these he wants us to love him with a certain type and measure[15] [of love]. If you ask what measure, this measure of love is a burning desire for what he has promised. This measure has a measure beyond my comprehension; it is rather without measure,[16] for the promises of God surpass every desire. What is surpassed is exceeded: its size is limited, and its limits give its measure. But however much we may desire the promise of God, we desire it less than we should, for there is no possibility of our desiring worthily that which is beyond all desire! Thus, if there is a measure to holy desire in what it *can* be, there is none in what it *should* be, but however much progress it makes, it ought to make more. In a certain way, therefore, there is no measure to burning desire, since there can never be too much of it.

In other things impatience should normally be reproved, but when we are waiting for such a great promise, burning impatience at its delay is something to be praised. The more one loves and the more one desires, the more one is tormented with

Pr 13:12

impatience at any delay, for the hope that is deferred
torments my soul.*

The bride, therefore, desiring her desire to be com-
mended to God by the merits and prayers of blessed
souls and of heavenly powers, says, 'I adjure you,
daughters of Jerusalem, if you find my beloved, tell

Sg 5:8

him that I am sick with love'.* And the Psalmist, as
if unable to bear the delay in patience, says: 'As the
heart desires the fountains of water, so my soul
desires you, O God. My soul has thirsted for God,
the living fountain.[17] When shall I come and appear

Ps 41:2–3[42:1–2]

before the face of God?'* Paul, too, as if burning
with impatience with this same desire, says: 'I am
hard pressed between two things: my desire is to die
and be with Christ, for that is something far better;
but to remain in the flesh is necessary on your account'.* Yet this same Paul, who is now so impatient

Ph 1:23

that he prefers death to being kept in suspense by
[continued] delay, says in another place: 'We wait

Rm 8:25

for it with patience'.*

So we see in a marvellous way the patient impatience of this holy and burning desire. The just suffer
torments in having to wait, but they are long-suffer-
ing and do not complain; and while enduring this
anguish indefatigably, they retain an unshaken hope
and bravely endure any adversities.

It is this feeling of holy desire which can be understood by the word 'soul' when it says 'You shall love
with all your soul'. And there is a good reason for
this. The soul is a spirit, and by the inspiration of
the Holy Spirit it continually desires and sighs until
it be refreshed in him for whom it aspires.[18] The
saints, therefore, very often mention [the word]
'soul' when expressing their desires. This is why the

Ps 62:2[63:1]

prophet says, 'For you my soul has thirsted';* and

again he says, 'My soul faints with desire for the
courts of the Lord'.* And another prophet says,   Ps 83:3[84:2]
'Your name, O Lord, and the memory of you are
the desire of my soul. My soul desired you in the
night, and my spirit [sought you] within myself'.*   Is 26:9

THAT GOD SHOULD BE LOVED WITH ALL
OUR STRENGTH IN HIS JUDGEMENTS

God should be loved in his judgements with all
our strength. To judge God's judgements is difficult,
for the judgements of God are a great abyss.* Never-   Ps 35:7[36:6]
theless, it is clear that when the prophet says to the
Lord, 'Look upon me and be merciful to me, accord-
ing to the judgement of them that love your name',*   Ps 118[119]:132
he is referring to one [sort of] judgement, and when
the same prophet says, 'Do not enter into judgement
with your servant',* he is referring to another [sort   Ps 142[143]:2
of] judgement.

In that judgement by which those already in the
fire are condemned, no one loves God, but no one
loves himself there either. In this present life,
however, God administers his judgements in various
ways, both on those he reproves and on those he has
chosen. Sometimes, in a marvellous manner, he con-
ceals his mercy and anger from them, and at other
times he shows them forth in such a way that what is
[actually] anger appears to be mercy and what is really
mercy appears to be anger. This is why the prophet
says, 'Who is wise and will take heed to these things?
Who will understand the mercies of the Lord?'*   Ps 106[107]:43
And referring to anger, he says to God, 'Who knows
the power of your anger?'*   Ps 89[90]:11

By his hidden judgement, God allows some of the
wicked their will and abandons them to their heart's
desires so that they might continue in their wicked

conduct. He raises up his enemies and honors them; day by day he heaps more and more good things upon them and does not chastise them with [other]

Ps 72[73]:5   men.* In so doing, he adds iniquity to their iniquity,†
†Ps 68:28[69:27]   so that those who are unclean may remain unclean††
††Rev 22:11   until their iniquity be brought to its full measure. In this [type of] judgement, God hides his anger under the form of what appears to be mercy from those who transform his mercy into judgement, so that their prosperity may become their destruction and they perish as they truly deserve, just as those who do not love God. This is why it is written: 'The pros-

Pr 1:32   perity of fools shall destroy them'.* Yet fools rejoice in their destruction! They do not know what he

Ps 65[66]:5   who is terrible in his counsels over the sons of men* intends for them, and they do not understand the deep thoughts of God, [those thoughts] of which it is written: 'How great are your works, O Lord; your thoughts are exceedingly deep! The foolish man will not know these things, nor will the fool

Ps 91:7[92:6]   understand them'.* But when the sinners spring up like grass and all the workers of iniquity appear so

Ps 91:8[92:7]   that they may perish for ever and ever,* then shall they understand what the Most High intends for them! Such is the outcome of that hidden judge- ment of God in which God hides his anger from those who do not share the troubles of men, who

Ps 72[73]:5   will not be chastised with [other] men.[19]*

There are, however, other wicked people who *are* chastised by God here below. But in their case, the chastisements do not cleanse them because they blas- pheme and complain in their impatience, and neither show reverence to him who chastises them nor ac- cept his correction.[20] Because they do not love God in God's judgements, these people, through their

impatience at his judgement, make that judgement
worse in that they go from torments [here] to torments [in the next world].

But when the good are chastised by God, some of
them love God in his chastisements, and others love
the chastisements themselves for the sake of God.
The former glorify God and praise him *when* they
are chastised, the latter *because* they are chastised.[21]
The former, who are patient in tribulation,* love
God in his judgements; the latter, who rejoice in tribulation, accept his judgements joyfully as if they
were blessings and rejoice in them. Of these it is written, 'The daughters of Judah rejoiced because of
your judgements, O Lord'.* By 'daughters', therefore, we are right in understanding those souls who
acknowledge God, who always glorify God in adversity, and who accuse themselves, saying: 'All that
you have done to us, Lord, you have done in true
judgement, for we have sinned against you and have
not obeyed your commandments. But give glory to
your name, and do with us according to the multitude of your mercies.'[22]

There are others who so love the judgements of
God that they do not wait for the correction of the
Father but judge and punish themselves. Each day
they look for retribution for those daily sins which
human infirmity cannot avoid. Of such as these the
Apostle says, 'If we would judge ourselves, we
would not be judged'.* Whoever judges himself and
punishes himself as a criminal is at one and the same
time the accused, the judge, and the executioner.[23]
[He is] a just judge, for he prosecutes the guilty; and
because he is himself the guilty party, he justly suffers; and while he justly prosecutes himself, he hates
his own soul and [thus] preserves it for eternal life.*

Rm 12:12

Ps 96[97]:8

1 Co 11:31

Jn 12:25

In his judgements God tries and instructs those he
has chosen in being patient; he trains them to endure their sufferings and strengthens them with
hope. 'Tribulation brings about patience, patience
trial, and trial hope. And hope does not disappoint

Rm 5:4-5
Ps 118[119]:43

us.'* Because of this, the prophet says to God, 'I
have great hope in your judgements',* indicating
that by undergoing the judgements of God in patience and by loving them, he is established not in
just any sort of hope, but in a firmer and more certain sort, and confident of a greater glory. The certainty of hope and the greatness of glory lighten the
weight of tribulation so that it may be borne more
composedly, or even loved. But as the Apostle says,
'The sufferings of this present time are not worth
comparing with the glory to come, which will be

Rm 8:18

revealed in us'.* And again: 'That which is at present
passing and trivial in our tribulation produces for

2 Co 4:17

us, beyond all measure, an eternal weight of glory'.*

Ps 118[119]:39

Someone who says to the Lord, 'Your judgements
are delightful',* knows how worthy of love are God's
judgements. And again he says, 'The judgements of
the Lord are true, justified in themselves. They are
more to be desired than gold and many precious
stones and sweeter than honey and the honey-

Ps 18:11[19:9-10]

comb.'* By these words we see that all the pleasure
which comes from possessing gold and silver and all
the sweetness of this present life—even if it be like
honey and the honeycomb—is less than the delight
with which God's judgements become sweet for the
soul that desires God above all things. To such [a
soul], all its sufferings are as nought, and it counts it

Jm 1:2

all joy when it meets with various temptations.*
'How great is the greatness of your sweetness, O
Lord, which you have hidden for them that love

you!'* Great indeed! I cannot say how great! You
are sweet in your judgements—but not yet for someone who says, 'I am afraid of your judgements'!*

Ps 30:20[31:19]

Ps 118[119]:120

THAT GOD SHOULD BE LOVED WITH ALL OUR MIND IN HIS COMMANDMENTS

The mind is what rules in a person and holds the
highest and principal place. Just as the father of a
family regulates everything in the house according
to his decision, arranging what needs to be done,
commanding the servants, and making judgements
on everything, wishing to be heeded and obeyed by
all in all things, so the vigorous activity[24] of the
mind should rule every movement and sense of
body and soul according to its decision. It should
order them, judge them, and take care that it is
obeyed in all things.

But just as the mind knows itself to be superior to
everything beneath it, so it should remember that of
necessity it has a strict obligation to be obedient to
God. The obedience which it demands from its in-
feriors it accords most justly and fairly to him who
is superior to it. But woe to that man who has not
obeyed God! The punishment of his disobedience
will be the triumph over him of death itself!

Death, however, is as hateful as it is terrible, and
because it is intimately linked to disobedience, disobedience itself deserves to be hated just as much as
death. It was through the sin of disobedience that
death came into this world. But if disobedience is
just as hateful as death since death arises from it,
why should we not love obedience as much as life,
since life arises from obedience and life continues in
it? It is obedience which submits to God and his
will, and life is in his will.[25]*

Ps 29:6[30:5]

The charity of God and obedience are bound each to each with an unbreakable bond and in no way separated from each other. The Lord shows us that there cannot be charity without obedience when he says, 'If anyone loves me, he will keep my word';* that is to say, he will observe my commandments, and in observing them, he will obey me. And he also shows us that there cannot be obedience without charity when he says, 'He who does not love me does not keep my words'.* If, then, he who loves obeys, and he who does not love does not obey, it follows that just as there cannot be charity without obedience, neither can there be obedience without charity.

Jn 14:23

Jn 14:24

Through charity, obedience sees God in his commandment, and through the commandment, charity directs obedience to God. Through the commandment God reveals his will, and charity enjoins obedience to the commandment. But whoever truly loves God also loves his commandment. For just as it is impossible for someone to love God and not to love his will, so one cannot love him and not love his commandments as well, since it is in them that his will is revealed and made known.

The love of obedience, therefore, is always joined to the love of God, just as the latter is always joined to the love of his will and the love of his commandments. Whoever loves the commandment of God and his will also loves obedience [and we can prove this in the following way:] God's will is that what he commands be done, and when he commands that it be done, his will is that he be obeyed. Thus, whoever loves God's will, which he commands to be done, loves to be commanded. But no one loves to be commanded unless he also loves to obey. If, then, there cannot be obedience to God without charity (that is, without the love of God), and if the love of God cannot exist without the love of his will, which he commands to be done, and if [the love of his will] cannot exist without the love of his commandment, nor the love of his commandment without the love of obedience, what can we conclude but that there cannot be obedience to God without both the love of obedience and the love of the divine commandment to which obedience is due?[26]

Let us look into this a little further and see if it is indeed the case. First of all, let us consider what the Psalmist means by these words which refer to the love of God's commandments: 'I meditated', he says, 'on your commandments which I loved',* 'and I lifted up my hands to your commandments which I loved',* 'and I shall strive in your statutes'.†[27] He shows [us here] that there are three ways in which he loves God's commandments: by meditation, by lifting up his hands—that is, by practical work[28]—and by striving.[29]

Ps 118[119]:47

Ps 118[119]:48
†*Ibid.*

We should love the commandments of God by meditating [on them] in accordance with this [saying]: 'Think always on the things which the Lord has commanded'.* In meditation, God's commandments become sweet, for we consider how beneficial they are, how upright, how faithful, and how they are established for ever and ever, made in truth and equity.*

Si 3:22

Ps 110[111]:8

There are some, however, who find them sweet and agreeable in meditation, but because they are lazy in putting them into practice, find them bitter and burdensome in action. This laziness is banished

Ps 118[119]:48

by him who says, 'I lifted up my hands to your commandments which I loved'.*

Again, there are a considerable number who seem to love God's commandments and to delight in them both in meditation and in action, but who are found to be lacking in courage and constancy when it comes to striving. This is banished by him who

Ibid.

says, 'I shall strive in your statutes'.* There is a sort of striving [involved] both in carrying out God's commandments and in meditating on them, but here by 'striving' we understand something which struggles against any difficulty—whether it be from temptation or persecution or adversity—which tries in some way to divert us from the righteousness of God's commandments. The love of God's commandments, therefore, finds its perfection in the love of meditation, of action, and of striving.

The love of obedience, however, proceeds from the love of the commandments, and anyone who does not love the commandments does not love obedience. What, then, shall we say? Are there not many who keep the commandments but who do not really want to be commanded, wishing instead that the commandments be abolished? Are there not many who do not fornicate and do not steal and do not attack their enemies but who really wish that God had not commanded these things, that they did not exist? Truly, there are many who wish that God had commanded nothing concerning these things, but who, nevertheless, refrain from [doing] them because he commanded that they should not be done. They fear him who so commanded, lest he punish them for doing something which he has forbidden.

People like this appear to keep God's commandments and to obey God [but] without loving obedience, and if this is so, then not everyone who is obedient loves obedience and not everyone who keeps God's commandments loves them. How, then, is obedience the inseparable companion of charity? And how can it be true that 'He who does not love me does not keep my words'?*

Jn 14:24

We must consider the fact that one sort of obedience can be distinguished from another by one's intention and one's attitude.[30] According to one's intention, obedience can be either true or counterfeit. True [obedience] is in the Truth—that is, in God—and guarantees the hope of reward; but counterfeit [obedience] only pretends to submit to God, and as a result of cupidity, it places the hope of its efforts outside the Truth. [Similarly], according to one's attitude, there is an obedience which is forced and another which is voluntary. It is fear which exacts the former, but passionate love which urges on the latter.

If we consider both attitude and intention in combination, then [we see] there can be a type of obedience which is both forced and true, [an obedience], that is, which is produced by fear of God and which is directed to God. This sort of obedience sometimes involves more fear and less love and, in other cases, more love and less fear, but it always derives something from both, for just as there is never a forced [obedience] without fear, so there is never a true [obedience] without love.

There is also a type of obedience which is both forced and counterfeit. This is produced by fear alone and is not directed to God. So too there is a type of obedience which is both voluntary and counterfeit, such as that of hypocrites. But there is also a type of obedience both voluntary and true, which arises from charity and which, through charity, stretches out toward God. It is this which God looks for,[31] and this that he loves; it is this that he commends by his commandment and his example; and as it is this that he loves, so it is this that he rewards.

But in the case of obedience which is forced and true, although it does not have the [full] freedom of charity because of the attitude of fear which drags it into doing what it does not want [to do], yet it has something of the freedom of charity because of the intention by which it directs itself [to do] what it does wish [to do]. Just as it is aware of its unwilling inclination, it also willingly brings into play its intention.[32] This type of obedience, therefore, is not always reproved but is to some extent approved. If someone is restrained from sin by fear of punishment, he avoids the punishment he deserves because he does not commit the sin which deserves the punishment, and because he directs his intention to God, he deserves something from God in whom he puts his hope. So long as he is restrained from sin by the fear of God, he shows his respect for the fear of God, and in a certain way he dedicates his fear to God and honors God in so doing.

In all fairness and justice, however, it is the obedience which is voluntary and true which should really be shown to God. Just as a rational creature should subject himself to his Creator so that he might will the things which [God] wills simply because He wills it, he should also, in addition to this, will that [God] wills whatever it is that he wills. Let me explain more clearly: if I will what God wills, but not because God wills it, then my will, because it is so much my own, is not yet formed in God's will. If, however, I will what God wills *because* he wills it, then my will has God as its origin and cause and is [consequently] good. But this is especially true if it is my will that [God] wills what he wills. If, however, my will were that he should *not* will what he wills, then however much I might will what he [wills] for the sole reason that he [wills it], I do not yet will it with all my will, because my will is that he should *not* will it, so that I need not will it either.

For example, if I love my enemy because God has so commanded and so wills, then in a certain way what pleases God also pleases me because it pleases God. Nevertheless, it does not please me in every way, since I do not yet love my enemy freely. In fact, I do violence to myself and divide myself against myself: part of me is willing, because loving one's enemies is a good thing and merits a great[33] reward, and part of me is unwilling, because it is difficult to forget an injury one has received and to stop oneself from grumbling about it. And although I may have no intention of seeking revenge in any way, and although my heart is ready to show kindness [to my enemy] when he asks for it or needs it, yet if my heart still whispers and murmurs secretly that I wish God had not commanded this and did not wish us to love our enemies, then I do not yet will fully and perfectly what God commands. But the extent to which obedience falls short of perfection is also the extent to which charity [falls short] of perfection, and if both charity and obedience are to be perfect, then whatever someone realizes he should do to please God, this he should be pleased to do. The reason it should please him is because it is pleasing to God, and its purpose is that God be pleased with him. There is but one purpose for both obedience and charity: to please God—but [only] in those things which are pleasing to God.

I have added this last [provision] because the wicked [also] want to please God, but in things which are pleasing to them and displeasing to God. Thus, there are many who do not love God but who believe that they love God and think that they want to please God. They think about those blessings and promises by which God pleases them, but they give no thought to the things in which they want to please God—the very things, in fact, in which God is displeased with them! They judge charity, not by the virtue of obedience, but by their own personal opinion.[34]

Obedience, however, is the companion of charity, and just as it struggles against a person's own self-will, so it always relies on God's will. And in that first and foremost standard of justice, that form of equity—namely, the will of God—the will of the rational creature is so formed that it still remains its own self, but because it has its source in God according to prevenient grace and strives towards God according to the direction of its intention, it is not unjust to speak of it also as the will of God. No one can derive from his own self the ability to be good, but only from him who says, 'Without me you can do nothing';* and in just the same way, he cannot will what is good except through him who works in you that you might will and accomplish, according to his good will.* When we speak of the power of God, we mean not only that which is in God and which is God, but also that which is given to man by God and which is in man; and in the same way,

Jn 15:5

Ph 2:13

when we speak of the will of God, we mean both that which is in God and which is God and also that which is in man—not, indeed, to the extent [that it derives] from man, but [to the extent] that it is from God. And in addition to all this, we also speak of the will of God [in referring to] whatever he wills be done by man—any act of righteousness or mercy, for example. The full meaning of the will of God, therefore, is, firstly, the will of God which does the commanding; secondly, the will of God in the person whom God commands; and thirdly, the will of God which God commands be done.[35] Authority appertains to the first; service to the second; and to the third, the proof of love.[36]

Obedience, therefore, comprises nothing but the love of God, for it directs itself to the will of God from the will of God through the will of God and returns to the will of God. The will of God which is in God works the will of God in man by the will of God in the commandment because of the will of God in God! The will of God in God, therefore, is the beginning and end of obedience, for someone who obeys in charity yearns for God as for his goal, and it was God who inspired him in the beginning. Inspired by God and yearning for God, he finds in God eternal rest from the labor which he frames in his commandment. *

Ps 93[94]:20

NOTES TO TRACTATE III

1. Title as in PL 417–418. The nature and content of this important tractate would seem to indicate that it dates from Baldwin's years as abbot of Ford.

2. For the etymology of *seraphim*, see Tr. II n. 3.

3. PL 420B has *ad orandum*; Thomas (35/120) reads *ad adorandum*, which is correct.

4. Thomas (35/122, n. 1) compares this with William of St Thierry, Med 3.4 (PL 180:212A): 'Where are you, Lord, where are you? And where, Lord, are you not?' (CF 3:103). The expression is indeed similar, but the context is quite different.

5. Thomas (35/122) omits an essential *non*. The text should read: *nisi ille fecerit non esse tuum* (as in PL 420C).

6. This is a Bernardine idea: see E. Gilson (trans. A. H. C. Downes), *The Mystical Theology of St Bernard* (London, 1940) 36.

7. PL 420D omits 'so far as it is now your own . . . your whole heart' by hom.

8. The term is *beneficia*, 'blessings, favors, kindnesses, benefits'.

9. *Affectiones*. Baldwin usually speaks of *affectus amoris*, not *affectio amoris*, but both words are very difficult to translate. *Affectiones* could be rendered by feelings, affections, types, movements, forms, or manifestations, depending on the context. See also n. 30 below for a further translation. *Affectus*, likewise, covers a wide range of ideas, but in this translation of the tractates we have normally rendered it by 'disposition' or 'inclination', and have provided the Latin wherever it occurs.

10. In the twelfth century, the term *sacramentum* was used in a much broader sense than it is today. As in the early church, 'everything which could be called a "mystery" was to Latin Christians a "sacrament"' (J. F. Bethune-Baker, *An Introduction to the Early History of Christian Doctrine* [London, 1903] 376). For Augustine, for example, a *sacramentum* was simply the visible sign of a sacred thing, whether or not the gift of grace was attached to it. Baldwin's view is not essentially different from this.

11. PL 421C (incorrectly) reads *orare* for *sperare*.

12. Baldwin is playing on words here: being in accord (*concors*) with God means being of one heart (*cor*) with God. We then love God from the heart (*corde*). He continues in this vein in the next sentence: 'remember' is *recordari*, 'to bring back to the heart'.

13. From *discordia* to *concordia*. Baldwin is still playing on the word *cor* 'heart'.

14. *Per hunc incipimus Deo concordare, et cor nostrum Deo dare.* Cf. nn. 12 and 13.

15. I have rendered *modus* here as 'type and measure' since the whole of this paragraph, deeply indebted to Bernard, plays on these two meanings of the word.

16. Baldwin is echoing the beginning of Bernard's *De diligendo Deo* I.1 (see CF 13:93).

17. Baldwin substitutes *fontem* for the Vulgate *fortem*.

18. In this sentence, Baldwin plays on the root SPIR-: *spiritus . . . Spiritus . . . suspirat . . . respiret . . . adspirat*.

19. PL 424C has *flagellantur*; Thomas's text (35/144) follows the Vulgate version of Ps 72:5 and reads *flagellabuntur*.

20. *Disciplina*. See Tr. I, nn. 31, 40.

21. The contrast is between *in flagellis* and *de flagellis*.

22. As Thomas indicates (35/147 n. 1), we have here a liturgical amalgam of Dn 3, 31, 29, 42.

23. *Minister judicis.*

24. *Vigor.*

25. There is a longer discussion on the ideas expressed in this paragraph in Tr. x.

26. Baldwin's argument here is logical, but complex. Expressed symbolically, what he is saying is: if A then B; if B then C; if C then D; if D then E; therefore, if A, then E and D.

27. For the Vulgate *exercebar* (which is imperfect), Baldwin substitutes the future *exercebor*.

28. *Operatio.*

29. *Exercitatio.* Baldwin explains what he means a little further on.

30. Lit. 'by one's *intentio* and one's *affectio*'. On the difficulty of translating *affectio*, see n. 9 above.

31. Or 'It is this which God demands'. The verb is *requirere.*

32. Lit. 'For just as it perceives its *affectio* unwillingly, so it directs its *intentio* willingly'.

33. PL 428C omits *magna.*

34. Lit. 'by the opinion of their own wisdom'.

35. This is a paraphrase of Baldwin's very concise Latin: *Est ergo voluntas Dei, et quae mandat, et cui mandat, et quam mandat fieri.*

36. *Experimentum amoris.* I.e. it is by one's obedience in doing the will of God which he commands be done that one demonstrates one's love for him.

TRACTATE IV
ON THE TWOFOLD RESURRECTION
WHICH IS OBTAINED BY
PERSEVERANCE IN OBEDIENCE[1]

Ps 107:2–3[108:1–2]

*My heart is ready, O God, my heart is
ready; I will sing and give praise in my
glory. Arise, psaltery and harp! I will arise
at dawn!**

WHAT OBEDIENCE can bring about,
where it goes, and where it leads, what
its goal is, and what its fruit is, is revealed to us by the glory of the Lord's resurrection.
The fruit of obedience is resurrection and life through
the obedience of Christ who is the resurrection and
Jn 11:25 the life.*

Christ died but once and only once was raised.
One unique resurrection corresponded to one unique
death. But for us, a single resurrection is not enough.
We are so utterly cast down by the debt of a double
death, we are brought so low, that we cannot find
contentment[2] by a single resurrection.

OF THE TWOFOLD RESURRECTION.[3]

A twofold resurrection is necessary for us: a first
[resurrection] and a second. 'Blessed is he who shares
Rev 20:6 in the first resurrection.'* The first resurrection is
partial; it is of the soul rather than the body. Yet in
a certain way it applies to the body too, but because
the latter is imperfect, it is only in part,[4] and that

which is imperfect always lacks something. 'But when that which is perfect is come, that which is in part shall be put away.'* The second resurrection will involve absolute perfection in which nothing whatever will be lacking.

1 Co 13:10

These two resurrections are distinguished [from each other] in the words of the Lord. [First of all] he says, 'The hour is coming, and now is, when the dead will hear the voice of the Son of God, and those that hear it shall live'.* As compared with eternity, this present life is like an hour. The dead are those who, through disobedience, are separated from God, who is the life of the soul. But because there is accorded us a time for repentance⁵ in the hour of this present life, those who hear the voice of the Lord in obedience will live. They will be raised from death to a good life and raised once more to the life of the blessed.⁶ Thus [the Lord] goes on to refer to the second resurrection: 'The hour is coming when all who are in the tombs will hear the voice of the Son of God'.* This will be the hour when the Lord will come down from heaven with the voice of the archangel and the trumpet of God,* and he will give to his voice the voice of power.* Then those who have done good will come forth to the resurrection of life; but those who have done evil, to the resurrection of judgement.*

Jn 5:25

Jn 5:28

1 Th 4:15
Ps 67:34[68:33]

Jn 5:29

For the good, who are raised to eternal life, there will be in the future a resurrection of life. But there will also be a resurrection of judgement for the wicked. They have no part in the first resurrection, for in the present hour they do not rise up to judge themselves. 'The wicked do not rise again in judgement; nor sinners in the council of the just.'⁷* The wicked are those who do not believe, and whoever

Ps 1:5

Jn 3:18

does not believe is already judged.* As for the sinners, even though they believe, they have no part in the first resurrection, for they live abandoned lives and do not rise again in the council of the just.

What, then, is this council of the just?[8] Listen to the prophet speaking to the Lord: 'Your commandments are my council!'* We therefore have little choice![9] We must judge ourselves. In no way can we avoid judgement! We either judge ourselves here and are therefore [judged] more leniently, or else judged in the future by a wrathful God and therefore more severely! But what does the Apostle say? 'If we would judge ourselves, we would not be judged by the Lord!'* The Lord will not render judgement twice for the same offence. The resurrection of life, therefore, is the second resurrection. But we see that the resurrection of judgement is neither first nor second: it is not the first, for nothing follows it, and not the second, for nothing precedes it.[10]

Ps 118[119]:24

1 Co 11:31

Both forms of our resurrection, the first and the second, have as their cause, their form, their model, and their sacrament, the resurrection of Christ. It is by faith in the resurrection of Christ and by imitating it that we are reformed, justified, sanctified, and raised from the dead, so that being dead to sin, we might live in righteousness.* We walk in newness of life,* waiting to be adopted as children of God, [waiting for] the redemption of our body.* In the second resurrection Christ will reform our lowly body and conform it to his body of glory.*

1 P 2:24
Rm 6:4
Rm 8:23

Ph 3:21

The first resurrection begins with obedience and finds its perfection in perseverance. The second begins with glory and is established in eternity. Whoever perseveres in obedience to the end will persevere in glory for ever, for, in a certain way, perseverance and eternity are similar. Just as eternity is a sort of perseverance of glory, so perseverance is a sort of eternity of obedience. 'For whoever perseveres to the end will be saved.'*

Mt 10:22

It is perseverance which is the glory, the perfection, and, as it were, the virtue of all the virtues. Now charity is also a virtue[11] which is much praised — a virtue, indeed, which deserves much praise for it is the life and virtue of the other virtues — but the virtue of charity is patience, and the virtue of patience is perseverance. Charity without patience is not true charity but an imitation, and imitation charity flourishes in good times but collapses in adversity. Patience without perseverance is inconstant and feeble; it is born in adversity, but it weakens in the course of time, and with prolonged effort it succumbs. But perseverance neither flourishes, nor falls, nor weakens, nor succumbs. It is as if all the other virtues were running in a race, but that which takes the prize is the straight course of perseverance.*

1 Co 9:24

Obedience which perseveres to the end experiences in the first resurrection as much as it truly deserves and in the second will experience the reward which it has earned. In the first, it strives for [the goal] which it wants to reach; in the second, it reaches [the goal] for which it earlier strove.

Of the Obedience of Christ

It was Christ himself who taught this sequence of obedience, perseverance, and glory. When he was in the bosom of the Father, he knew the advantages of obedience and perseverance in obedience and wanted us to know them. He therefore reflected and resolved in his heart to subject himself to the

Ps 68:12[69:11]

yoke of obedience, to assume the habit of humility, to garb himself in sackcloth, to cover his soul with fasting, to take for his vestment a garment of goat-hair,* to give himself up to abuse, to commit himself to obedience, and to persevere in obedience to his death.

What he determined, he did. And just as Abraham left his homeland, his kindred, and his father's house for the land which God had promised him, as he left it all in obedience to the voice of God, so too the Son of God went forth from the highest heaven and his Father's house into the land which his Father had promised him when he said, 'Ask of me, and I will give you the nations for your inheritance and the uttermost parts of the earth for your possession'.*

Ps 2:8

When he came into the world he was clothed in a seamless garment. It was woven [in a single piece] from top to bottom and was given to him by his mother, who wove it with the hand of Wisdom and the finger of God. It was a robe which his Father had prepared for him, but [a robe in which] his mother also cooperated. She was a strong woman, who put out her hand to strong things, and her fingers took hold of the spindle.* She sought wool and flax* and from the choicest material, in a new way, with new skills, made a new garment, a unique product, the like of which no-one on earth can make.

Pr 31:19
Pr 31:13

When Jesus had assumed this garment, it was as if he were girded for total obedience and filled with zest and zeal for his complete submission to humility, and then he said to the Father, 'My heart is ready, O God, my heart is ready!'*

Ps 107:2[108:1]

He said that his heart was ready, but he did not state what it was ready for, and so the phrase, though twice occurring, appears incomplete. The doubling of the phrase, however, is a confirmation of obedience, and the incompleteness of the phrase is a manifestation of perfect obedience. In promising obedience, he bears witness that his[12] heart is completely ready and shows us that there is nothing for which it is not prepared. It is as if he says, 'Father, command what you will! If there is anything you want me to do, my heart is ready. If there is anything you want me to suffer, my heart is ready. If you want me to be scourged, behold! I am ready for the scourges!* If you want me to keep your commandments, I am ready, and I am not troubled in keeping your commandments.'*

Ps 37:18[38:17]

Ps 118[119]:16

This was not the case with Peter, when he said, 'I am ready to go with you to prison and to death'.* But Christ was a rock more steadfast in obedience than Peter[13] and he became obedient to the Father to his death.* 'His heart is ready to hope in the Lord: his heart is strengthened; he will not be moved until he looks down upon his enemies.'*

Lk 22:33

Ph 2:8

Ps 111:7–8[112:8]

After he had declared his obedience, Jesus revealed to us his glory, saying, 'I will sing and give praise in my glory; arise, psaltery and harp!'* The psaltery and harp [symbolize] the joy and exultation of his glorious resurrection, and the song and the psalm [symbolize] praise and thanksgiving for this same glory. Christ will sing in his glory. Now Christ, as the Apostle says, is the power of God and the wisdom of God,* but the Wisdom of God speaks of the Father thus: 'Before he made anything I was with him forming all things. I was delighted every day, playing before him at all times.'* What a vision! What sweet and ineffable joy! In heaven to see the Son of God playing before the Father and to hear him singing—there, where sing the stars of the morning

Ps 107:2–3[108:1–2]

1 Co 1:24

Pr 8:23, 30

Jb 38:7

and all the sons of God shout for joy!* Who of the faithful would not clap his hands in the hope of such a blessed vision, would not dance in his heart, would not raise his voice in exultation?*

Ps 46:2[47:1]

Jesus sings in his glory. But to whom does he sing, and what does he sing? He sings to the Father, he sings to the angels, and he will also sing to us.

To the Father he sings eternal eulogies of praise, psalms of triumph and psalms of exaltation, and a new song, the song of songs, which none can sing save Jesus alone: 'I will extol you, O Lord, for you have sustained me'.* And he sings this: 'For me you have turned my mourning into joy. You have torn up my sack-cloth and have surrounded me with gladness, so that my glory may sing to you, and I may feel no remorse. O Lord my God, I will give praise to you for ever.'*

Ps 29:2[30:1]

Ps 29:12–13[30:11–12]

To the angels he will sing: 'Rejoice, Jerusalem! Celebrate a feast-day, all you that love her!'* One great angel, falling like lightning from heaven,* caused great ruin and drew in his train[14] a third part of the stars.* But Christ, in rising from the dead, will fill up the ruins,* rebuild the walls of Jerusalem,† and complete the number of its citizens. Then there will be joy and exultation among the angels, for if they rejoice over one sinner who is penitent,* how much more [will they rejoice] over the thousands upon thousands who will join them and be like them? 'For the chariot of God is attended by tens of thousands, thousands of them that rejoice.'*

Is 66:10

Lk 10:18

Rev 12:4

Ps 109[110]:6

†Ne 2:17

Lk 15:10

Ps 67:18[68:17]

Finally, Jesus will sing to us. He will sing a song of joy, a song of delight, saying, 'Come, you blessed of my father, possess the kingdom prepared for you from the foundation of the world'.* In the ears of those that hear it, this utterance will be like a song,

Mt 25:34

a melody sung in sweet and delightful tones. Oh, if
only he would let us hear such a voice! If only it
would caress our ears! If only it would come to us!
If only it applied to us,[15] so that we would never be
unworthy of hearing such a wonderful song.[16]

In the meantime, [we pray] that the voice of Jesus
inviting us to him may grow strong in our hearts.
Even now he sings his invitation, saying, 'If anyone
will come after me, let him deny himself, and take
up his cross, and follow me'.* The author of life   Mt 16:24
invites us to life: he calls us from labor to rest, sing-
ing ceaselessly, 'Come to me all you who labor and
are burdened, and I will refresh you'.* All who hear   Mt 11:28
this voice shall live*—even if they are dead. This is   Jn 11:25
the voice[17] that could say but once, 'Lazarus, come
forth!',* and immediately raise from the earth a   Jn 11:43
man dead and buried for four days. Woe to those
who are found to be more deaf than a man four
days dead when the Lord calls to us: 'Come to me,
all you who labor', etc.

Let us cry to each other and exhort [each other] by
our mutual example, 'Come, let us praise the Lord
with joy! Come, let us adore and fall down before
God, and weep before the Lord that made us';*   Ps 94[95]:1, 6
'And let him who hears, say "Come!"'* [Inspired]   Rev 22:17
by the singing of Jesus, let us also sing in the ways of
the Lord, for great is the glory of the Lord.*   Ps 137[138]:5

OF THE SPIRITUAL HARP[18]

Christ, in rising from the dead, awakes the psaltery
and harp. He wakes them for himself, and he wakes
them for us as well. How could we hear the psaltery
and harp unless he awakened them? Whatever we
are within is our own doing;[19] it is lamentable and a
matter for mourning and sorrow. Since the time of

Adam's transgression our harp has been turned to
mourning; joy is eclipsed in our heart, and it is
lamentation, not song, which befits our misery.
Like the children of the exile in the midst of Babylon,
we have hung up our instruments.* 'I shall go to the
gates of hell':* such is the voice of man in the condition of his first birth.[20] But if we are raised in Christ,
then in the first resurrection, glory is given to us,
and psaltery and harp are awakened.

Ps 136:2[137:1]
Is 38:10

On a harp there are many strings arranged in a
certain order, and by the harpists' skill they are so
modulated and tuned that when the harp is sounded
there is one concordant sound from many notes,
one sweet consonance, one melodious harmony.
But if it should happen that one note is somewhat
out of tune,[21] if it sounds out separately and dis-
turbs the concord of the others and disrupts the harmony, the harpist immediately brings into play his
tuning-key[22] and skillfully corrects it. He either
sharpens it or flattens it until harmony is restored
and the string which was previously out of tune is
once more in accord with the others. The harpist,
therefore, is always careful to watch out for this, so
that we do not hear any discord or dissonance
which could offend our ears.

This also applies to our conduct with regard to
each other. The senses of the body and the senses of
the heart which [we have] within us are just like the
strings of a harp. The senses of the heart are like the
limbs of our body, and the way in which we use
and move the one is similar to the way in which we
use and move the other. In the heart there are different thoughts and affections and intentions, different ideas and different opinions, different wishes
and different desires, and it is these which, in us, are
either dissonant or consonant, either in disagreement

or agreement, either discordant or concordant. At the dawn²³ of our resurrection—at the beginning, that is, of our conversion from the vain ways of the world—all these begin to be ordered within us and arranged in their places by the laws of holy obedience, the exercise of daily discipline, and the rule of reason. And if it should happen that something disordered or undisciplined suddenly breaks out—either from the resurgence of an old habit or because of our weak human condition—we immediately correct it with the tuning-key of penitence and discipline so that everything within us is [once again] composed, tranquil, and harmonious. All is then obedient to reason alone, until there is spiritual harmony and spiritual joy, peace and joy in the Holy Spirit,* when the flesh is subjected in obedience to the Spirit, as in the spiritual harp. The joyous harmony and harmonious joy is the music of harpers playing on their harps.*

Rm 14:17

Rev 14:2

If someone strives for peace in others while not being at peace in himself, he does not yet play his own harp, even though he seems to play on the harp of others. But if he is not in accord with himself, with whom can he be in accord? With whom can he be in harmony, if he is at variance with himself, inconsistent with himself, always quarrelling with himself, and always contrary to himself? With whom can he be at peace if he is always disturbed and unquiet, like the raging of the sea which is never at rest?* 'There is no peace for the wicked, says the Lord.'* None of the wicked, therefore, plays upon this harp, but the sound of rejoicing and salvation is in the dwellings of the just.* This is the rejoicing of the just, to whom is said, 'Rejoice in the Lord, you just!'† and 'Give praise on the harp'.*

Is 57:20
Is 48:22

Ps 117[118]:15
†Ps 32[33]:1
Ps 32[33]:2

But why does it say elsewhere, 'Sing praise to the Lord on the harp, on the harp'?*²⁴ What is the

Ps 97[98]:5

meaning of this repetition? Is it because one harp [represents] our own individual conduct, and the other our mutual interaction, one with another? Indeed it is! There are many strings on a harp, and they are not all tuned to the same note, but it is possible to combine a number of them in concord and harmony to produce, as it were, one single sound. Similarly, all of us together are like a harp, each of us separate, but each [responding] to each, as string responds to string. And as often as one of us applies himself with holy zeal and sets an example to another, or, through some service of charity and humility, shows himself worthy of love,²⁵ it is like one string responding to another in the playing of a harp.

No instrument you can think of can produce a more joyous and delightful melody than the sweet and pleasing fellowship [we can enjoy] in the company of the holy assembly. [A fellowship] in which, in Christ and for Christ, each in turn strives to attune himself to the other and in which, to preserve its peace, each adapts himself in all things to the actions of others in humility and patience. Here is no one puffed up with pride, no one consumed with envy, no outbursts of anger, no quarrels or discord, no murmurs of impatience.²⁶ We do not find here perverse distrust, and nothing shameful is ever mentioned. 'Behold', said the Prophet, 'how good and how pleasant it is for brethren to dwell together in unity.'*

Ps 132[133]:1

Those who think that there is more pleasure [to be found] in the vanity of the world than in the truth of Christ are clearly and completely wrong. 'Let them rejoice and be glad', said the Lord, 'who are well pleased with my justice.'* If anyone experiences

Ps 34[35]:27

this, he will not deny it, but man shall say: the just
shall receive the fruit of their works.*

Ps 57[58]:11

The entirety of the reward due to the just for
keeping God's commandments is not, however, reserved for the future. On the contrary. 'In keeping
them there is a great reward. For the commands of
the Lord are right, rejoicing hearts',* and 'at your
right hand there are delights for evermore'.* His
right hand is liberal and generous; it bestows such
pleasures as the world does not know and gives a
peace which the world cannot give.²⁷ But only to
those who do not love the world.*

Ps 18:12, 9[19:11, 8]
Ps 15[16]:11

1 Jn 2:15

See how it is that now, even now in this present
time, [although only] in part, we see clearly how
good it is and how joyful, how useful and beneficial,
how sweet and how delightful, for brethren to dwell
together in unity.* Those whom the love of Christ
has gathered together as one love each other mutually, and each obeys the other in turn. And if they
are awakened daily to the love of God by the examples and encouragements they give each other, if
they serve God with one accord, and with one heart
sing eternal praises to him with chosen lip,* if all
desire the same and are all averse to the same, if all
feel the same and have the same understanding, if
they have one heart and one soul, are they not a
spiritual harp, and do they not rejoice in God and in
themselves? 'Blessed is the people that knows this
jubilation!'*²⁸

Ps 132[133]:1

Zeph 3:9

Ps 88:16[89:15]

Of the Spiritual Psaltery

At the dawn of our resurrection, Christ awakes
for us not only the harp, but also the psaltery. And
even though I have here spoken first of the harp,

which seemed to me to need some discussion, it is the psaltery [which he awakes] first. 'Awake', he says, 'psaltery and harp.'* As Father Augustine tells us, the sound-board of the psaltery is on the top, whereas that of the harp is on the bottom.[29] The harp, as we have already shown, is that joyful harmony [which we have] either within ourselves or with our brethren. The psaltery is peace and harmony with God and in God. Of this peace the Apostle says, 'Since we are justified by faith, let us have peace with God'.* By the sin of disobedience man began to be at odds both with God and with himself, and by the just judgement of God, he who did not want peace with God did not find peace in himself. As it is written, 'You have set me against you, and I am become a burden to myself'.* Man, therefore, who did not wish to be united with God, is divided in himself, for disobedience separates the soul from God and is the death of the soul. But in the first resurrection that death is swallowed up in victory,* for it is by obedience that the soul is restored to life and united with God.

The soul, therefore, occupies a sort of middle position between God and the flesh; it is united to God above itself and united to the flesh below itself. The former union can be dissolved by the will but not by force; the latter can be dissolved by force, but not by the will. The soul cannot leave the body, even if it wants to, unless it has been wrenched away by the force of some tremendous pain, but in the case of a soul which is more perfectly united with God, there is no force, no violence, no intensity of pain which can bring about a separation. 'Who shall separate us from the love of Christ?' says the Apostle. 'For I am sure that neither death, nor

Ps 107:3[108:2]

Rm 5:1

Jb 7:20

1 Co 15:54

life, nor angels, nor principalities, nor powers, nor
things present, nor things to come, nor might, nor
height, nor depth, nor any other creature shall be
able to separate us from the charity of God.'* All of
these things, or even any one of them, had the
power to separate Paul's soul from his body, but not
all of them together [could separate it] from the
charity of God.

My beloved brethren, you who are so zealous for
God, see how strong is this union, how it cannot be
broken by any cause, save only the will of the soul
itself. 'He who is joined to the Lord is one spirit
[with him].'*

It is written that the soul of Jonathan was joined
to the soul of David, and Jonathan loved him as his
own soul.* David and Jonathan made a covenant,
and Jonathan stripped himself of the garment he
was wearing and gave it to David, and the rest of his
garments too, even his sword and his bow and his
girdle.* If Christ is the true David, why then do we
not see in Jonathan, the friend of David, one who
truly emulates[30] Christ? He abandoned all for the
sake of God and even gave his garments to him with
whom he joined himself.* This was the sign of the
covenant he made with David. But was Christ ignorant of the way to make a covenant? Is it not he
who, through the Prophet, says to certain people, 'I
will make their work in truth, and I will make a perpe-
tual covenant with them'?* The soul of Jonathan
was joined, was 'glued', to the soul of David—and
with what glue but the glue of love?[31] By the glue of
charity the soul of a just person is so glued to God
as to be joined to him inseparably. This is why the
Psalmist says: 'It is good for me to be joined to my
God'.*

Rm 8:35, 38–39

1 Co 6:17

1 S 18:1

1 S 18:3–4

2 Tm 2:4

Is 61:8

Ps 72[73]:28

The same [Psalmist], however, considers both the union of soul and body and also that of the soul and God. Of the former he says, 'My soul has cleaved to the floor',* and of the latter he says to God, 'My soul has cleaved to you'.* The flesh is the floor of this house of clay in which we dwell, we who have an earthly foundation. The soul cleaves to this foundation by inclination, but if it is too attached, it becomes subjected to it and dies. It becomes so far separated from God that it holds no longer the middle place, but the lowest of all, as if it were now buried in the earth and entombed beneath the floor. Thus, after the Prophet said, 'My soul has cleaved to the floor', he added, 'Give me life according to your word!'*

[The soul] receives life, however, only if it is subjected to God and not the flesh. One who is just, therefore, can truly say: 'My soul has cleaved to you'.* It has cleaved to you and preferred you to itself; it has neglected itself for you, so that it may love you more than itself. But it is not for its own sake that it loves you like this; it is for your sake that it loves itself![32] O Lord, God of my salvation,* this I pray: draw me after you in such a way* that my soul may cleave to you!

This union of the soul and God is far closer than the other [union]; it is much more binding and, as it were, much more inward, for God is in the soul and the soul is in God. The soul is also in the flesh, but the flesh is not in the soul. The soul is certainly in the flesh, and in the flesh it lives and senses. But the flesh is not in the soul. It does not live in it, and it does not sense in it, even though it receives from it its capacity for living and sensing. It is the soul which gives life

Ps 118[119]:25
Ps 62:9[63:8]

Ps 118[119]:25

Ps 62:9[63:8]

Ps 87:2[88:1]
Sg 1:3

to the body and bestows upon it movement and sensation. By movement, it carries out its tasks and attends to itself by using the body to do what it wants. By sensation, it is able to perceive pleasures and sufferings, either painfully or pleasurably. For the five senses of the body, each in its own individual way, have a knowledge of sensible objects and are brought into play in experiencing pain or pleasure. But whereas the flesh and the soul have their own individual delights and discomforts, which they feel in themselves either pleasurably or painfully, they rejoice together and suffer together at the changing course of things, both good and bad. The soul is consumed with misery at the things which the flesh suffers in anguish and is overjoyed at those which give the flesh delight and pleasure. But when, as often happens, the soul feels a sense of delight at the unlawful pleasures of the flesh, it becomes jealous of its own integrity and separates itself from them by the restraint of reason. In a marvellous manner, it wills in a certain way, or wants to will, what it does not fully will because of its disapproval; and when the desires of the flesh are contrary to those of the spirit, and those of the spirit to the flesh, then, in some extraordinary way which cannot be explained, the soul, as it were, is divided against itself: it wants to satisfy the will of the spirit and wants just as much to satisfy the will of the flesh. It is troubled, therefore, and tormented within itself. It longs to carry out the will of the flesh and yet withholds its approval or consent. It loves the flesh so much that it grieves over its vicissitudes, and it is troubled when its will—which it is not itself willing to carry out—is not satisfied.

OF THE FIVE SPIRITUAL SENSES[33]

When it is wonderfully united to God by the love of obedience, the soul lives and senses in him and by him, and it draws a sort of analogy with the things it knows through the bodily senses. Thus, by the grace of a most inward inspiration, it senses God within itself and touches him spiritually by faith, smells him by hope, tastes him by charity, hears him by obedience, and sees him by contemplation.

OF SPIRITUAL TOUCH

Touch refers to faith, for it is faith which grasps things.[34] Thus, the woman in the Gospel who was suffering from a flow of blood believed that she would be cured if she touched but the hem of Jesus' garment. She may not have known that she symbolized the touch of faith, but when, in her belief, she touched it, the Lord said, 'Who touched me?' And when his disciples were astonished that Jesus, who was so hedged in by the crowd, said that he had been touched, he added, 'Somebody touched me'.*

Lk 8:45–46

And when he had been raised from the dead, he said to Mary, 'Do not touch me, for I am not yet ascended to my Father'.* It was not the spiritual touch that he forbade, but the corporeal, for if Mary had touched the man and therefore, because she put too much faith in the corporeal touch, did not believe that Jesus was the equal of the Father, the spiritual touch [of faith] would have been hindered by the corporeal. In [her] heart, Jesus had not yet ascended to equality with the Father, since she did not yet believe that he was indeed his equal. If, in her heart, Jesus had already ascended to the Father,

Jn 20:17

then there is no doubt that Mary, at that moment, would have touched Jesus with the hand of faith. But because it was after this that Mary touched Jesus spiritually, he forbade that touch which could have hindered or weakened faith. Nevertheless, his refusal to let her touch him was not absolute. It was deferred until the time of his visible or spiritual ascension, so that Mary would then know herself that she truly touched Jesus when, by the hand of faith, she began to comprehend his divinity and his equality with the Father. For the touch of faith not only apprehends the humanity of Christ, but by handling it reverently,* it also comprehends the whole of his divinity.

Cf. 1 Jn 1:1

It was not unusual for Mary to touch Jesus, nor was she aware of having recently offended Christ in some way so that [as a result] she should believe that he had forbidden her such a familiar approach. But when he said to Mary 'Do not touch me', he did not say it in the same way as was said to certain others, 'Do not touch my anointed!'[35]* The pursuit of malice is one thing, and the service which stems from devotion another.

Cf. Ps 104[105]:15

In Mary the sinner, we sinners find a double consolation, both when she was permitted to touch Jesus and when she was forbidden to touch him. Do not despair of forgiveness! It is true that we have sinned much[36] and in many things we all offend,* but Mary sinned [too], and yet Jesus permits her to touch him and admits her to the grace of [his] friendship. See how this raises our hopes! It was not granted us to see Christ in the flesh or to handle him with our hands,* but yet we need not despair. To Thomas he said: 'Blessed are they that have not seen and have believed';* and to Mary too he said: 'Touch

Jm 3:2

1 Jn 1:1

Jn 20:29

Jn 20:17

me not'.* See how this also raises our hopes and
offers us an abundance of consolation! The touch
which he permitted Thomas has the power to dispel
doubt and establish faith in the resurrection, but the
touch which he forbade Mary also, in a certain
way, provides consolation for us, because it was not
granted us to touch Jesus either. To the former he
gave permission since it was necessary for someone
who did not yet believe; to the latter, permission
was refused, since it was unnecessary for someone
who already believed. Even then Mary believed in
the resurrection. What she did not believe in was
the glory of Jesus in his equality with the Father, a
glory which would be declared to the world by his
wonderful ascension. But because she was being led

Rm 1:17

from faith to faith,* she was then told of the glory
of the ascension, so that she who was [already]
aware of the resurrection would know in advance of
the ascension yet to come. For Mary, therefore, the
bodily touch — that with which she touches the feet

Cf. Lk 7:38
Mt 28:9

of Jesus* — is not necessary; but when Jesus said to
the women, 'I give you greeting',* Mary was given
permission to touch him for a certain mysterious
reason. The touch which was required of her was
the spiritual [touch], that with which she touches his
head — in other words, his incomprehensible divinity
in which he is the equal of the Father in all things.

It is clear from all that we have so far said that the
spiritual touch refers to faith. It is one of the five
senses by which the soul is united with God and
perceives God. The soul perceives God in five ways
and in five ways is perceived by God. There is therefore a total of ten ways, for the ten-stringed psaltery
is provided with ten strings. This is the delightful

psaltery which accompanies the harp,* [the psaltery]
which Christ raised up with himself when he rose
from the dead, saying, 'Awake, psaltery and harp! I
will arise at dawn.'*

The soul perceives God, as we have said, by
touching him with the hand of faith, and God perceives the soul by touching it with the hand of various graces. He touches it, for instance, [in moving
it] to tearful penitence,³⁷ and he lays low the swelling
of pride as though it were a mountain.* This is why
it is written: 'Touch the mountains, and they shall
smoke'.* The smoke which is sweetest to the Lord
[rises] from a contrite and humble heart,* but it is a
smoke which is bitter to the eyes and wrings from
them tears of remorse. [God] touches the place of
the leprosy to heal it,* he touches and caresses the
head with manifold consolations, he touches the
eyes to enlighten them, he touches the cheeks to
make them rosy, he touches the neck to make it like
jewels,* he touches the breasts so that they will not
be dry and without milk, and he puts his hand
through the opening that our heart may be moved.*
Finally, the bridegroom touches the whole of the
bride with the sort of freedom of those who are
married; he talks with her, he joins himself to her
with kisses, he clasps her in his embrace. But yet his
touch is the purest [of touches] and purifies by its
touch, and whatever he touches is kept wholly
chaste, inviolate, and untouched. For the bridegroom
is full of zeal* for the bride to whom he has be-
trothed himself in faith, as it is written: 'I will betroth
you to me for ever. I will betroth you to me in justice
and judgement, in mercy and commiseration. I will
betroth you to me in faith.'*

Ps 80:3[81:2]

Ps 107:3[108:2]

Is 40:4

Ps 143[144]:5
Ps 50:18[51:17]

2 K 5:11

Sg 1:9

Sg 5:4

1 K 19:10

Ho 2:19–20

OF THE SPIRITUAL SENSE OF SMELL

It is also through [the sense of] smell that the soul perceives God and is perceived by God. It smells the sweetness of God[38] by hope and by longing for God. This is the hope that his promise will be fulfilled, as the blossom is fulfilled in the fruit, for the scent of the blossom is the hope and expectation of the fruit. In hope we await the promises of God, which are fragrant as perfumes and sweetly redolent. In the midst of the afflictions of this present life we breathe in the fragrance of his promises for our comfort, and by their fragrance we are drawn to persevere to the end unremittingly. Otherwise we might wander from the path and be diverted from our proposed undertaking.

This is why the bride says to the bridegroom: 'Draw me after you; we will run to the odor of your perfumes'.* The bride scents the virtues of the bridegroom as if they were precious perfumes, but she scents them in the hope of imitating them. Since she is stimulated by the example of the bridegroom, she hopes in some way to follow the tracks which he leaves. But she does not presume to follow him in this way by herself, as if by her own power. She perceives the fragrance by which she knows he is present, and in the hope that he will come to her aid, she says, 'Draw me after you; we will run to the odor of your perfumes'.

If we offer [ourselves] as a living sacrifice, pleasing to God, in an odor of sweetness,* if we burn the frankincense of devotion or the incense of pure prayer on the glowing coals of charity in the censer of our hearts, if the smoke of the perfumes ascends before the face of God,* then he smells the sweetest

Sg 1:3

Rm 12:1

Rev 8:4

of savors,* and perceives the devotion of a soul which burns in itself with holy desire, a devotion which enables the soul in its turn to perceive him.[39]

Gn 8:21

Of the Spiritual Sense of Taste

It is through love, as if through taste, that [the soul] perceives and is perceived. Christ says, 'My food is to do the will of my Father',* and he shows us elsewhere what the will of his Father is: 'This is the will of the Father who sent me—that I should lose nothing of all that he has given me'.* It is clear from this that God is fed and refreshed by his love of our salvation, and when the soul tastes the sweetness of God,* it is this love which feeds and refreshes it.

Jn 4:34

Jn 6:39

Ps 33:9[34:8]

Of the Spiritual Sense of Hearing

It is through hearing that God perceives and is perceived when he hears and is heard. But he is heard through obedience,[40] for if he is obeyed, then he hears and grants our prayers and supplications, petitions, wishes, and desires.

We say to God, 'Hear my words, O Lord',* and God says to us, 'Listen to the words of my mouth'.* If you hear God, God hears you; but if you do not hear him, he does not grant [your prayers]. This is why it is written: 'If anyone refuses to hear the Law, his prayer shall be an abomination'.*

Ps 5:2
Ps 77 [78]:1

Pr 28:9

Of the Spiritual Sense of Sight

It is through sight that God perceives and is perceived. It is said of the just, 'The eyes of the Lord are upon the just',* and the just man says, 'My eyes are always [turned] towards the Lord'.* The wicked,

Ps 33:16[34:15]
Ps 24[25]:15

Ps 81[82]:5

Ps 53:5[54:3]
Pr 15:3

Am 9:4

however, walk in darkness* and do not see God, and of them it is written: 'They have not put God before their eyes'.* 'But the eyes of the Lord see the good and the evil wherever they are.'* They gaze upon the just with a tender and caressing glance, but to the wicked he says, 'My eyes are upon you for evil, and not for good'.

As we have shown already, the spiritual harp is constructed from the senses of the body and the senses of the soul, mutually harmonized through the obedience of the flesh subject to the spirit. [Similarly], the ten-stringed spiritual psaltery is constructed from the five spiritual senses by which the soul senses God and consents to God[41] and the five ways in which God perceives the soul spiritually. When God touches the five upper strings on the psaltery, he sings praises to the soul; and when the soul touches the five lower [strings], it sings praises to God, delighting God and finding its delight in God.

Jn 3:8

God touches the psaltery when he breathes his grace upon it. He is the Breath of Life[42] and breathes where he will, and the soul hears his voice.* Then, so as to make the lower string respond to the upper string, [the soul] returns thanks for the grace it has received,[43] touching him who touches it, scenting him who scents it, tasting him who tastes it, hearing and contemplating him who hears and contemplates it.

Sg 2:14
Ph 2:13

But it is God who comes first to us and sings to us the first song. [It is God] who, accompanied by measured harmonies, like a harpist playing his harp, says, 'Let your voice sound in my ears, for your voice is sweet'.* God works [in us] both to will and to accomplish,* and by moving the soul inwardly so

that it believes and hopes and loves and obeys, he
enables it always to see him whom it loves and perceive him who perceives it; in other words, [the soul
is so moved] that it can always give its consent to
the will of God.[44]

It is not, therefore, to no purpose, not without
reason, that the Psalmist five times repeats [his invi-
tation] to sing praises to God. 'Sing praises to our
God', he says, 'sing praises. Sing praises to our King,
sing praises. God is the king of all the earth, sing
praises wisely.*   Ps 46[47]:6–7

There is also a specific reason for his adding at the
end [the word] 'wisely'. 'The fear of the Lord is the
beginning of wisdom.'* Someone who sings praises   Ps 110[111]:10
wisely is someone who rejoices in the Lord, but
who always fears the danger of falling. 'For blessed
is the man that is always fearful'.* This is why the   Pr 28:14
Prophet says: 'Let my heart rejoice so that it may
fear your name',* and again, 'Love the Lord with   Ps 85[86]:11
fear, and rejoice in him with trembling'.* Thus,   Ps 2:11
although it is proper for the soul to perceive God
through fear, this fear should not separate it from
the five spiritual senses which we discussed earlier.
It is united with each and regulates and maintains
the overall spiritual harmony so that it does not
relapse into the danger of discord through careless-
ness and laxity.

Let us return now to the text with which we began.
It is the voice of Christ professing obedience and offering service to God his Father: 'My heart is ready,
O God; my heart is ready'. We may see in this repetition a two-fold obedience: that of the soul subjected to God and that of flesh humbled even to the
shame of the cross. But what follows is the voice of
Christ rejoicing in the glory of his resurrection: 'I

will sing and give praise in my glory. Arise, psaltery and harp!' Christ had a double glory and a double joy: the glory of the soul (which is the psaltery on which he plays) and the glory of the flesh (which is the harp with which he sings), and he therefore praises God on the ten-stringed psaltery and with his singing upon the harp.

For us who have been raised with Christ, this same saying[45] can be applied both to our first resurrection and our second. It is the voice of someone who repents, who returns to obedience and promises obedience: 'My heart is ready, O God; my heart is ready'. It is ready to perform good works, ready to sustain the wicked, ready to begin, ready to persevere, ready for the obedience of the soul which should be in your service, O God; ready for the obedience of the flesh which should be subject to the spirit.

Those who are obedient and serve God are given a double joy in accordance with their double obedience: [the joy which comes] from the obedience and peace of the flesh with regard to the spirit (which is called the harp) and [that which comes] from the peace and obedience of the spirit with regard to God (which is called the psaltery). With these spiritual instruments, man is justified by God through penitence, and since he is raised from death to life, he sings and gives praise in his glory: 'I will sing', he says, 'and give praise in my glory'.

The first resurrection has its glory: the glory of the flesh and the glory of the soul. Let us consult the Apostle on each of these glories. Of the present glory of the flesh he says, 'God forbid that I should glory, except in the cross of our Lord Jesus Christ',* and again, 'If I must glory, I will glory in the things that concern my infirmity'.* But of the glory of the

Ga 6:14

2 Co 11:30

soul he says, 'Our glory is the testimony of our conscience',* and again, 'We glory in the hope of our
adoption as children of God'.46*

2 Co 1:12
Cf. Rm 5:2

The second resurrection will also have its glory:
the glory of the soul in the vision of God, when it
shall see God in his glory and the glory of the flesh
in its incorruption, when what is corruptible shall
put on incorruption and what is mortal shall put on
immortality.* Each of the saints will have a double
vestment. They will be clothed in white and hold
psaltery and harp. They will sing and give praise in
their glory, singing together eternal praises to God.
Their mouth shall be filled with gladness and their
tongue with joy,* to the praise and honor of our
Lord Jesus Christ, who is above all things,
God, for ever blessed.
Amen.*

1 Co 15:54

Ps 125[126]:2

Rm 9:5

NOTES TO TRACTATE IV

1. Title as in PL 429–430. It is fairly certain that this tractate dates from Baldwin's years at Ford. The brief allusions to the nature and benefits of the common life (see nn. 26 and 28) are elaborated at length in Tr. xv.

2. Thomas (36/16) reads *contenti esse*; PL 429C has *beati esse*.

3. This subtitle occurs in the manuscripts, but not in PL.

4. Thomas's text (36/18) accidentally omits *ex parte est*. PL 429C is correct here.

5. An expression borrowed from the liturgy. See Thomas 36/19, n. 2.

6. The second half of this sentence has been omitted in PL 429D by hom.

7. Ps 1, 5 with the tense of *resurgere* changed from future (*resurgent*) to present (*resurgunt*).

8. Baldwin is playing on words here: *consilium* means both council / assembly and counsel / advice.

9. Lit. 'Our situation is straitened'.

10. I.e. the resurrection of judgement may take one of two forms: (a) if we judge ourselves, we will not be judged by God (judgement is not followed by judgement); or (b) if we do not judge ourselves, God will judge us (judgement is not preceded by judgement). But in neither case are there two judgements.

11. PL 431A omits *virtus*.

12. For *cor suum*, PL 432A reads *cor meum*.

13. There is a play on words here: *Petrus* 'Peter' is linked with *petra* 'a rock', as in Mt 16:18.

14. Lit. 'His tail drew the third part of the stars' (Rv 12:4). The text is referring to the seven-headed, ten-horned dragon.

15. Or 'if only it reached us'. The verb is *pertinere*.

16. Lit. 'May we not deserve to be separated from such a good hearing'.

17. Thomas (36/36) has *vox una*; PL 433B reads *vox tua*.

18. PL 433C (incorrectly) has *creatura* instead of *cithara*. See Thomas 36/38, n. 1.

19. Lit. 'Whatever is in us is from us'.

20. I.e. his natural birth. The second birth, in which we are raised in Christ (= the first resurrection), is baptism.

21. *Raucius*.

22. The text reads *plectrum*, but it is difficult to see how it could be referring to a plectrum in the normally accepted sense. The medieval *cithara*, unlike the *psalterium*, was played with the fingers, not a plectrum, and in any case, in neither instrument was a plectrum used to adjust the tension of the strings. A T-shaped tuning-key, however, appears in a remarkable number of portrayals of medieval harps and harpers, and it may well be that Baldwin's comments in this paragraph reflect the fact that medieval harpers had great difficulty in keeping their instruments in tune. Since the strings at this time were of animal gut, this is not surprising. For an illustration of a tuning-key being used on a ten-stringed *cithara*, see D. Munrow, *Instruments of the Middle Ages and Renaissance* (Oxford, 1976) 21.

23. This is an allusion to the basic text of Baldwin's sermon, 'I will arise at dawn'.

24. The PL text (434C) is corrupt here.

25. Lit. 'renders himself loveable'.

26. This same passage appears word for word in Baldwin's fifteenth tractate: see Tr. xv, n. 18.

27. A liturgical phrase deriving from Jn 14:27.

28. Once again, similar ideas and similar expressions may be found in Tractate xv: see Tr. xv, n. 18.

29. See Augustine, *Enarratio in Psalmum* 56. 16 (PL 36:671–672) and *Enarratio in Ps*. 32. II. I. 5 (PL 36:280–281).

30. *Verus Christi aemulator*. An *aemulator Christi* is someone who zealously imitates Christ: see Tr. x, n. 2.

31. The idea of *gluten amoris / dilectionis* occurs fairly frequently in twelfth-century spiritual writings. We also find it in Augustine (*Confessiones* IV. x. 15; PL 32:700), but here, Baldwin is echoing the biblical text of 1 S 18: 1 'Anima Ionathae *conglutinata est animae David*' ('The soul of Jonathan was knit to the soul of David' in RSV).

32. Baldwin is thinking of the fourth degree of love in Bernard's *De diligendo Deo* x. 27. See CF 13:119–120.

33. This subtitle is omitted in PL 437BC.

34. The verb is *comprehendere*, 'to grasp, seize, take hold of', either physically or mentally.

35. Ps 104[105]:15 reads literally, 'Touch not my christs (*christos meos)'*. *Christus* is here being used with its etymological meaning of 'annointed'.

36. A phrase from the liturgy. See Thomas 36/63, n . 1.

37. There are three variant readings here: (a) following MS Troyes 876: *Tamquam ad lacrimosam poenitentiam* . . . (see Thomas 36/66); (b) following MS Troyes 433: *Tangit cor ad lacrimosam poenitentiam* . . . (see Thomas 36/67, n. 2); and (c) following PL 438D: *Tangit tamquam ad lacrymosam poenitentiam* . . . .

38. PL 439B omits *Dei*.

39. Lit. 'by which he too is perceived'.

40. 'To hear' (*audire*) is linked etymologically with 'to obey' (*obedire = ob-audire*).

41. The association of *sentire* and *consentire* occurs a number of times in Baldwin. See Tr. IV, n. 44; Tr. VI, n. 35; and Tr. IX / iv, n. 5.

42. The Latin simply has *Spiritus est* (Jn 4: 24), but I have rendered it as 'Breath of Life' so as to bring out Baldwin's play on words.

43. A play on words impossible to render satisfactorily into English: 'having received grace (*gratia*), one returns thanks (*gratia*)'.

44. Baldwin's thought is less logical in English than it is in Latin. Once again, there is a play on words: . . . *sentientem sentiens, hoc est voluntati Dei semper consentiens*. Cf. n. 41 above.

45. Thomas (36/80) has *ipsa vox*; PL 441B reads *prima vox*.

46. Rm 5:2 actually reads 'Gloriamur in spe *gloriae* filiorum Dei'. Baldwin has borrowed his *adoptionis* from Rm 8:15.

ON THE REST WHICH CHRIST
HAS SOUGHT AND PREPARED
FOR HIMSELF AND FOR US[1]

*In all these things I sought rest, and I will
abide in the inheritance of the Lord. Then
the Creator of all things commanded and
spoke to me.[2] And he that made me rested
in my tabernacle, and he said to me, 'Let
your dwelling be in Jacob and your inheritance in Israel, and take root in my elect.'**

Si 24:11–13

WE SEE in [the twenty-fourth chapter of
the book of] Ecclesiasticus the Wisdom
of God, in whom all things are renewed
and restored, declaring and relating certain of his
mighty achievements, wonderful and marvelous,
and then adding [the words], 'In all these things I
sought rest'.

Christ is the power of God and the wisdom of
God. But God is a certain supreme peace and supreme
rest, for he is always the same, always immutable
and unchanging. With him there is no change,*
since he is not changed from what he was, nor any
shadow of variation,* since he will not be changed
from what he is. Variation, indeed, is the changeable condition of a changeable thing, and it cannot
in any way be applied to God. He is not affected by
the rise and fall of different passions nor found to be
subject to a succession of variations. Just as he is

Jm 1:17

Ibid.

always that which he is, so he always remains the same.[3]

He is therefore always stable and at rest, and he who cannot be at variance with himself has no need to seek rest within himself. But yet[4] he says, 'In all these things I sought rest'. For whom, then, has he sought rest? For himself, or for us? Or is it rather both for himself and for us? This is clearly the case. In everything God has done for us since the creation, he sought rest for himself in us and [rest] for us in him. Everything which he created or founded or made for man was done to glorify man in him or to glorify himself in man and to enable each of them to find that rest which is sought in so many ways, God pleasing man in all things, and man displeasing God in nothing.

If we consider the course of time from creation [onwards], we find that sometimes God effects things but does not labor;[5] sometimes he labors but does not effect things; and sometimes he effects things by laboring or labors by effecting them. In creating the world, God effects something but does not labor, and on the seventh day [therefore] he does not rest from labor but from effecting things. In this he has provided us with an illustration of how, before sin [came into the world], he effected things without labor and afterwards rested. For this reason he placed man in Paradise to effect things in it and to preserve it.* After [the advent of] sin, however, God labors in the perverse conduct of men but effects nothing, since he is not the maker, but the hater, of wickedness. Thus, through Isaiah, he condemns the deeds of certain wicked men, even though they seem to have been done in his honor: 'I am weary with the labor of enduring them'.* And

Gn 2:15

Is 1:14

Is 43:24

Ps 73[74]:12

Is 1:16

1 P 5:6

Is 66:21

Mt 11:29

Ps 4:9[8]

Rv 14:13

1 Tm 2:4

Mt 11:28

elsewhere, through the same prophet, 'You have served me with your sins and have caused me weary labor with your iniquities'.*

But in coming into the world, God both effects things and labors. He effects salvation in the midst of the earth,* and he labors even to death, and through [his death] he brings about the end of his own labors and equally [the end] of ours.

[On the one hand], therefore, there is the labor of enduring our sins and [on the other] the labor of suffering on account of our sins. God rests from the labor of endurance when he brings about in us what is taught through the prophet: 'Cease to act perversely',* for at our conversion6 we begin to be humbled under the mighty hand of God,* to be at peace with the Lord, and to tremble at his words. In this way, he too rests in us, as he himself bears witness, saying, 'Upon whom shall my spirit rest, but on one who is humble and at peace, and who trembles at my words?'* And we rest in him, as he says again, 'Learn from me, for I am gentle and humble of heart, and you shall find rest for your souls'.* God rests from the labor of suffering, as he himself says: 'In peace will I sleep and rest in him who is ever the same'.* And we too shall rest from our labors after death: 'Blessed are the dead who die in the Lord. Now and from henceforth, says the Spirit, may they rest from their labors.'*

'In all these things I sought rest.'7 It is as if he says, 'In all my works I have sought rest for myself: for myself in all, and for all in me, to the full extent of my capacity.' 'For God wants everyone to be saved and to come to the knowledge of the truth.'*

But although he says to all, 'Come to me all you that labor and are burdened',* it is not in all that he

finds rest. He finds rest in those who were known
in advance as belonging to the Lord's inheritance,
and he therefore adds, 'I shall abide in the inheritance of the Lord'.* 'Blessed is the nation where
God is the Lord, the people whom he has chosen
for his inheritance.'* This inheritance is that of
which it is written, 'The Lord has chosen Sion; he
has chosen it for his dwelling. Here will I dwell for I
have chosen it. This is my rest for ever and ever.'*

Si 24:11

Ps 32[33]:12

Ps 131[132]:13–14

This is the inheritance which the Father gave to
[the Son] when he asked him for it. He said to him,
'Ask of me, and I will give you the nations as your
inheritance and the uttermost parts of the earth for
your possession'.* But the Son's request was to lift
up his hands on the cross and to utter this prayer:
'Let my prayer be directed as incense in your sight,
and the lifting up of my hands as evening sacrifice'.*
Thus, by the Father's command and injunction, the
Son gained for himself the possession of this inheritance by his blood. Therefore he now says, 'Then
the Creator of all things commanded and spoke to
me'.* [The word] 'then' refers to time, not to eternity,
and it is as if he says, 'When the time is fulfilled, and
I gain the inheritance in which I have remained,
long[8] awaiting and desiring it, then I said, "Behold, I
come."'* It is then that the Creator of all things
commanded and spoke to me. He commanded me
as a servant, as one less than he according to humanity, and he spoke to me as a son, as his equal according to divinity.

Ps 2:8

Ps 140[141]:2

Si 24:12

Ps 39:8[40:7]

Just what he commanded, however, or what he
said is not clearly stated but must be deduced from
what follows. The same thing occurs elsewhere.
When it says, [for example], 'Command your
strength, O God,'* there is no statement of what he

Ps 67:29[68:28]

wished to command of his strength (that is, of Christ), but we understand from what follows that [he wanted] to confirm what he has already effected in us. And in another place, when we read, 'He spoke, and they were made; he commanded, and they were created',* what he said and what he commanded is shown from the context but is not plainly stated. In the same way, then, we understand [from the passage we are at present discussing] that God the Father, Creator of All, commanded and said to Christ that he should be created after the manner of men. This is why he says through Isaiah, 'Let justice spring up together: I the Lord have created him'.*

Pss 32[33]:9, 148:5

Is 45:8

Furthermore, in order to make known to us the nature of this command, the Son himself makes mention in this same passage of the Father, the Creator of all, saying of him, 'He that made me rested in my tabernacle'. It is as if he said, 'By so commanding me, the Creator of all created me and rested within me'. [God] also says of him, 'This is my beloved Son, in whom I am well pleased'.* By his tabernacle he means the humanity he assumed, [the tabernacle] in which he fought so valiantly and vanquished the powers of the air,[9] the tabernacle in which the Father himself also rested, since God was in Christ, reconciling the world to himself.* The Father rested in the Son to establish the beginning of the rest he desires and afterwards to perfect the rest he desires through the mystery of the incarnation.

Mt 3:17

2 Co 5:19

The way in which the Son himself should prepare his rest in his inheritance is made clear to us when he says, 'And he said to me, "Let your dwelling be in Jacob and your inheritance in Israel, and take root in my elect."' The Son [thereby] shows us that there

are three things which the Father has said to him
and enjoined upon him, and, if you like, we can
relate these three things to [the passage] we quoted
earlier: 'Then he commanded and spoke to me'. In
this passage we have only a brief allusion to the incarnation, but we are now told more precisely what
it was that his Father commanded and said to him.
And even though this earlier passage does contain
the two phrases 'he commanded' and 'and he said',
the reference is so brief and fleeting that he now
repeats 'and he said' to reveal exactly what was said
and what was commanded with regard to the preparation of his rest in his inheritance.[10]

Thus, there are three [virtues], faith, hope, and
charity, and by them the hearts of the elect are prepared for Christ to rest in them. And to these three
[virtues] correspond very neatly the three expressions [from the verse we are at present discussing]:
'your dwelling', 'your inheritance', and 'your root'.

'Your dwelling' appertains to faith; as the Apostle
says, 'May he grant you, according to the riches of
his glory, to be strengthened by his spirit with might
in the inner man, so that Christ may dwell by faith
in your hearts'.* 'Your inheritance' corresponds to   Eph 3:17
hope, since an inheritance which is promised is not
yet seen, not yet possessed in actuality, but only
held in hope. The inheritance of the just is Christ,
and meanwhile [in their time on earth], they inherit
in hope him to whom the Father says, 'Make your
inheritance in Israel', which is the same as saying,
'Become the inheritance of Israel'. And he adds,
'Take root in my elect', which corresponds to charity.
This is why the Apostle says, 'being rooted in charity'.*   *Ibid.*

By these three virtues God prepares for himself
rest in his inheritance and in the people whom he

Ps 32[33]:12

Dt 32:9

has chosen for his inheritance.* 'The portion of the Lord is his people, and Jacob the lot of his inheritance.'* Therefore, have faith and hope and charity, and you will be of the house of Jacob, of the people of Israel, of the number of the elect, and Christ will dwell in you, and you will have him as your inheritance. He will take root[11] in you so as to remain in you forever, and he will rest in you as in his inheritance.

Si 24:11

1 Co 3:9

'In all these things I sought rest.'* The Wisdom of God, which works all in all things,[12] is Christ, who works in us. For the most part he works without our help, but sometimes, since we are God's helpers,* it seems that we assist him. With us he works in us what we, through him, work in him; and in the same way he speaks in us what we, through him, speak in him. Thus the works and words of the just are the works and words of Christ. This is why Peter says, 'If anyone speaks, [let him speak] as the words of God. If anyone ministers, [let him do it] as by the power which God administers.'* If any right thoughts are suggested to our heart or [right] words to our mouth, they are God's and not ours—or if they are ours in some way, they do not [derive] totally from us. He knew this who said, 'Such is the confidence we have through Christ to God. Not that we are sufficient of ourselves to think that anything comes from ourselves: our sufficiency is from God.'* So too the Psalmist says, 'In God I will praise my words'.* And when he says, 'There is no speech in my tongue',* it is as if he says, 'It is not in my tongue but rather in God that I bring forth words worthy [of him]'. Whenever we bring forth something worthy of him, it is he himself who speaks, and it is by his gift that [such words] are brought

1 P 4:11

2 Co 3:4–5
Ps 55:5[56:4]
Ps 138[139]:4

forth. 'Do you seek a proof', asks the Apostle, 'that
it is Christ who speaks in me?'* It is Christ, therefore, who speaks in his saints, Christ who works in
his saints, as it is written, 'Lord, you will give us
peace, for you have worked all our works for us'.*
And the Apostle says, 'He works in you to will and
to accomplish, according to his good will'.*

2 Co 13:3

Is 26:12

Ph 2:13

This passage, 'In all these things I sought rest',
therefore, applies in such a way to Christ, working
and speaking in all the just, that it also applies to all
the just themselves, and it applies to all the just in
such a way that it applies no less to Christ! When a
just man seeks rest for himself, Christ also seeks rest
for himself in that just man, having first given him
the power to seek his rest in Christ.

Rest, wherever it may be [found], is something
much craved and desired. All entreat it in their
prayers; all long for it, both good and bad; all desire
it and yearn for it; it is sought by everyone in his
toil. Everyone engaged in study, every skilled ar-
tisan, every manual worker—all of them—, in accordance with the desire they seek, strive for rest
and aim for rest, although their searches do not
always lead them to it. Those who are involved
with farming, those occupied with the pursuit of
arms, those concerned with the world of business,
all those, in short, who are engaged in any of the
many different sorts of study and labor and busy
themselves with them—all of them, in all these
things, yearn for rest and seek for rest. They strive
for anything which they think will please them and
in which they may rest with pleasure. All a man's
work and equally all his leisure, all his activities and
all his free time are turned to this end and look to
this goal.

A rest which is [too] extended often turns into boredom, and after the boredom of inactivity, we want to rest all over again by busying ourselves with labor. In this way we seek rest even when we flee it! We seek it in our labor, through our labor, and after our labor, but for those who do not enter the path which leads to its attainment, there is no end to their labor, no rest from their searching. The wicked, therefore, seek rest in all these things, but they do not find rest. 'Grief and misfortune are in their ways, and the way of peace they have not known.'*

Ps 13[14]:3

The just man, however, also seeks rest in all these things, but in order to find it, he first finds where rest may be found and says, 'In all these things I sought rest', etc. Here is rest! Here, in the inheritance of the Lord, where the just man determines to remain for his repose. And what is the inheritance of the Lord but the communion of the saints, of which it is written, 'The portion of the Lord is his people; Jacob is the lot of his inheritance.'*

Dt 32:9

To someone determined to remain within the Lord's inheritance, God himself, full of compassion for the things he created, goes forth to meet him, as to one returning from the paths of error. He receives the runaway servant who has returned to him, subjects him to his lord, and then, to enable him to find rest through obedience, enjoins on him a command. [The text], therefore, says, 'Then the Creator of all things commanded and said to me,' and what he commanded and what he said follows soon afterwards.

At this point, however, there is interposed another [passage] which reads, 'He that made me rested in my tabernacle'. The great hope of the just man is to find the rest he seeks, for in the very first

moment of his conversion to God, God, being
pleased with his intention [to live] a better life, rests
in the heart of his convert so as to make his convert
rest in him.[13] It is impossible for anyone to rest in
God unless God rests in him and unless the Spirit of
the Lord rests upon him. Therefore he now[14] says,
'He that made me rested in my tabernacle', that is,
in me, as if in a tabernacle. The voice of the Son
himself tells us that the just man is like God's dwelling-place: 'My Father will love him', he says, 'and
we will come to him and make our dwelling with
him'.* Or again, 'He rested in my tabernacle' means   Jn 14:23
[that he rested] in my heart, for the just man dwells
in the tabernacle of his heart where God also dwells.
But the wicked, who do not dwell within themselves in this way,[15] are exiles from their own heart.
They are therefore called back to their heart through
the prophet saying, 'Return, you transgressors, to
the heart!'*   Is 46:8

'He that made me rested in my tabernacle.' There
can be no doubt that this passage, which applies to
each and every one of the just, applies in a special
way to the most blessed Mother of God. In her
womb she bore her God and the Creator of all and
she therefore claims this saying for herself with a
unique right and says, 'He that made me rested in
my tabernacle'. 'For a man is born in her, and the
Most High himself has created him.'*   Ps 86[87]:5

When someone who is just has turned to God,
God, by grace, dwells and rests within him, so that
by receiving his commands with reverence and being obedient to him, he might, through obedience,
be worthy to rest [in God]. The rest we desire is
prepared by obedience to his commands, and it is
attained by the merit of obedience after the labor

Ps 93[94]:20

Ml 1:2–3

Lm 1:3

Ps 105[106]:35–6

Sg 2:2

Rm 12:18
Ps 119:7[120:6]

which God has framed in his commandment.*

To find rest, therefore, he is told,[16] 'Let your dwelling be in Jacob', in the people, that is, whom I have loved. 'For I have loved Jacob but have hated Esau.'* It is just as if he says, 'Live your life among the good, and let your dwelling be with the just'. There is no rest among the wicked; as it is written, 'Judah has removed her dwelling-place because of her affliction, and because of the greatness of her bondage she has dwelt among the nations and has found no rest.'*[17] And of some it is written, 'They were mingled among the nations and learned their works and served their idols, and it became a stumbling-block to them.'* We should therefore flee the company of the wicked—always with the soul, though not always with the body; always by our different way of life, but not always by removing ourselves physically.[18] For it often happens that when good and wicked are living together communally, the wicked are reformed, and the good become better and purer. The lily springs up among thorns,* and the just man grows among the wicked like a lily. He is pricked by the spines and suffers tribulation at the hands of the wicked, just as Jacob [did] at the hands of Esau, the innocent [afflicted] by the guilty, the just by the unjust. But yet, so far as he is able, he is at peace with everyone* so that he may say, 'I was at peace with them that hated peace'.*

In a metalworker's workshop, a file is essential. [It is used] to scrape the rust from iron until it becomes gleaming and polished. The same is true of a wicked man who lives his life as part of a community. Even though he injures himself and seeks to injure others, those he persecutes he also 'files' and purifies.

What then? Does the just man who says, 'I have

dwelt with the inhabitants of Cedar', * also dwell in
Jacob? Indeed, he does, with the soul if not with the
body, for he walks simply, * as did Jacob. Jacob was
a simple man, but nonetheless astute,[19] so astute
that he supplanted Esau [once] by purchasing his
birthright and supplanted him a second time by rob-
bing him of his blessing. But [these actions were]
not unjust! The blessing was lawfully due to him,
and Esau despised his birthright, for he went away
thinking little of the fact that he had sold it. Since he
was born first, he hastened to his inheritance in the
beginning, and he was therefore without a blessing
at the end. * 'When he wanted to inherit the blessing, he was rejected; he found no place for repentance, even though he sought it with tears.'*

If, then, a person acts in all things with simplicity
so as to injure no one and [acts] in all things astutely
so as not to injure himself, if he is neither supplanted by anyone nor cheated of his right, such a
person is Jacob, and to the best of his ability, he preserves unharmed and unimpaired the laws and cus-
toms of fraternal fellowship.

A peaceable way of life in the midst of our brethren
is, therefore, recommended for us, and although
[such a life] may be less pleasant for the good [who
dwell] among the wicked, it is often more useful.
But for the good [who dwell] among the good, it is
both useful and full of delight. There is nothing in
human life better than mutual love nor anything
sweeter than holy fellowship. To love and be loved
is a sweet exchange, the joy of one's whole life,[20] the
recompense of blessedness. What can be lacking in
the sweetness of this good and pleasant dwelling, *
[this place] where God dwells and where he rests?
'God is in his holy place, God, who makes those

Ps 119[120]:5

Gn 25:27, Pr 10:4

Pr 20:21

Heb 12:17

Cf. Ps 132[133]:1

Cf. Ps 67:6–7
[68:5–6]

who share the common life to dwell in his house.'²¹ *

The unity of the religious life is a symbol and in some ways an expression of that celestial fellowship in which, through the communion of love, things which are particular to each separate individual are found to be common to all.²² Here indeed is the merit, but there is the reward; here is the figure, there is the truth, although the figure itself is not without truth. Here our rest is begun, there it is perfected. Perfect rest cannot be found in this place of affliction, this place of pilgrimage. For us, the fullness of rest is not to be found outside our inheritance.

[The text], therefore, adds, 'Let your inheritance be in Israel'. Jacob himself is Israel. He is himself the inheritance of the Lord, and the Lord is his inheritance. Esau is a malicious man who hates his brother, and if any one of the just supplants Esau, so that in

Ps 14[15]:4

his sight anyone malicious is brought to nothing, * he is himself Jacob. Whoever is 'strong against God'²³ and acts courageously, whoever holds firm to God²⁴ and always sees God in his fear, his desire, his hope, and his intention, this man is Israel.²⁵

But Jacob, just as Israel, is himself the inheritance of the Lord. It is written of Israel, 'Israel is the work of my hands and my inheritance',²⁶ and of Jacob,

Ps 46[47]:4

'He has chosen for us his inheritance, the beauty of Jacob whom he has loved'. * 'He has chosen', he says, 'for us', for it is we who profit from what he has chosen. He has chosen for us,²⁷ but it is his inheritance that he has chosen. And what is this inheritance but the beauty of Jacob whom he has loved? The beauty of Jacob is the form of faith and righteousness which Jacob shows as being proposed for all, as being something which all should imitate. He consented to dwell for a time in Egypt, but he did

not want to remain there after he had died. He
wanted instead to be carried to the land which had
been promised him, and he [thereby] indicates that
his inheritance should be sought, not in Egypt-in
the world, that is—nor in this life, but [at death],
when God will give sleep to his beloved.*

Ps 126[127]:2

The inheritance of Israel is none other than that
of which the prophet says, 'O Lord, [you are] my
portion',* and 'The Lord is the portion of my inheritance'.* But as for Esau and those lovers of the
world whom he symbolizes, because of the food of
base desires and because of a single meal, once
[eaten] and soon finished, they despise and lose the
right to their inheritance. Of them it is written,
'They set at nought the desirable land'.* But Jacob
despised this food, astutely acquired the birthright,
and thereby inherited the blessing as well.

Ps 118[119]:57
Ps 15[16]:5

Ps 105[106]:24

This inheritance is gained by the love of God.
Outside this inheritance rest is sought in vain. To
them that seek it, therefore, it is said, 'Let your inheritance be in Israel', that is, 'Strive and struggle to
have your inheritance in Israel, not in Egypt; not
among the nations who do not know God, but
among the people of God'.28

Those who seek rest, then, should seek only the
inheritance of Israel, and since it is the one who perseveres to the end who will be saved*, [they should
seek it] with perseverance. There is added, therefore, 'Take root in my elect'. Just as cupidity is the
root of all evil, so charity is the root of all good.29
Of the former it is said, 'I have seen a fool strongly
rooted, and I cursed his beauty immediately'.*
Anyone who prefers the things of this world to
those of eternity is a fool, and he is certainly strongly
rooted—but only in his own estimation and that of

Mt 10:22

Jb 5:3

those like him! 'They trust in their own strength and glory in the multitude of their riches',* and 'They have called happy the people that have these things'.* But [God] says, 'I cursed his beauty immediately', and with this the Psalmist agrees: 'God will destroy you for ever. He will pluck you out and remove you from your dwelling place, and your root from the land of the living.'*

Therefore, lest love of God slip back into lust for the world through inconstancy of soul, and the love of your neighbor degenerate into hatred or contempt for your neighbor because he has pestered you with unjust actions, it is rightly said to someone who loves God and his neighbor, 'Take root in my elect'. By these words, we are taught to fix our roots immovably in both these forms of love and to persevere to the end, so that one day we may be able to say, 'I took root in an honorable people'.*

The people of the just, however, are designated in three ways and, as it were, by three names: 'in Jacob', 'in Israel', and 'in my elect':[30] Jacob according to the simple astuteness in which he walks simply, supplanting every attempt [to move him from his path] so that he will not himself be supplanted and lose his right; Israel when he is so strong that he can hold even God in check[31] and so blessed that he sees him; his elect because he is loved first while he himself has not yet loved.[32] He is loved and elected for the rest which God has prepared for him, [the rest] which will be bestowed upon him at its proper time and which will find its perfection in a threefold joy: in the communion of a most blessed fellowship; in the vision of God's divine majesty; and in the immutability of unending eternity. This is why it is written, 'They will receive double in their land,

Ps 48:7[49:6]

Ps 143[144]:15

Ps 51:7[52:5]

Si 24:16

everlasting joy will be theirs'.* The love of one's
neighbor corresponds to the first [of these forms of]
joy; the love of God to the second; and to the third,
the constancy of persevering, that is, of loving even
to the end.

Is 61:7

Let us therefore love our neighbor, either in God
if he is good or for the sake of God if he is wicked.
Let us love him so that we may thereby dwell in
Jacob—in other words, that we may remain in the
communion of the just and always be far from the
communion of the wicked, so that when we live
among them or with them, we may never be [counted
as one] of them. The law of this dwelling in Jacob is
the love of our neighbor, and by this [love], fraternal unity is preserved among the just so that it
may lead to communion in the celestial fellowship.
Let us love God with all our heart and with all our
soul. Our inheritance will then be in Israel, and we
will seek no other inheritance but the vision of God
himself, for he swore to Abraham our Father that
he would grant it to us.* Let us persevere in the love
of God and our neighbor to the end, so that there
will be no end to our eternal rest in the kingdom of
God.

Lk 1:73

OF THE THREE FORMS OF DISQUIET

Let us consider now the three forms of disquiet
which hinder the rest we long for. They continually
trouble us and force us to think of them nearly all of
the time. We are disquieted [firstly] by the evil of
time, that is, by the everchanging character of earthly
existence;[33] [secondly] by the evil of the heart, that
is, of our own cupidity; and [thirdly] by the evil of
man, that is, by the wickedness of others.[34] O evil
upon evil! The second upon the first, and the third

Mt 6:34

upon the second! 'Sufficient for the day is the evil thereof!'* The evil of time has [already] sufficed to make us miserable enough, but the perversity of others and our own iniquity oppress us beyond all measure, and our misery is more than enough. Did I say that we are miserable? Say rather that we are in the very depths of misery, completely and utterly miserable!

Where shall I escape such great and manifold miseries? Where shall I turn to find rest? In all [these] things I sought rest, but that which I sought everywhere, I found nowhere. O rest, where are you, and where shall I find you? I know that I will not find you unless you come to me. O Lord God, you alone are the repose of souls, and there is no peace for us from all this misery save through you and in you. As for me, [when I sought] to find rest in you, I turned to your inheritance in which you are at rest, and I said, 'I shall abide in the inheritance of the Lord'. This I said with my mind's resolve, my heart's desire, and the vow of my profession. Grant me now that I may say, 'He that made me rested in my tabernacle'. Build in me your tabernacle and rest in me, that I may rest in you. For this is your rest: to effect our rest. Work therefore in me, that I may love you before all things and above all things, that I may desire nothing apart from you, nothing at all, save only you or for your sake. Thus will I find peace, and in my heart will be rest from evil cupidity, from the evil of my heart, and from all the cares—so many, so wicked, so bitter—which devour my heart like birds with bitterest bite.*

Dt 32:24

What blessedness I could claim—or rather, [what blessedness] I would feel in my heart—if I flamed with desire for you alone and, burning and yearning, could with the prophet say, 'What have I in heaven, and what do I desire on earth but you?'* And if I could say this, why not add immediately and joyously, 'Away! Away! all these vain cares of mine, and all my worries, for man is disquieted in vain.* Away with my anxieties! Give place to my peace and my rest! For you are the God of my heart, and God is my portion for ever!'*

Ps 72:24[73:25]

Ps 38:7[39:6]

Ps 72[73]:26

O Lord God, repose of souls, if you grant me rest from evil cupidity, which is the root of all evil, how can another's wickedness injure me once I am not ruled by my own iniquity? If Esau says, 'I will kill my brother',* if he persecutes Jacob and drives him across the Jordan with [only] his staff,* leaving behind his father and mother and homeland, [if he forces him] to ask of and hope in God alone for food to eat and a garment to cover him, and to be exiled and to be a servant for the course of so many years so far from his own borders, even then, what can he really do to Jacob?³⁵ For you are his strong helper, O God of Jacob.*

Gn 27:41

Gn 32:10

Ps 45:8[46:7],
Is 17:10

Strengthen me, O God, in your love and in the love of my neighbor whom you have directed me to love for your sake. Strengthen me, I beseech you, that for your sake I may be able to love even those who hate me. And if my enemy is my brother and I am truly afraid of him, [grant] that I may not hate him in any way but may strive to appease his anger with gifts,³⁶ returning good for evil, so as to calm his rage and find favor with him, leading him to love me by my submission, so that from being my enemy he may become my friend, never conquered by evil but conquering evil with good. And if so forceful a love grows strong within me, then, through you the whole course of human wickedness will cause me no disquiet.

But as for the evil of time, when will that cease?
How long will that endure? While we are enslaved
by time, subject to this mutability, there will be no
peace for us from its evils. The righteousness of the
perfect cannot free them from this disquiet [which
stems] from time until every imperfection of this
mortality is destroyed by death. Yet by the power
of your charity, O Lord, in those whom you have
perfectly justified, there is even now, here in this
present time, peace from the evil of man and from
the evil of the heart, for justice and peace have kissed.*
But the evil of time has not yet ceased, and for the
just, that is quite sufficient. But for the wicked,
there is yet more evil to come.[37]

Ps 84:11[85:10]

When the wicked seek for things which are vain
and needless and harmful, they make their own
chains heavier, and to the evil of the day, to the
misery of our common infirmity and our common
needs, they add the misery of an evil will, of their
concern with things needless and harmful. To seek
what we need to alleviate our common misery is
[already] onerous and burdensome and wretched,
but to wear oneself out in affliction of body and
spirit* for things which are useless and harmful is
to heap misery upon misery.

Cf. Qo 4:16

This misery [which results] from self-will is more
of a burden to those who take more delight in self-
will, for [self-will] itself is something we all need and
is therefore common to good and bad alike.[38] It endures for the whole course of time until the end, so
that in it we might be exercised in your love, O
Lord, and persevere until the end. But when the evil
of time has, with time itself, ceased, you will crown
our perseverance in love with the perseverance of
eternity, and those who fail in these times [while

waiting] for that time will then rest in you fully and unchangeably and never more fail. 'For you are always the self-same, and your years will not fail.'* Ps 101:28[102:27]

Finally, O Lord, I beseech you to hear this little prayer of mine, so profitable for me, and no difficulty for you. Hear me, and do not refuse me.* This is 1 K 2:16 my prayer: Do not set my portion with those to whom you swore in your wrath and said, 'They shall not enter my rest',* but 'Let me rest in the Ps 94[95]:11 day of tribulation, and go up to our people who are girded'.* Say to my soul on the day of my death, 'Rest in peace'.[39] Amen. Hab 3:16

NOTES TO TRACTATE V

1. Title as in PL 441–442. This treatise also dates from Baldwin's time at Ford, and, as in Tr. IV, there is a brief discussion of the common life (n. 22) which is elaborated in Tr. XV.

2. To understand Baldwin's exegesis, the phrase *et dixit mihi* must be translated in this way. At this point, we are only told that the Creator said something; we are not yet told what he said.

3. *Sic semper est ut semel est.*

4. Thomas (36/94) has *et tamen*; PL 441D (incorrectly) reads *iterum*.

5. The contrast here is between *operare* and *laborare*, but to render these verbs as 'to work' and 'to labor' fails to bring out the difference between them. Hence my translation (see also n. 12 below). The principle is actually augustinian: for Augustine, as John Burnaby points out in his *Amor Dei. A Study of the Religion of St Augustine* (London, 1938) 57, *labor* 'does not mean "work", which he never disparages,—there was work in Paradise!—but "toil" which is for him indisputably one of the world's evils'.

6. Baldwin is using *conversio* here to refer to one's entry into the monastic life. See DLF s.v. *conversio* #6.

7. Thomas (36/98) omits the *itaque* which appears in PL 443B.

8. PL 443D omits *diu*.

9. I.e. the demons. See Eph 2:2.

10. This is an awkward passage in Latin, and I have paraphrased it to bring out the sense. A literal translation would be: 'Having mentioned his incarnation in a parenthesis (*interpositio*), he now finally adds what it was that the Father commanded and said to him. And although above he said both, viz., "he commanded" and "and he said", nevertheless, because of the parenthesis, he repeats "and he said" in order to reveal what was said to him, or commanded, for the preparation of his rest in his inheritance'.

11. Thomas (36/106) reads *mittet*; PL 445A has *mitte*.

12. In this passage, 'to work' (*operare*) is to be taken in the same sense as in the passage at n. 5 above.

13. For Baldwin (and his confrères) a 'convert' meant, literally, someone who had turned again to God, and most especially someone who had done this by entering monastic life. See also n. 6 above.

14. PL 446C omits *nunc*.

15. Lit. 'the wicked who do not remain *apud se*'.

16. Thomas (36/118) has *dicitur ergo*; PL 447A reads *dicitur ergo ei*.

17. The passage from 'as it is written . . .' to '. . . has found no rest' has been omitted in PL 447A by hom.

18. Lit. 'but not always by corporeal separation'.

19. In describing Jacob as *simplex* but *prudens*, Baldwin is echoing Mt 10:16, 'Be wise (*prudens*) as serpents and simple as doves', but in the circumstances, *prudens* is better rendered as 'astute' than 'wise'.

20. Thomas (36/122) reads *totius vitae*; PL 447D (incorrectly) has *fons vitae*.

21. Ps 67:6–7 (Vulgate) actually reads 'God [is] in his holy place; God, who makes men of one manner (*unius moris*) to dwell in a house', but since Baldwin is referring to the common life of a monastic community, I have amended the verse a little in order to make this clearer.

22. The ideas expressed in this last sentence are elaborated at considerable length in Tr. xv.

23. This is the etymological meaning of Israel (= Jacob) according to Gn 32:28.

24. *Deum sustinens*. This is an allusion to Jacob's wrestling-match with the angel, when the latter 'did not prevail against Jacob' (Gn 32:25). *Sustinere*, however, not only means 'to hold in check', but also 'to hold onto in hope', i.e. to await, to yearn for (see, for example, Ps 32[33]:20).

25. The correct meaning of Israel is given at n. 23 above, but a popular and false etymology, deriving from Philo, is to be found in Ambrose, Augustine, and other canonical authorities. E.g. Augustine, *Enarratio in Ps.* 75, 2; PL 36:958.

26. According to the Vulgate text of Is 19:25, Israel is certainly God's inheritance, but the work of his hands is actually the Assyrian. There is, however, liturgical authority for attributing both phrases to Israel (see Thomas 36/127, n. 3).

27. *Nobis elegit* has been omitted from PL 448B by hom.

28. Thomas (36/128) has *in populo Dei*; PL 448D reads *in populo Israel*.

29. Baldwin is quoting Augustine, *Enarratio in Ps.* 90.1.8; PL 37:1154 (and elsewhere).

30. The subject of the sentence is actually 'the people of the just'.

31. See n. 24 above.

32. Baldwin is echoing 1 Jn 4:19 (an important text for the Cistercians) and playing on words: he is his elect (*electus*) because he was loved (*dilectus*) first.

33. Lit. 'the evil of time, that is, of all this mutability'.

34. PL 449D omits this third form of *malitia*.

35. Lit. 'What can he [do] against Jacob?' Jacob's inner purity guards him against Esau's malice.

36. As Jacob sought to appease Esau (see Gn 32:20).

37. *Quod autem amplius est, a malo est, et malorum est.*

38. Self-will (*voluntas propria*) is self-centered or egocentric will. To a certain extent, this is essential—after all, we must use our will to keep alive—but the more we concern ourselves with self-will, the more we alienate ourselves from God. God's will and self-will vary in inverse proportion. For a useful discussion, see Gilson, *Mystical Theology of St Bernard*, 55–58.

39. A liturgical phrase from the office for the dead.

TRACTATE VI
ON THE POWER OF
THE WORD OF GOD[1]

*The Word of God is living and effective,
more piercing than any two-edged sword,
reaching to the division of soul and spirit, of
joints and marrow, and a discerner of the
thoughts and intentions of the heart. No
creature is hidden from his sight, but all are
open and laid bare to the eyes of him with
whom we have to do.**

Heb 4:12–13

WHAT GREATNESS OF POWER,
what wealth of wisdom in the Word
of God is shown by these words of the
Apostle to those that seek Christ, who is himself the
word, the power, and the wisdom of God.* In the

1 Co 1:24

beginning, this word was with God, coeternal with
him; in his time he was revealed to the prophets,[2]
proclaimed by them, and received humbly in the
faith of his believing people.

We have, therefore, the word in the Father, the
word in the mouth, and the word in the heart.[3] The
word in the mouth is the expression of the word
which is in the Father and also the expression of the
word which is in the heart of man. The word in the
heart of man is either the understanding of the word
or faith in the word or the love of the word when
the word is either understood or believed or loved.
When these three are united in one heart so that the

152

word of God is at one and the same time understood, believed, and loved, then Christ, who is the
word of the Father and of whom the Father himself
says, 'My heart has uttered a good word',* dwells in
[the heart] by faith. And with wonderful condescension he who is God in the heart of the Father descends even to the heart of man and is there conceived
and formed in a new way, as the Apostle says to the
Galatians: 'My little children, with whom I am
again in labor, until Christ be formed in you'.*

Ps 44:2[45:1]

Ga 4:19

When Christ is proclaimed, we hear the word of
God. That is to say, we understand it and therefore
believe it (for faith comes from hearing*) and therefore love it. There can be no love of the word without faith in the word, nor faith in the word without
hearing the word; for whoever loves believes and,
by an inward revelation of the Spirit who breathes
where he will, whoever believes hears the words, as
it is written, 'You hear his voice'.* [This is true]
whether [we hear it] outwardly as a result of someone's preaching or inwardly as a result of the Spirit
telling us the same things, for unless he is there to
teach us inwardly, the tongue of the preacher labors
in vain.

Rm 10:17

Jn 3:8

Our understanding should be employed in two
ways, either with regard to the beginning of faith or
to its end, for when the word is proclaimed, then
unless we understand it in some way, we do not
believe it. It is this understanding, inspired by the
Spirit, which is called 'hearing', and the Apostle
[refers to it when he says]: 'Faith comes by hearing'.*
The same apostle also shows us that 'hearing' can be
interpreted as 'understanding' when he says, 'He
that speaks in tongues speaks not to men but to God,
for no one hears him',* that is, no one understands

Rm 10:17

1 Co 14:2

him If someone speaks a foreign language to people who do not understand it, then as far as they are concerned, he is a barbarian, and since they do not understand him, they are not edified.* Understanding, therefore, is essential to the beginning of faith, that we may understand what is being proclaimed and what we should believe.

There is another [sort of] understanding which applies to the end of faith, to its consummation, and it is said of this that 'Unless you believe, you will not understand'.⁴ Although it seems that this refers to future knowledge, there is no doubt that we can also understand it [as referring] to the progress of faith in those who have exercised their senses* to achieve a more comprehensive knowledge of the reason for faith,⁵ those who are always ready to give an answer to all who ask the reason for the faith and hope which is in us.*

The word of God, with which the words of my sermon are concerned, is living, and the Father granted to him that he should have life in himself as [the Father] has life in himself.* On this account, he is not only living, but life; as he says of himself, 'I am the way, the truth, and the life'.* Because he is life, he lives in such a way that he is able to give life, for as the Father raises up the dead and gives them life, so the Son also gives life to whom he will.* He gives life when he calls a corpse from the tomb and says, 'Lazarus, come forth!'* When this word is proclaimed, the voice of him who proclaims it gives to the voice which is heard outwardly the voice of power* which is heard inwardly, and it is by this [voice] that life is given to the dead and the children of Abraham raised up from these stones.⁶ This word, therefore, is living in the heart of the Father,

1 Co 14:11

Heb 5:14

1 P 3:15

Jn 5:26

Jn 14:16

Jn 5:21

Jn 11:43

Ps 67:34[68:33]

living in the mouth of him who proclaims it, and
living in the heart of him who believes and loves it.

Just as this word is living, there is no doubt that it
is also effective.* It is, in fact, an all-powerful word.   Cf. Heb 4:12
When it said, 'Let there be light',* then immediately   Gn 1:3
it was light. When it said, 'Let there be lights [in the
firmament of the heavens]',* then immediately the   Gn 1:4
lights appeared. Whatever it said should come to be
came to be without the slightest delay. This word
runs swiftly,* and in the course of its swiftness there   Ps 147:15
suddenly appeared the lights of the heavens, the vast
reaches of the earth, and the depths of the seas.
With this word, nothing is impossible.* It is effective   Lk 1:37
in the creation of things, effective in governing the
world, effective in redeeming the world. Is there
anything more effective, anything more powerful?
'Who shall declare its powers? Who shall set forth
all its praises?'* It is effective in operation; it is effec- Ps 105[106]:2
tive when it is proclaimed; 'it shall not return in vain,
but shall prosper in everything it was sent to do'.*   Is 55:11

It is effective and more piercing than any two-
edged sword when it is believed and loved, for what
is impossible to him who believes,* and what is dif-   Mk 9:22
ficult for him who loves?[7] When this word speaks,
its words transfix the heart like the sharp arrows of
the mighty.* They enter in like nails hammered   Ps 119[120]:4
home* and enter so deep that they pierce our in-   Qo 12:12
most parts. This word is more piercing than any
two-edged sword; it cuts more effectively than any
strength or power; it is more subtle than any human
sagacity or shrewdness; it is more acute than all the
subtleties of human wisdom and all our learned
words. But the power which lies in strength is also a
two-edged sword, and the acuity of reason is again a

two-edged sword, and so too the subtlety of our [learned] words.

If anyone asks [why we say this about] strength or power, the reason is obvious. There are two powers by which this world is governed: royal power, and priestly dignity;[8] and of these it is written: 'See, here are two swords'.* The king bears a sword, but the most that this sword can do is shown us by the Lord when he says, 'Do not fear those who kill the body and are not able to kill the soul',* and again, 'Do not be afraid of those who kill the body and after that have no more that they can do'.* This sword has two edges and cuts with both. It cuts the body and kills it, and although it also cuts the soul by the amount of pain [it causes], yet it does not kill it. By the pain [it inflicts] it can separate it from the body, but it cannot separate it from its life, which is hidden in God.* It dissolves the union of body and soul, but it does not dissolve the union of the soul and God. 'Who shall separate us from the charity of Christ?' says the Apostle. 'Shall tribulation or distress or famine or nakedness or danger or the sword?'* It is as if he had said, 'Certainly not the sword!' This sword can do much, but it cannot go that far.

More piercing, therefore, than this sword which cannot [separate the soul and God] is that word which has been entrusted to the power of the Church, [the word] which can destroy both body and soul in hell-fire!* For those in authority in the Church also have a sword in the power of the word of God. Is it not written that 'Two-edged swords are in their hands'?* Is it not written that 'A sword is in their lips; who has heard?'* And if it is said of the wicked that 'Their tongue is a sharp sword',* how much

Lk 22:38

Mt 10:28

Lk 12:4

Col 3:3

Rm 8:35

Mt 10:28

Ps 149:6
Ps 58:8[59:7]
Ps 56:5[57:4]

more of a sword is the tongue of Peter, a sword which is twice as sharp!

In addition to this, the penetrating insights of human genius and the human senses, together with the subtlety of our words, are also a two-edged sword, [a sword] of most subtle discernment,⁹ which makes a division between the true and the false, the good and the bad, the honest and the dishonest, and all the other opposites which are subject to its shrewd and skillful investigations. From this there derives the whole of worldly philosophy and human wisdom.

The latter, however, being ignorant of the limits to which it could go, has dared to attempt an examination of the things above it, things to which it could never attain if left to itself. It has busied itself with arduous and abstruse investigations into the nature of God, the origin of the world, the condition of the soul, and the quality of righteousness and blessedness, and [in so doing] has been able neither to find the way of truth nor to attain to the wisdom of God which is hidden in mystery.* The Wisdom of God, therefore, says, 'I will destroy the wisdom of the wise, and the prudence of the prudent I will reject',* and again, 'I will catch the wise in their own craftiness'.* And the prophet [says]: 'The wicked have told me fables, but they are not your law, O Lord'.* Whatever elaborate investigations the wise of this world attempt, and however subtle they may be, the more they disagree with the word of God, the more they differ from the truth. They are like fables which contain in themselves nothing but error and vanity.

The word of God, however, is truth and is like a two-edged sword, a two-edged sword more piercing

1 Co 2:7

1 Co 1:19
1 Co 3:19

Ps 118[119]:85

than any other. It examines all things—even the depths of God—with a discernment as subtle as it is true. When we think of a two-edged sword, therefore [we may think of it in terms] of either power or wisdom, but the word of God, who can do all things and who examines all things, is more piercing [than any sword], for he is the power of God and the wisdom of God.

1 Co 12:6

Since this word works all in all* in a wonderful way, it also works in a still more wonderful way in the hearts of the saints; [it does so] by the effect of its grace—through fear and love, that is, and the other holy virtues—as if [it had spoken to the heart] certain secret words. [In this way] it shows them its power and its wisdom, piercing all their inmost parts and reaching to the division of soul and spirit.

To elucidate this more clearly, we should note that [the words] 'soul' and 'spirit' are used in three ways: according to nature, according to sin, and according to grace. They are used with reference to nature when they are understood in accordance with what they are naturally, or what they have naturally, what they have from the beginning of their creation. So when it says, 'The first man, Adam, was

1 Co 15:45

made a living soul',* or 'The rational soul and the flesh make one person',[10] we take this as referring to the soul according to nature. [Similarly], when it says, 'Who knows a man's thoughts, but the spirit

1 Co 2:11

of a man that is in him?'* we understand this to refer to the spirit according to its essential nature. But when it says, 'Whoever hates his soul in this

Jn 12:25

world keeps it to eternal life',* this is understood of the soul not only according to nature but also according to sin. And when it says, 'He remembered that they are flesh; a spirit that goes and does not return', * this is to be understood of the spirit according to sin. When it says, 'Whoever loves iniquity hates his own soul', * we should understand that [the psalmist] is not [speaking of] a hatred of sin, but of nature or grace. When it says, 'The Lord keep you from all evil, may the Lord preserve your soul', * soul is here to be understood according to nature and grace. And when it says, 'If by the spirit you put to death the deeds of the flesh, you shall live', * this is to be understood according to grace.

Although in their essential nature soul and spirit are the same, they are sometimes regarded as different and distinguished [from each other]. Such is the case with the Apostle when he says: 'May God himself sanctify you in all things, so that your spirit and soul and body may be preserved sound and blameless at the coming of our Lord Jesus Christ'. * And [the same is true] in the passage we are at present discussing: 'Reaching to the division of soul and spirit'. Here we see that soul and spirit are united as two distinct things, and this union, therefore, seems to be in need of some sort of distinction. And as far as I can see, the spirit pertains to the better and more worthy part, since it lives its life for God. As for the soul (which is itself also spirit), when it lives well it lives for God, in accordance with the saying of the prophet, 'My soul shall live for him', * and this is the life of grace. When it lives wickedly, it lives for itself, for it is a slave at the beck and call of self-will, and this is what the life of sin is.

There is still the life of nature [to be considered], that which the soul provides for the body so that its members can perform their duties, [the life] which supplies motion and sensation. Life according to nature is common to both the good and the wicked;

Ps 77[78]:39

Ps 10:6[11:5]

Ps 120[121]:7

Rm 8:13

1 Th 5:23

Ps 21:31[22:29]

life according to sin is only usual for the wicked; life according to grace, by which we cleave to God, appertains only to the good.

In the passage we are discussing, it is not inappropriate to take [the word] soul in accordance with the life of grace, [the life] by which we cleave to God, since it is written that 'Whoever cleaves to God is one spirit [with him]'.* Nor is it unsuitable to take [the word] soul in this passage as referring either to temporal life, by which we live naturally, the good as well as the wicked, or to a sinful and undisciplined life, which is lived in wickedness by the wicked alone.

1 Co 6:17

This passage, therefore, where the word of God is said to be living and effective, and more piercing than any two-edged sword, and to reach to the division between soul and spirit, suggests to us that there are two sorts of martyrs: those who are slaughtered for Christ in the flesh and those in whom the will and desires of the flesh are in opposition to the spirit.*

Ga 5:17

When the flesh is slaughtered, when it is killed by the sword of the persecutor, does not the living word of God, through the love and fear of God, reach to the division of soul and spirit? Does not Christ say, 'I lay down my soul for my sheep'!* And does he not say, 'Into your hands I commend my spirit'?* And when Stephen, the first martyr, laid down his soul for his friends, did he not say, 'Lord Jesus, receive my spirit'?* Does Paul not say, 'Bonds and afflictions wait for me, but I fear none of these things, and I do not count my soul more precious than myself'.* He said 'myself' to indicate the spirit which cleaved to God and 'soul' to indicate the temporal life which he despised for the sake of God.

Jn 10:15

Lk 23:46

Ac 7:58

Ac 20:23–24

This is the soul of which it is said, 'Do not be anxious about your soul, about what you should eat',* and again, 'Is not the soul more than food?'*

Mt 6:25
Ibid.

Thus, when the sword of the persecutor mangles the bodies of martyrs and divides and sunders their members, the sword of the spirit, which is the word of God, makes an inner division between soul and spirit. The fear or love of God is greatly strengthened inwardly, and for the sake of confessing the truth or the defence of justice, it remains steadfast and immoveable to the point that it despises [the temporal life of] the soul.

It is a similar situation—though not one of equal glory—in spiritual combat, when we resist the flesh whose desires are contrary to the spirit and renounce our self-will. Whoever lays aside the pride of self-will lays down his soul for God. This is the soul of which it is written, 'Whoever does not hate his soul cannot be my disciple.'* You see how the word of God is more piercing than any two-edged sword and can reach to the division of soul and spirit.

Lk 14:26

There are certain desires and intentions[11] which cling to the soul only weakly and superficially: they lack deep roots and are like the hair on our body, which can easily and painlessly be shaved off with a razor. Yet when we renounce such desires as these for God's sake, God rewards us for this with no mean recompense, for not a hair of your head shall perish.*

Lk 21:18

There are others, however, which are deeply rooted and cling much more firmly, and it is wholly impossible—or at least very difficult—to cut them off without blood and pain. Thus, just as a visible sword, which the hand can wield, inflicts a painful wound and a wounding pain when it cuts and divides

things which are joined together, so too the sword
of the spirit cuts with both edges—here through
love, there through fear—and divides up all the
things which our love embraces[12] as if [it, too, were
dividing] things which are joined together; it uses its
power to despise what it loved [at one level] so as
not to lose what it loves more.

Anyone who loves God also loves his own flesh,
[the flesh] which no one has ever hated.* The love
of a just man embraces both of these [loves], but not
to the same extent, since the more he loves God,
the less [he loves] the flesh. Thus, when he is
threatened by a persecutor, he despises the life of
the flesh so as not to lose the life which is hidden in
Christ.* But when we give up our concern with
preserving the body through the love or fear of
God, it is like breaking off a limb which is very
tightly attached, and we suffer great pain. The same
is true of self-will. By our desire—though not by
our consent—we embrace both this and God in our
love, and when we cut it off for the sake of God,
the sword of the spirit divides up things which are
joined together and inflicts a very painful wound.

Eph 5:29

Cf. Col 1 3:3

Of the Way in which the Soul is
Divided Asunder

As we have noted earlier, this sword reaches to
the division of soul and spirit and divides from one
another the soul (which is natural or carnal life) and
the spirit (which is spiritual life). But this sword also
reaches to the divisions within the soul itself and, in
a similar way, even to the divisions within the spirit,
but I think that [for the moment] we should say
more about the divisions of the soul.

The soul is a certain simple nature, indivisible in

its essence, united with each individual body in a
personal unity, a single [soul] with a single [body],
one with one, and thus, as is rightly said, the unique
with the unique. But when this soul, according to
God, loves someone it knows it should love for the
sake of God, it unites itself by the disposition of
charity[13] to the one to whom it joins itself in charity,
and thus, by these feelings of love,[14] it becomes
divided in itself:* it lives not only in its own body,   Cf. 1 Co 7:34
[the body] to which it is personally united, but in a
certain way it divides its life and feeling off from itself [and shares them] with those to whom it joins
itself in love.

Thus, it feels not only the good and evil things
which pertain to itself alone, but by rejoicing with
others and suffering with them, it also feels what
they feel and makes their feelings its own. The
sword of the spirit, therefore, does not only cut
with the pain of one's own personal suffering, but
also with the pain that one suffers with someone
else. And it can happen that the pain we suffer with
another is more severe than our own suffering. It is
often the case [for example] that a mother who suffers with her son when he is ill suffers more than the
son himself suffers. It is love that does this, [love]
which transfers to itself the sufferings of another,
[love which seeks] to increase these sufferings so
that it may itself suffer more than the other suffers,
[love] which sometimes seeks to suffer alone, so that
the other will not suffer at all.

In its compassion and fellow-suffering, the soul
which suffers with another is in a certain way divided
from itself and in itself. When the one it loves suffers, it gives itself up to him, it pours itself out from
itself,[15] so as to share his suffering with him. By this

willingness to suffer with him, it unites itself to him
so that it may suffer in his place; it pours itself into
him by its desire to suffer with him[16] and somehow
manages to become part of him. It is as if it were living with him whose pain it feels.

Thus, when old Simeon had delivered his proph-
ecy about Christ by saying, 'Behold, this [child] is
set for the fall and rise of many in Israel, and for a
sign which shall be spoken against', he immediately
spoke to the Blessed Virgin and added, 'And a sword
shall pierce your own soul'.* That is, a sword shall
pierce your soul, as if it were his.[17] But we can also
understand it in this way: a sword shall pierce your
own soul, that is, your own personal soul. Speaking
in this way, as do certain holy doctors [of the
Church], the Apostle says, 'With fear and trembling
work out your own salvation',[18]* that is, your own
personal salvation.

Now just as the Mother of God loved more than
all the others and was loved more than all of them,
so she suffered with her son when he was dying as
if, in truth, it was she herself who suffered. The
greatness of her suffering [matched] the greatness of
her love, for she loved her son more than herself,
and therefore, feeling his pain within herself, she en-
dured in her own soul[19] the wounds he received on
his body. For her, the suffering and passion of Christ
was martyrdom, for the flesh of Christ was in a certain way her own flesh; his flesh [had come] from
her flesh, but the flesh which Christ had assumed
from her she loved more in Christ than in herself.
But the more she loved it, the more she suffered,
and suffered more in her soul than a martyr in his
body. She therefore shines forth with a special sort
of glorious martyrdom. There were certainly other

martyrs who consummated their martyrdom with their own deaths, but she, from her own flesh, supplied the flesh which would suffer for the salvation of the world, and during the suffering of Christ— and by reason of this suffering—her soul underwent such violent pain that her martyrdom, as it were, was consummated in that of Christ, and one could believe that she, after Christ, deserved the supreme glory of martyrdom.

A Further [Discussion] on the Division of Spirit and Soul in Mary

There is something else which we should consider at this point, since it pertains to the division of soul and spirit. When the Mother of God realized that the salvation of the world would be brought about by the death of her only-begotten son, she wished for his death but also suffered because of it. She wished for it for the sake of her own salvation as well as ours, but she suffered because she was a mother, the mother of Christ's weakness, and herself weak. The sword of the Spirit, therefore, made a division between the sadness of her soul and the joy of her spirit which rejoiced in God her Saviour.* This is the sword which divides father and son, brother and brother, husband and wife, friend and friend, soul and spirit, soul and soul, spirit and spirit, love and love, hate and hate, love and hate, peace and peace, war and war, peace and war. 'I came not to send peace', says the Lord, 'but the sword'.*

Who can know all the divisions of soul and spirit which lovers who are wounded by charity must needs feel in themselves, a number so great that even they cannot count them? The divisions of soul

Lk 1:47

Mt 10:34

and body are many and various, and just as the
word of God touches the heart in many different
ways, so there are many different ways in which it
reaches to the division of soul and spirit.

OF THE WAY IN WHICH THE SPIRIT IS DIVIDED ASUNDER

What we have said already concerning the way in
which the soul is divided asunder can itself lead us
to an estimation of the way the spirit is divided
asunder, but I would like to glance at the division of
the spirit [a little further] so as to give the wise an
opportunity to become yet wiser.*

Pr 1:5
Jn 4:24
1 Co 6:17

God is spirit,* and he who cleaves to God is one
spirit [with him].* But since the human spirit is
totally divided and dispersed within itself, it can
only be collected together and united by joining itself to God, who is one and simple. Yet even when
it joins itself to God, it divides itself up, for in seeking to join itself to him and be joined to him more
closely, it joins itself to him in a whole variety of
different ways.[20] But who is capable [of enumerating
these]? Who can count every single rapturous out-
pouring[21] of awe, wonder, amazement, meditation,
or contemplation? Who can count all the pricks of
his conscience, the joys of devotion, the bursts of rejoicing, the extent of his yearning, his sobs and his
sighs, his burning desires, and earnest prayers? Only
he who counts the days of the world and the drops
of rain,* he alone, can comprehend and count them!

Si 1:2

The mind which is fixed in the love of God is subject to countless loving passions and is drawn [to
God] in countless ways; but although its affections
interchange and alternate in a marvellous manner,

its love still remains constant and immoveable. When it changes within itself in so many different ways, it is certainly divided [in its approach] *to* God, but it is not divided *from* God. Nor is it separated from itself since its love remains constant in all its various forms. The sword of the spirit, therefore, reaches to the division of the spirit.

When this sword persecutes the old man [in us], it is not satisfied with just killing him: it slices up whomever it kills, cuts him to pieces, and reaches to the division of joints and marrow, until the body of sin is totally destroyed. So it was that the sword of Samuel did not only kill the obese Agag but cut him to pieces.* We should examine with the greatest care, therefore, how this sword divides the joints and then how it reaches to the division of the marrow.

1 S 15:32–33

Whether we consider the life of a sinner sin by sin —limb by limb, as it were—or bring them all together at once before the eyes of the heart, we find that there are both joints and marrow. Just as one body is composed of a multitude of interconnected members, so a life which is totally wicked [is composed] of a multitude of sins. The joints of the members are the connecting-points of the [various different] sections, for sin is joined to sin either by the movement of self-will or the severity of God's judgement.

A person who sins and who thinks to remain in sin by living wickedly commits certain sins, and then [commits] further [sins] as a result of others: some [he commits] to pave the way for others to follow; others to hide or excuse or defend what he has already done. [He commits] some after pausing to weigh up the matter carefully; others by a sudden impulse of his will, as when a temptation presents itself or there appears an opportunity too good to be missed.

The connections between these sins, whether they are a result of premeditation or a chance opportunity, are like the joints of our limbs, and just as in the case of the body, they make it possible for the life of the sinner to develop and grow and increase until his iniquity is complete. But in accordance with what these sins demand and deserve, and as a result of the just decree of divine judgement, the sinner who scorns repentance and resists the divine will is left for a while to his own will and allowed to fall from sin to sin, since the cause of his later transgressions is his neglect in repenting of his earlier ones. And when iniquity is added to iniquity, it comes to the point that the sinner is excluded both from justice and from the kingdom. This is why it is written, 'Add iniquity to their iniquity, and let them not come into your justice. Let them be blotted out of the book of the living, and with the just let them not be written.'* Such is the end of those who despise the riches of God's goodness†. By their piling up of sin upon sin, they horde up for themselves the wrath of God, until the wrath of God is revealed from heaven upon all unrighteousness.*

Penitence, therefore, should not be neglected, for by it the living and effective word of God, through the fear [it inspires] of a terrible and dreadful judgement, severs the joints of our old life, the ligaments of our former conduct, like the joints of a body. It reaches so far into the division of the joints that all the bonds of sin are broken, and there is no link by which any one sin is joined to any other. This is why the prophet says, 'Break the bonds of wickedness; loose the burdens which weigh you down'.*

Ps 68:28–29
[69:27–28]

†Rm 2:4

Rm 1:18

Is 58:6

The word of God, therefore, divides the joints
when, through the contrition[22] of our heart, it
breaks into pieces all that we have wickedly joined
together in our perverse way of life, just as [the
Lord] tears to pieces a calf of Lebanon.* [It divides
the joints] when it tears apart all the things which
stick together so tenaciously, when it rips off from
their joints all the limbs of the old man and leaves
no member unseparated or unsevered from its joints.
These are the members which are listed by the
Apostle when he says, 'Mortify your earthly
members: immorality, impurity, lust, evil concupiscence, and covetousness'.*

Ps 28:5[29:6]

Although a single sin is only one member of the
body of sin* or of the body of the old man, it is
also possible to refer to each [sin] itself as a body,
since each is brought to perfection in its various
parts just as a body is completed by its joints. The
Lord shows us that we can refer to sin as a body
when he says, 'If your eye is evil, your whole body
will be evil'.[23]* It is not unreasonable to apply this
to the sinner's whole life, for if someone lives only
for himself and for his own advantage, and considers only himself in deciding how he should live,
we can understand [this whole life] to be wholly
dark. On the other hand, it is also correct to believe
that this [passage] can refer to one particular sin, for,
when one's purpose in doing something is perverted
by the vice of error or wickedness, even what seems
to be done rightly is reckoned among the works
of darkness.

Col 3:5

Rm 6:6

Cf. Mt 6:23

This body [of sin] has its joints sundered and
divided when the whole mass of sin is smashed to
bits by the testimony of a trustworthy conscience,
when the quality, quantity, form, and cause of sin,

together with everything that accompanies it, is, as it were, impeached before God, when our whole heart is shaken within itself by everything that arouses shame or fear, when it is inflamed with the love of God in the hope of forgiveness and is brought contrite to God as a burnt-offering, bit by bit, as a sacrifice cut in pieces. The sword of the spirit, therefore, reaches to the division of the joints and reaches even the division of the marrow.

The marrow supplies the bones with nourishment, and in the whole of the body we can find nothing more inward than the marrow. The marrow of the body, therefore, is whatever is deepest in our thoughts, our affections, and our works. But what lies deeper in our desire than that which we desire most of all? What lies deeper in our hope than that which we hope for beyond all else?[24] What lies deeper in our love than that which we love most of all? What lies deeper in all the thoughts and affections of our heart than that which occupies the highest place in our affections and our thoughts? But since I am speaking of sins, the thing which we seek, the thing which lies deepest, seems to me to be none other than the pleasure which sin provides. At the beginning of sin, in its course, or at its end, the sinner craves and desires nought but this one thing: the pleasure which he feels, or which he hopes to feel, by sinning. It is true that one often seems to enjoy sinning for reasons other than pleasure, but the motive of pleasure must always be there, either directly or indirectly.[25] Sometimes, too, one enjoys sinning when there is no immediate pleasure,[26] but one never enjoys sinning without intending that such pleasure should arise! What, then, lies deeper in sin than pleasure? What is more worthy of being called the marrow of sin? In every sin it is sought above all else, even if it is not found.

Let us now turn our discussion from sin to righteousness. What is more worthy to be called the marrow of righteousness than the fat which lies deep within it, that innermost pleasure which righteousness brings?

OF THE THREE TYPES OF FAT WHICH PERTAIN TO THE GOOD

If we consider the bodies of healthy animals and the kinds of fat we find in them, there appears [first of all] a sort of external fat which adheres to the flesh, and then another [sort of] fat which is internal and adheres to the vital organs, something which is usually called the soft fat or tallow, and finally another [sort of] fat which fills the bones: this is entirely fat, and it is this which is the marrow.

In the first stages of righteousness, the soul of the just also has a certain sort of fatness insofar as it finds its delight in the law of God;* but [this fat], as it were, adheres to the flesh, for having been weighed down by the former habits of the flesh, it is not yet free to aspire to the perfection of righteousness. When it has climbed a few steps [along the path] of righteousness, it begins to feel that it has now made some headway in its progress, and it desires to be filled with that internal fat which adheres to the vital organs. We are shown that this is so by him who says, 'Let my soul be filled with tallow and fatness'.* Certainly it desires to be filled with tallow, to be fattened so completely within itself that its burnt-offering might be fat;* [to be filled and fattened] until it attains the perfection of righteousness and finds the plenitude of its pleasure in the love of [God].

Rm 7:22

Ps 62:6[63:5]

Ps 19:4[20:3]

Then, as if it were fattened to the very marrow, it can say, 'I will offer up to you burnt-offerings full

Ps 65[66]:15

of marrow'.*

1 Co 7:31

There are certain of the just who use this world* in such a way that they prefer to be without things which are unlawful and forbidden rather than to have them, but with regard to things which are lawful, they prefer having them to being without them. Thus, they use the things which are permitted them by [God's] indulgence and have wives, possessions, and the other things granted to human weakness, things which may be used — if one wishes to use them — without endangering one's salvation.

There are others who, to some extent, wish to do without the things which are permitted, insofar as they do not wish to have either a wife or possessions.[27]

But there are others who, in striving for perfection, renounce everything which is permitted, as far as this is possible for human weakness. These, in accordance with the counsel of the Apostle, have food

1 Tm 6:8

and [clothes] to cover them, and with these they are content.* They are as much fatter [and richer] in spiritual goods as they are found to be thinner [and poorer], for the sake of God, in the goods of this world.

Righteousness, therefore, has external fatness, internal tallow, and marrow; the more interior it is, the more profound it is, and the more perfect it is.

From another point of view, it is possible to refer to the pleasure of righteousness as the marrow not only in the case of those who are perfect in righteousness, but also in the case of those who are beginners in righteousness, or making progress in it. For there is no righteousness so insignificant or so meagre that it does not have joined to it some degree of fortitude — a degree proportionate to its insignificance — and in this fortitude [it finds] its pleasure, as marrow [is found] in the bones.

Of the Three Types of Fat which Pertain to the Wicked

Iniquity also has its fat, its tallow, and its marrow in those who are fattened with the love and abundance of worldly things, those who are rebellious and puffed up with pride, who give little obedience to God, those who grow fatter and fatter with their ever-increasing iniquity, their intemperate use of the things they have in over-abundance, and their voluptuous habits. Then, as both their pride and their practice of vice increase, they are fattened by their very love of iniquity until finally, as if completely bloated with the fat of presumption, they are so proud of themselves that they openly scorn God. They are so swollen that they forsake God their maker and abandon the God who is their salvation, as it is written, 'The beloved grew fat and rebellious; he grew fat and swollen and gross',* and again, 'They have shut themselves up in their fat; their mouth has spoken pride'.* And once again, 'Their iniquity has come forth, as though from fatness; they have passed into the affection of the heart. They have thought and spoken wickedness; they have spoken iniquity on high'.* So it is that iniquity begins, as it were, on the surface of the heart, then little by little enters insidiously into its interior, until finally the marrow of iniquity becomes like the oil in his bones.*

In the soul, there is something which craves evil,[28] something which consents to it so as to bring about that which is craved, and something which moves

Dt 32:15

Ps 16[17]:10

Ps 72[73]:7–8

Ps 108[109]:18

Rm 6:13

the bodily members as instruments of iniquity to sin* so as to complete the act in accordance with the wish expressed by our craving and our consent.

In this same soul, there is also something which finds pleasure in this action—the action, that is, which it craves to do, to which it consents, and into which it moves itself [in such a way] that the body also moves with it in its service so as to bring about that which pleases it, since the object of all this is pleasure. Thus, there is something in the soul which is in command of all these and to which they provide pleasure.[29] First [we have] craving, then consent, then the movement [from intention] into action, and then the final goal: the pleasure that the action [produces].

When all four of these give us pleasure at the same time—craving, consent, movement into action, and the action which results from the movement—the reason why they please us and the goal [to which they aim] is the pleasure which is sought and coveted in the action. There are therefore five things: craving, consent, movement into action, the action which results from the movement, and the pleasure produced by the action. But only four of these are found in the soul: craving, consent, the movement into action, and the pleasure produced by the action. The action itself is not in the soul, but by the power and will of the soul, the body, by a voluntary movement, uses itself to act externally for the sake of that pleasure which it seeks either in this very action or as a result of it. I say 'as a result of it' so as to include all those actions which do not themselves, perhaps, give us pleasure, but which are done to bring about something else which will give us pleasure.

When these three together—craving, consent, and the movement into action—give us pleasure because of the action or because of the pleasure which the action produces, we can see that it is not the action with which they are associated alone that gives us pleasure, but these three [factors] which precede it also please us because of the pleasure brought about by the action [which they produce]. Craving, therefore, has its pleasure, since craving itself pleases us.

That the Craving for Wickedness is not under Our Control

One often comes across people who crave for things to which they are wholly averse and totally opposed; they feel a craving for many sorts of wickedness, but they do not consent to them.[30] But although it is granted to such as these to restrain themselves from going further, they cannot stop [the craving] from arising or command it to keep quiet. The craving for wickedness is not within man's control, for when it is quiet, it does not rise up by his decision, and when it has arisen, he cannot quieten it or even stop it from increasing further.

For this reason, the just man—although he has been freed by the Lord* and released from the yoke of sin—is not yet free to the extent that he is not yet completely freed from concupiscence of the flesh which stirs him in its craving for wickedness. He is free, in fact, to the same degree that he has evil concupiscence in his power, [the power] by which, through the grace of God by whom he has been freely justified, he can stop himself from going so far as to give his consent to the act. Such is the grace given to someone who has been justified. But although he

1 Co 7:22

has been justified, although he has been established in this freedom with the help of God's grace and is able thereby to refuse his consent when he is tempted by concupiscence, he cannot—as we have said before—stop concupiscence from rising up before he is stirred with unlawful craving. Nor is it in his power to stop it increasing in any way, nor to quieten it immediately. The grace of such power is not yet granted to man, even though he be justified. But by disciplining himself long and assiduously, it is possible for a just man to obtain the grace by which this concupiscence rises up but rarely, increases to only a small extent, and dies away more swiftly.

In the case of the sinner who is a servant of sin because he consents to sin, the more he desires concupiscence to be stirred within him—even when it is not actually stirred—the more firmly is he bound by the bonds of his servitude. There are some who have sunk so deep into iniquity that they carefully think up ways to invite sin and deliberately encourage it so as to satisfy their will. Their desire is to bring about a condition of habitual depravity, even when they are not disposed to sin.[31] They are so well trained in sin[32] that they want to sin even when they cannot sin. So pleasing to them is evil concupiscence and its stirrings—evil craving, that is, or its disposition [to evil][33]—that far from wishing such things were absent, they desire them to increase more and more in themselves; this is the very depth of iniquity. Concupiscence is the cause and the beginning of the sin which follows it, just as pleasure is the goal at which the craving for sin and consent to it are aimed. Concupiscence is as hateful as death, for it leads to death through the pleasures of sin; as it is written, 'When concupiscence has conceived,

it brings forth sin. But sin, when it is full-grown,
brings forth death'.*

Jm 1:15

The just, therefore, justly hate concupiscence as
they do death, and they justly fight against it with
all their power and all the warfare of spiritual discipline, so that even if they cannot totally eradicate it,
they can at least weaken it. The more the just hate
this concupiscence, the more they love righteousness. The less there is of concupiscence of the flesh
whose desires are contrary to the spirit,* the more

Ga 5:17

there is of concupiscence of the spirit whose desires
are contrary to the flesh. Just as unrighteousness
begins from concupiscence of the flesh, so
righteousness takes its origin from concupiscence of
the spirit. Thus, to hate the concupiscence of the
flesh and to love the concupiscence of the spirit is
[already] a form of righteousness, and without this
no one can be righteous or just—neither he that
begins, nor he that makes progress, nor he that
achieves perfection. The more progress he makes
and the closer he comes to perfection, the more he
hates the one and loves the other.

That there are Three Things which Perfect the Pleasure which comes from Concupiscence of the Spirit

There are three things which bring to perfection
this love and this hatred: the desire for righteousness,
the resolve, and their execution. Desire on its own,
which lacks resolve and execution, is a useless
desire. When it touches a sinner's heart, it goads
him for a moment, but when he is tempted, it is so
fickle that it vanishes away. Of such a kind, perhaps, was the desire of Balaam the soothsayer, for
when he considered the tabernacle of Jacob he was

Nb 23:10

goaded to say, 'Let my soul die the death of the just, and my end be like theirs'.* Many are the criminals and profligates and malefactors who have this sort of desire; for a moment, they are goaded to righteousness, but because they condemn themselves by returning to their sins, it is all in vain.

There are others who have the desire for righteousness together with the resolve [to pursue] a better life, but they postpone that which they intend for a long while and either set no time limit to this delay or set yet a further time limit when the last has expired, and then when the second time limit has arrived, they take the opportunity to set a further limit and thereby seek [to provide themselves with] a delay which has no limit at all. But should their scheme be interrupted by death,[34] then neither their desire nor their resolve [to pursue] this postponed righteousness will free them from the punishment due to unrighteousness. Thus it is essential that those who desire the life of righteousness and who are resolved [to pursue it] should put their desire and their resolve into execution. It is one thing to intend to go all the way to Jerusalem and show on one's face that one is already going there,* and quite another to have an idle desire to make the journey and then, by endlessly postponing it, never to set out.

Cf. Lk 9:53

The execution of our holy desire and holy resolve consists in our body and soul taking an active part in the combat of the concupiscence of the spirit and the concupiscence of the flesh, giving our consent to righteousness with the former and never permitting the latter to assent to unrighteousness. The desire and resolve for righteousness, together with their tireless pursuit, brings to perfection our holy hatred of concupiscence of the flesh, [that concupiscence] which, by its desire and resolve for wickedness, in-itiates unrighteousness and which has neither the desire nor the resolve for pursuing the good to its final goal.

But whereas the desire and resolve for wickedness is enough to make a person wicked, the desire and resolve for the good is not enough to make him good, although [it is true that] without these there is no one good and no one who is not wholly wicked. Those who have neither the resolve [to pursue] the good nor the desire for it love evil concupiscence beyond all measure, and it is not in their case as if they were led into this propensity for evil, this affec-tion for it, by being tempted within themselves. They themselves, of their own accord, pass over into this affection apart from any temptations. Of such as these it is written, 'Their iniquity has come forth, as it were, from fatness; they have passed over into the affection of their heart',* and again, 'They were consumed with concupiscence in the desert'.*

Ps 72[73]:7
Ps 105[106]:14

This concupiscence, then, unless it is resisted, first of all robs us of our consent to the good and then of our resolve [to pursue] the good and our desire for it, until [finally] it subjects to itself the whole of our will and the whole of our reason. There is then no movement or stirring of the will towards good, nor does the spark of reason,[35] the little light we have, reveal itself; the whole heart is hardened and dark-ened, and the lamp is extinguished in Israel.* When the will is not moved to desire the good, nor the reason moved by the resolve [to pursue] it, then concupiscence is the victor; it has subjected both to itself and celebrates a glorious triumph, [a triumph

Cf. 2 S 21:17

made] all the more glorious because neither [desire nor resolve] murmur or fight back.[36]

If a person has been so utterly vanquished by victorious concupiscence, so blinded that he loves it, [then] it follows that he hates the concupiscence of the spirit which is directly opposed to it. He hates righteousness, he hates consenting to righteousness, he even hates to desire righteousness, he hates not desiring evil, he hates not consenting to evil concupiscence, he hates not sinning, he hates abandoning sin, he hates repentance, he hates the truth which refutes [his ideas], he hates the wisdom which suggests more profitable things to him, he hates the discipline [which leads] to peace, he hates the grace of God and comes little short of hating God himself. But if the course of his iniquity does indeed lead him to hate God for no cause,* then he descends ever lower and lower until he falls into the unforgivable sin, which shall be forgiven neither in this world nor in the world to come.* In this way evil concupiscence, victorious and dominant, hurls its slave down from sin to sin and leads him from a love of himself to a hatred of God, until the pit closes its mouth upon him.*

One cause of this great evil is the pleasure which sin [provides], the other is the concupiscence of sin, [our desire for it]. The former gives the reason *for* which [this evil arises]; the latter the means *by* which [it arises]. The latter initiates the matter, the former brings it to perfection. The latter, by its unlawful representations, leads us away from good and attracts us to evil; the former seizes what has been led away and attracted, and imprisons it. The latter precedes our consent to sin as its cause; the former follows it in succession.

Ps 34[35]:19, 68:5[69:4]

Mt 12:32

Ps 68:16[69:15]

Of the Body and Soul of the Old Man

In a single human being there can be distinguished
body and soul. In the body we can see flesh and
bones, and in the bones, the marrow; but we believe
that the power of moving the body is held by the
soul. In just the same way [we see that] in putting
together a single sin, our old man (which can be called
with good reason the man of sin or the son of perdi-
tion)* has, for the flesh of sin, concupiscence. This
accords with what the Apostle says: 'The desires of
the flesh are contrary to those of the spirit'.* For its
bones it has consent, for the strength of sin lies in
consent, as the strength of the body [lies] in its
bones, and for marrow, it has pleasure. For its soul
it has that which is highest and most excellent in the
mind, which presides over that which craves, that
which consents, and also that which feels pleasure.
Craving, consent, and pleasure can either please it
or displease it, and without its connivance, craving
is not led to consent, the body is not moved into action, and the action [which results] from this movement, [the action] in which pleasure is so avidly
sought, is not brought to fulfilment.

When the mind which presides over all is pleased
by all and finds pleasure in all,³⁷ it does not feel
pleasure only in the action, but apart from the
pleasure [which comes] from the action, there is also
the pleasure which the mind feels in craving and
consent—but it feels pleasure in the craving only
after it has given its consent. For if it finds no enjoyment in consenting, then it finds either no enjoyment or very little enjoyment in craving. But when
it enjoys consenting, it also enjoys bringing [its

2 Th 2:3

Ga 5:17

intentions] to fulfilment. Thus, since all these three
factors, desire, consent, and action, give pleasure to
the mind, the mind finds pleasure in all three.[38]

Now although it may appear that the pleasure
found in craving pertains to craving itself rather
than to consent—to the fat of the flesh, that is,
rather than to the marrow of the bones—yet for this
very reason we see that it can also refer to consent,
since craving gives no pleasure whatever unless it is
accompanied by consent. Thus, we find that it is
not only the pleasure which comes from action
which is [symbolized by] the marrow, but also the
pleasure of craving, the pleasure of consenting, and
every other pleasure which the mind experiences,
for it is by the latter's command[39] that everything is
arranged to procure for it its wicked pleasure. But
since these forms of marrow are hidden so deep
within bones which are themselves deeply hidden,
who is the man or whose the sword that can divide
them, save that of him who can crush the bones of
Ps 74:11[75:10]   sinners and break their horns?* He it is who
humbles the proud to dust and ashes, who scatters
the clouds like ashes, who sends forth his ice like
Ps 147:16–17   morsels,* who, by his strength, brings out those
that were bound, and likewise those that provoke
Ps 67:7[68:6]   him, that dwell in the tomb.* It is he who can
waken the dead, he alone who has the power to
change all these guilty pleasures into the bitterness
of penitence, so that all those things which wickedly
pleased us now displease us, until the body of sin is
destroyed to its very marrow.

'AND A DISCERNER OF THE THOUGHTS AND
INTENTIONS OF THE HEART. NO CREATURE IS
HIDDEN FROM HIS SIGHT, BUT ALL ARE OPEN AND
LAID BARE TO THE EYES OF HIM WITH WHOM
WE HAVE TO DO'

The Lord knows the thoughts and intentions
of our heart: there is no doubt that in himself [he
knows] all of them, but in us he knows those whose
nature he makes us perceive by the grace of discernment.[40] The spirit in man does not know all that is
in man, and when it feels his thoughts, either giving
or refusing them its consent, what it feels does not
always correspond to reality. When someone looks
at the things in front of the eyes of his mind, he
does not see them accurately because his eyes are
darkened. So it often happens that when another
person or the tempter does something which has
every appearance of piety, his own thought judges it
worthy of the reward of virtue, although in the eyes
of God it certainly deserves no such thing.[41] There
exist certain imitations both of true virtues and of
vices which delude the eyes of the heart and which
so beguile the keen-eyed mind with their illusions
that what is really not good may have every appearance of being good, and what is really not wicked
may have every appearance of being wicked. This is
a part of our misery and our ignorance: we have
much to suffer and much to fear! Thus it is written:
'There are ways which seem right to men, but their
end leads to hell'.[42]

1 Jn 4:1

To avoid this danger, blessed John gives us this advice: 'Test the spirits to see whether they be of God'.* But who can test whether the spirits are from God save he who is granted by God [the grace of] discernment of spirits, who can thereby examine with accuracy and true judgement spiritual thoughts, affections, and intentions? Discernment is the mother of the virtues,⁴³ and it is essential for every individual, whether it be for governing the lives of others or the direction and correction of one's own [life]. But the only word that can introduce this into our senses is that living and effective [word] who is the discerner of the thoughts and intentions of the heart. This word organizes our life in accordance with a certain, specific pattern and directs it towards a certain, specific end. By being thus organized in this way, we ought always to love God in all that we plan to do, so that all that we do is done according to him and also for his sake. Do you want to know what I mean by 'according to him' and 'for his sake'? Listen, [and I will explain] both: [firstly] the whole of our life should be organized according to the pattern [laid down] by God's commandments,⁴⁴ [and secondly] every one of our actions should be directed to the end of God's promises. We are not permitted to do other than what [God] commands or permits or advises; nor should we hope for anything other than what he has promised, simply because he has promised it. Our righteousness is formed by God's commands and counsel; our hopes are raised by the truth of his promises. Our thought about what we will do is upright if it is ruled by God's command; our intention is devout if it is directed simply to him. It is in this way that the whole body of our life

or of any one of our actions will finally be full of
light, provided that our eye is simple.* And the eye   Mt 6:22
is both an eye and simple because it sees what it
should do by means of upright thought, and by
means of its devout intention, it does simply what it
should not do with duplicity. Upright thought does
not admit error; devout intention excludes deception. This, therefore, is true discernment: the union
of upright thought and devout intention. But do
not be surprised if I refer to discernment as union
when [the word] discernment itself implies divi-
sion.⁴⁵ This union does, in fact, involve division:
whoever unites these two things divides the light
from the darkness. Error and deception are dark;
righteousness and pious devotion are light in the
Lord.

But a person who tries to divide upright thought
according to God from devout intention for the
sake of God when he is choosing what he should do
and the goal for which he should hope has an eye
which is partly blind, and therefore he either walks
in darkness or does not know where he is going.*   Jn 12:35
Whoever acts wickedly walks in darkness, and
whoever does not direct his steps to God does not
know where he is going. We should not commit
wicked deeds for the sake of God, nor should we
perform good actions without God in mind. A vain
intention corrupts a work of devotion, and a devout
intention does not excuse a work of iniquity.

Everything, therefore, should be done in the light
of discernment, as if it were in God and before
God, for no creature is hidden from his sight:*   Heb 4:13
nothing corporeal, nothing animal, nothing
spiritual, nothing which God made for man or in

man, nothing which is made in man or by man in opposition to God. Whatever there is in man – part of which man sees and part of which he does not – is revealed in its entirety to God. The human heart is a great abyss, and in its secret places all kinds of darkness are hidden. There are there creeping things without number,* but God, who sees in secret† and brings to light the hidden things of darkness,†† sees all things, so that out of many hearts thoughts might be revealed.* Nothing, whether visible or invisible, escapes him, for all are open and laid bare to his eyes.* There are many things which are now hidden and concealed by mysterious silences and policies, fabrications and deceptions, trickery and deceit, cunning words and deeds, subterfuges and excuses, simulations and dissimulations. But there is nothing covered which shall not be revealed.* All that is now so skillfully concealed will be stripped of its covering by that word with whom we have to do.⁴⁶ It is to him that we should render account, an account to which is credited the whole course and conduct of our life.

The Lord is so attentive to the ways of each and every individual and counts their steps so [carefully] that neither the most insignificant thought nor the most inconsequential word which serves to demean us remains unexamined. What, then, can I say to defend myself? What excuse can I offer on my own behalf? All that I can do is to say with the prophet, 'You have understood my thoughts from far off; my path and my line you have searched out. You have foreseen all my ways, and there is no speech in my tongue.'* O good Jesus, I am inadequate to render account; accept, then, my prayer as my account,

Ps 103[104]:25
†Mt 6:6
††1 Co 4:5
Lk 2:35

Heb 4:13

Mt 10:26

Ps 138:4[139:3-4]

and do not enter into judgement with your
servant, for in your sight there
is no one living who shall
be justified.*

Ps 142[143]:2

NOTES TO TRACTATE VI

1. This is a title of convenience, and does not occur in the manuscripts. In the course of this lengthy tractate, Baldwin sometimes uses the term *sermo*, and sometimes *verbum*, for 'word', and it is not always possible to distinguish between them in English translation. In addition to this, when he speaks of the 'word' he often implies two things at the same time: the word of God in scripture and the word of God as Christ. It is important to bear this in mind when reading the text. Finally, both *sermo* and *verbum* can signify rather more in Latin than 'word' in English, and Baldwin is therefore able to play upon words (literally!) in ways which are impossible to render satisfactorily in translation. The tractate most probably dates from Baldwin's years at Ford.

2. Thomas (37/22) has *prophetis*; PL 451B (incorrectly) reads *apostolis*.

3. This threefold division of the word is also to be found in SA 766 C-D (SCh 94:556–558).

4. This is the O.L. version of Is 7:9; Baldwin's source for it was most probably Augustine (e.g. *De Trinitate* XV. II. 2; PL 42:1058, *Sermo* 272; PL 38:1246). This text appears elsewhere in Baldwin's writings (e.g. SA 703B [SC 93:300]).

5. A full explanation of what Baldwin understood by *ratio fidei* would be out of place here, but his approach on the whole was extremely cautious and conservative, and is well exemplified by the following passage from SA 653B–C (SCh 93:116): 'We cannot give a reason for everything that the ancients have handed down, but in those things they have transmitted which are not contrary to reason, the very authority of the ancients should be sufficient reason for us. Our very faith, without which it is impossible to please God, relies more on authority than human reason. So when Peter tells us that we should give a reason to all who ask for the faith and hope which are in us, I cannot think of any better reason to give for our faith than the authority of Scripture or the authority of the ancients—at least, of those ancients who have not been found to be in error on any point of faith, and whom we know have pleased God by virtue of [their faith]'.

6. Since this is based on Mt 3:9, the reading *laudibus* in PL 452D is an error for *lapidibus*.

7. Thomas suggests that this idea has its roots in Augustine (see 37/33, n. 1, and 40 / 134, n. 1, citing *De bono viduitatis* XXI. 26; PL 40; 448, and *Sermo* 70. III. 3; PL 38: 444), but although the principle is the same, the actual source of the expression is Cicero, *Orator*, x. 33. Bernard also quotes it (see Palm I. 2; PL 183: 255C [SBOp 5:44]), and it would seem to have been a phrase which was fairly well known at the time.

8. Thomas (37/32–34) has *sacerdotalis dignitas*; PL 453C reads *sacerdotalis auctoritas*.

9. This follows the reading of MS Troyes 433 which Thomas prefers (see 37/36): *tamquam gladius anceps subtilissime quasi per discretionem dividit* . . . PL 454B substitutes *subtilissimi corporis* for *subtilissime quasi*. Discernment (*discretio*) is of considerable importance for Baldwin (and many other twelfth-century writers) and he elaborates on it in the final section of this present treatise. Cf. also nn. 43 and 45 below.

10. A phrase from the Athanasian Creed.

11. Lit. 'certain wills (*quaedam voluntates*)'.

12. *Quae communiter amantur.*

13. *Per affectum caritatis.*

14. *Per affectiones amoris.*

15. *Se illi indulget et se transfundit extra se.* Transfudit in Thomas's text (37/54) is merely a typographical error.

16. *Per affectum condolendi.*

17. This only becomes intelligible when we consider the peculiar Latin rendering of Lk 2:35: *et tuam ipsius animam pertransibit gladius.* It is, in fact, a literal translation of the Greek, but what is in Greek a perfectly sound construction does not work in Latin. The *ipsius*, then, may be understood in two ways: (a) 'your soul, of himself', i.e. your soul, as if it were Christ's soul; or (b) 'your soul of itself', i.e. your very own soul. The latter, of course, is what the Greek says, and which Baldwin here prefers.

18. Baldwin is quoting Ph 2:12 in the O.L. version which appears in a number of patristic writers. E.g. Augustine, *Epistola* 157, IV. 29 (PL 33:688), *De sancta virginitate* xxxviii . 39 (PL 40:419).

19. Both here and in the phrase 'suffered more in her soul' a few lines further on, the term is *mens.*

20. This is a fairly loose translation of the Latin in order to bring out the meaning.

21. *Excessus.* This is a very important term, but it is clear that in the present context, Baldwin is using it fairly broadly. We may contrast Tr. VIII, n. 18.

22. *Contritio* is derived from *contero* which means 'to grind up' or 'separate into small pieces'. A contrite heart, therefore, is a heart which is broken up or divided into pieces.

23. Mt 6:23 with a second *nequam* substituted for the Vulgate *tenebrosum.*

24. PL 460D omits *maxime.*

25. A loose translation to bring out the sense.

26. PL 460D omits *nulla* in *cum nulla adest delectatio.*

27. The whole of this sentence has been omitted in PL 461C.

28. *Quod malum appetit.* Baldwin's name for this factor is normally *appetitus*, and thus accords with early scholastic usage.

29. As is clear from his later comments, Baldwin is referring to the *mens.* See n. 37 below.

30. Baldwin's argument centers around *sentire* and *consentire* (cf. Tr. IV, nn. 41, 44) and he provides a detailed explanation of what he means later in this present tractate.

31. *Qua desiderant consuetae turpitudinis effectum, et tunc cum nullum habent affectum.*

32. Thomas (37/84) reads *acuant*; PL 463C has *amant.*

33. *Appetitus malus, vel affectus.*

34. PL 464B omits *morte.*

35. *Scintilla rationis.* A well-known term deriving from Augustine, *De civitate Dei* XXII, 24, 2; PL 41, 789. It is this 'spark' which distinguishes man from the animals, and characterises us as created in the image of God.

36. PL 464D omits the last part of this sentence.

37. See n. 29 above.

38. This is an explanatory rendering. The Latin simply says, 'that which all these please finds its pleasure in all these'.

39. Thomas (37/96) reads *nutu*; PL 466A (incorrectly) has *motu*.

40. As Baldwin explains in his CF 597C, '[God] is said to know when he makes us know'. It is an augustinian idea.

41. This is a fairly loose translation to bring out the meaning.

42. This curious text appears to be based on the O.L. version of Pr 16:25 (which Baldwin could have found in Ambrose, Jerome, or even the *Rule of St Benedict* [RB 7, 21]), but it also shows traces of Pr 14:12 which, in the O.L., is very similar.

43. Baldwin is here echoing RB 64, 19.

44. PL 466D omits the whole of this first point.

45. *Discretio* derives from *discerno* 'to separate, divide', and hence, 'to distinguish, discern'.

46. A play on words which cannot be rendered satisfactorily into English: . . .*suis tegumentis nudabit sermo ad quem nobis sermo.*

TRACTATE VII
ON THE ANGELIC SALUTATION[1]

Hail, full of grace, the Lord is with you;
Blessed are you among women. *

Lk 1:28

THE MATTER OF OUR SALVATION begins with a salutation,[2] and the commencement of our reconciliation is consecrated by a proclamation of peace. The herald of salvation and messenger[3] of peace was sent from God and came to the Virgin, and this lover of virginity greeted her with a strange new greeting—[a greeting] which had never been heard from eternity until that moment—and thus conferred upon her at one and the same time both the favor of a new greeting and the acclaim of a new commendation. For a woman to be greeted by an angel is indeed new and rare! Although Hagar and the wife of Manoah enjoyed seeing an angel and speaking with him, the angel did not greet them.* But now a woman is greeted by an angel. Now the time draws near when women may be greeted by the Lord himself, saying to them, 'All hail'!*

Gn 21:17, Jg 13:9–20

Mt 28:9

The Virgin reflected on what manner of greeting this might be.* Let us, too, reflect upon it as best we can and consider its nature. It is not the sort of greeting [you give to someone you meet] on the road, but a greeting which leads [us] back to [our] homeland. 'Greet no one on the road',* says the Lord.

Lk 1:29

Lk 10:4

If someone deliberately flatters you and fawns on you and agrees with everything you say to ingratiate himself with you in vain things, or makes a great show of his friendship for you, or sings your praises — this is one who greets you on the road. Beware of him! Beware of those who give you this sort of greeting.[4] And woe to you if you become the slave of such a one! Woe to you if those who seek your soul

Ps 69:3[70:2]
Mt 23:7
2 Co 1:12
Ps 88:38[89:37]
Ps 21:26[22:25]

rule over you!* Do not be enamoured of greetings in the market-place.* Let the testimony of your conscience be enough for you,* and the faithful witness in heaven,* to whom you should say, 'With you is my praise in a great church'.*

We [need to] distinguish two sorts of greeting because there are two distinct sorts of salvation. There is a vain salvation, of which it is written,

Ps 59:13[60:12]

Ps 68:14[69:13]

'Vain is the salvation of man',* and there is a true salvation, of which it is written, 'Hear me in the truth of your salvation'.* But this [angelic] greeting [which we are now discussing], whether it be a yearning prayer for a salvation much desired or the proclamation of salvation given and received, does not proffer false friendship on the part of him who gives the greeting, nor does it proclaim false praise of the Virgin. But just as virginity is always dear to the angels, so the praises he utters of the Virgin are truly sincere, and he begins by praising her fullness of grace, saying 'Hail, full of grace!' O saving greeting, spoken by the angel, instructing us in how we should greet the Virgin. O joy of the heart, sweetness to the mouth, seasoning of love! What place can there be for anger where there is fullness of grace? For fullness of grace renders the [first] sin void and restores nature. It was sin which corrupted nature and gave rise to anger, but God, in his anger,

has not suppressed his mercies.* He has poured out
grace and turned away his anger. That sex which he
condemned and cursed⁵ in the first woman, he
now, in the blessed Virgin, fills with the grace of his
blessing and the oil of his mercy. This is the cruse of
oil;* this is the vessel of Gideon filled with dew;†
this is the golden jar containing the manna of surpassing sweetness which rained down from heaven.*
Who can conceive the nature and the abundance of
the grace which filled her who is named first among
women, who alone is called full of grace, who gave
birth to the only-begotten Son, full of grace and
truth?*

We read that Stephen, the first martyr, was filled
with grace⁶ and strength,* but we believe that [the
Virgin] was still more full of grace in accordance
with her greater capacity to receive it. She could
contain in both her heart and mind him who was
the author of grace, him who is so great and so im-
mense that the whole world cannot contain him.⁷

We have heard that when blessed Elizabeth was
filled with the Holy Spirit,* she recognized a greater
grace in the Virgin and was amazed that she visited
and greeted her. 'How is it', she said, 'that the
mother of my Lord should come to me?'* Since she
had been greeted herself, she was right to greet her
through whom salvation had to be imparted, for in
this way she rendered thanks to God, who gives salvation to kings* and who commands the saving of
Jacob.* For [Mary] was full of grace, in good measure, pressed down, shaken together, and running
over,* for the reason that through her the grace of
God might abound in us. God chose her in advance
in a unique way and accorded her the grace of being
endowed with a triple grace—the grace of beauty,

Ps 76:10[77:9]

1 K 17:12
†Jg 6:38
Heb 9:4

Jn 1:14

Ac 6:8

Lk 1:41

Lk 1:43

Ps 143[144]:10
Ps 43:5[44:4]

Lk 6:38

the grace of favor, and the grace of honor—so that
she should be made beautiful, gracious, and glorious.

OF THE TRIPLE GRACE OF BEAUTY, FAVOR, AND HONOR[8]

The grace of beauty shines out in an attractive
face, and according to the definition of blessed
Augustine, an attractive face is regularly formed,
with a good color and a cheerful expression.[9] The
regularity of the features, their proportion, unifor-
mity, composition, and the way in which the corresponding parts are arranged and matched, plays no
small part in beauty. Eyes which are different or un-
equal, or a distorted visage, or lips which do not
meet properly are displeasing, and if any part [of the
face] differs from its corresponding part by its deformity or irregularity, it detracts from the beauty of
the whole. Any part which is greater or less than it
should be or is out of proportion with its corresponding part disfigures the grace of beauty.

The praise of true beauty belongs to the mind
rather than the body. Yet in a certain way it belongs
to the body as well, for it often happens that what a
chaste heart conceives inwardly is manifested outwardly and becomingly through the agency of the
body. But whatever is not born from purity of heart
shows its impurity, since all the glory of the king's
daughter comes from within.* Yet not all her glory
[remains] within! It often comes forth from her inmost [parts] and glorifies outwardly the King of
Glory* who is in heaven.

This interior beauty, however, [also] loves regularity and balance.[10] For where there is no cause for irregularity, irregularity is always unseemly. If you
judge what is good and evil in yourself in one way

Ps 44:14[45:13]

Ps 23[24]:7 ff

and in your neighbor in another, then your two eyes are not the same. If you are proud before God but humble before men, the two sides of your face are out of proportion. If you speak well of your neighbor to his face and denigrate him behind his back, or if you praise God in prosperity but grumble in adversity, your two lips are ill-matched. The whole of this deformity stems from the sin of pride, which always loves imbalance and irregularity in our conduct, just as humility restores the balance to things unbalanced.

In the case of the Virgin, we are looking for the precise way in which the features of her face are proportioned, for [her face] is so attractive and so praiseworthy that a more attractive or more praiseworthy cannot be found among all the daughters of Sion.* And in what better way can we speak of the regularity of her features than in the balance of humility and honor, of condescension and dignity? It is written, 'The greater you are, the more you should humble yourself in all things'.* If you stand out from the crowd, become one of the crowd; if you are always in command, do not think it beneath you to be subservient.

Consider yourself, and consider your Master. And [consider too] the occasion on which he confesses that he is the Master—truly so, since that is what he is.* Consider what he said and what he did. 'I have not come', he says, 'to be served, but to serve.'* And he explained what he meant like this: 'Whoever is the leader, let him become as the servant; and whoever is greater among you, let him become as the younger'.* So much for what he said. Do you know what he did? He humbled himself at the very feet of his own disciples! Who was it who did this?

Sg 3:11

Si 3:20

Jn 13:13
Mt 20:28

Lk 22:26

Is 66:1, Ps 109[110]:2   He for whom the earth is a footstool for his feet.*
Rv 1:17   He who says, 'I am the first and the last':* the first
                          in dignity, the last in humility. He has given us an
1 P 2:21   example, therefore, that we may follow in his steps*
Ps 131[132]:7   and worship in the place where his feet have stood.*
Ps 94[95]:6   Come, let us worship and fall down before God;*
Gn 16:9   let us humble ourselves beneath him and with him,*
Ps 33:19[34:18]   for he will save the humble of spirit,* those, that is,
Jn 4:23   who worship in spirit and in virtue.* The place of
                          worship is the virtue of humility. Here his feet
                          stood. How did they stand? In humility he came,
                          and in humility he persevered. He emptied himself
                          and took the form of a servant, and on behalf of his
                          servants, the Lord endured the shame of the cross
Ph 2:7–8   and became obedient to the Father even to death.*
                          What is the height of humility, if not this? How
                          beautiful is this balance of the highest dignity and
                          the highest humility!

                          O faithful soul, if you are guarded against pride
                          by this example, and thus, through humility, follow
                          in your Master's footsteps, then to you is said,
                          'How beautiful are your steps in sandals, O prince's
Sg 7:2   daughter'.* 'Listen, daughter, and incline your ear,
                          that you might be humble, and the king will greatly
Ps 44:11–12   desire your beauty'.* Who is the king but he who
[45:10–11]   alone is king? If you incline your ear to him, if you
                          humble yourself, he will find you desirable and
                          more than desirable and worthy of his love, and the
                          more you [humble yourself], the greater you will
                          be. The more you humble yourself, the more you
                          magnify the Lord.

                          She, therefore, who we believe humbled herself
                          so much more than any other that she was to that
                          extent more worthy, she who alone says, 'My soul
Lk 1:46   magnifies the Lord',* she magnified him more who

had herself been more magnified and raised to such
eminence that she alone can say, 'He who is mighty
has done great things for me';* and having been
magnified more, she magnified God more because
she humbled herself more and bore witness herself
to her own humility, saying humbly, 'He has regarded the humility of his handmaid'.* Elizabeth,
too, was a witness, for when the Mother of God
visited her, she extolled equally her happiness, her
dignity, and, in that great dignity, her humility. For
great humility in great dignity is always admirable,
and so too [is] great humility in great power, or
great humility in wisdom, eloquence, or virtue. In a
word, in anything great, great humility is the bal-
ancing feature. It arranges and orders the face and
conforms and regulates everything so that all the
various parts are in harmony.

Lk 1:49

Lk 1:48

OF THE GRACE OF BEAUTY

The grace of color, both of whiteness and rosiness,
adorns the grace of beauty. Color means propriety,
but there are two forms of propriety: propriety
which stems from chastity and propriety which
stems from modesty.[11] Chastity and modesty are
the white lily and the red rose. Chastity bestows
upon the face its whiteness; modesty bathes the
cheeks in its redness. Modesty is the guardian of
chastity as well as its glory and adornment. Each of
the senses of body and mind has its chastity and its
modesty. There is a chastity of the eyes and a
modesty of the eyes; there is a chastity of the ears
and a modesty of the ears; and with each of the
senses, modesty is normally the companion of
chastity. The senses are considered chaste when
they are uncorrupted. This is why the Apostle says,

2 Co 11:3

'As the serpent seduced Eve by his cunning, I am afraid that your senses may be corrupted and fall from the simplicity which is in Christ'.* There is a holy modesty which blushes at shameful things; there is a holy chastity which preserves itself unstained. There was a man who said, 'I made a covenant with my eyes that I would not so much as think about a woman'.* See how chaste were his eyes! But if someone looks at a woman and lusts after her,* his eye is nothing but shameless, and an eye with no shame is the messenger of a mind with no shame. Corruption of the senses and shamelessness go together hand in hand. Integrity of the senses is the seal of chastity.

Jb 31:1
Mt 5:28

The integrity of the Virgin, however, and the chastity of her mind and body were such that she was wholly virgin, wholly undefiled, wholly unstained, in none of her senses corrupt, in none of her senses impure. She blushed at all things shameful; she condemned all things wicked; she desired all things seemly; she abominated all things dishonorable. The perfection of virginity is the inviolate integrity of all one's senses, and every detraction from this integrity is a sort of deflowering of virginity. This is the radiant color, the whiteness of chastity combined with the rosiness of modesty, which shines on the face of the Virgin and adds to the grace of her beauty. She was so radiantly colored, therefore, with chastity as well as modesty, that in her was realized that which is written, 'A holy and chaste woman has a double beauty'.[12]

Heb 1:9

'Full of grace.'[13] Her cheerful expression further added to her grace, and her face was gladdened with the oil of exultation.* With total devotion and the full fervor of charity, she offered herself to God in an odor of sweetness. More than all the daughters

of Sion who rejoice in their king,* her spirit rejoiced
in God her saviour.* See the beauty of her face:
how the grace of regularity formed it, how the grace
of whiteness and rosiness illumined it; how the grace
of cheerfulness gladdened it. Yet not only is her face
beautiful, but she is wholly beautiful, and he who
found in her his joy bears witness to this when he
says, 'You are wholly beautiful, my love, and in you
there is no stain'.* See how full is the grace of her
beauty!

Cf. Ps 149:2
Lk 1:47

Sg 4:7

Of the Grace of Favor

No less than this is the grace of favor. She is loved
and praised and honored by all. For men and for
angels, she is, after God, the first [object of] love and
praise and honor. The whole church of the saints
proclaims her praises: 'The daughters of Sion saw
her and declared her most blessed; the queens and
concubines praised her'.* Nor does she herself pass
over in silence this grace of such great favor: 'All
generations', she says, 'will call me blessed.'*

Sg 6:8

Lk 1:48

Of the Grace of Honor

It is not in my power to tell you how great was
the grace of honor bestowed upon her. Everything
in her is worthy of praise. Whatever is hers alone,
whatever she shares in common—both extol her
with special praise. Even the things she has in common she has in a unique way, for whatever she
shares with others, she herself possesses more than
all others in a manner surpassing all excellence. She
remains unique, therefore, even in the things in
which she is not unique! She is chaste, she is humble, she is sweet and kind. And although there are
others [who have] similar virtues, they do not [have

them] in the same way, or to the same extent. She surpasses all, and in all things she is the Mistress of the World, the Queen of Heaven, of men, and of angels, the Mother of God and his daughter, his sister, and his bride, his friend, and his neighbor. She is his mother by her fertile virginity, daughter by the grace of adoption, sister by the grace of communion, bride by the trust of betrothal, friend by the exchange of love, neighbor in being near to him in likeness.[14] She is more lovable than all, more honorable than all,[15] beautiful beyond beauty, gracious beyond grace, glorious beyond glory.[16]

'The Lord is with you.'[17] But is there any special glory in her being told, 'The Lord is with you'? After all, the angel said to Gideon, 'The Lord is with you, O strongest of men'.* And the Psalmist says, 'The Lord of hosts is with us',* and Christ says to us, 'Behold, I am with you always, even to the end of the world'.* And Isaiah says of Christ, 'They shall call his name Emmanuel, God with us'.* But he had prefaced what he was going to say with 'Behold, a virgin shall conceive and bear a son, and they shall call his name Emmanuel'. How could he come to us to be with us unless he comes to the Virgin? To her he came first so as to be with her and in her and from her, so that through her he should be in us, since he is the God of Jacob, our protector.* For the reason that the God of Jacob took our nature from her was so that he might always be with us, saying, 'My delight is to be with the children of men'.*

But if God's delight is being with the children of men, can you imagine his delight in being with her who is his alone, whom he chose in advance to

Jg 6:12
Ps 45:8[46:7]

Mt 28:20
Is 7:14

Ibid.

Ps 45:12[46:11]

Pr 8:31

administer such delight? That he is with us, therefore, sharing in our nature and sharing with us his grace that we may be sons and heirs of God, brothers and joint-heirs of Jesus Christ,* is the great gift and great good which, after God, we owe in a unique way[18] to her to whom was said in a unique way, 'The Lord is with you'.

Rm 8:17

Having been made the agent and collaborator in the divine plan, she gave us the salvation of the world, for she brought forth for us the Saviour who is himself the world's salvation.[19] She could not, however, do this alone, and therefore she offered her service, revealed her role as mediator, and brought forth in our midst the Mediator who could indeed bring it about, and it is for this reason that she was rightly told, 'The Lord is with you'. You are to effect a sublime work; through you the salvation of the world is to be achieved, and the rod of the oppressor is to be broken, as it was in the day of Midian.* That for which you have been chosen surpasses all human power and wisdom, but the Lord is with you, and for him nothing is impossible.* Thus, when Gideon was about to free the children of Israel from Midian, he was told, 'The Lord is with you, O strongest of men'. Strength is mentioned here specifically because it was a work which demanded strength, and strength was given by God himself, who is a strong helper.* [Similarly], in the work of our salvation, [a work] which begins from fullness of grace and is consummated in fullness of grace, fullness of grace is specifically mentioned, and praise is ascribed to the Author of grace who, with the cooperation of the Virgin, is revealed as the author of this work.

Is 9:4

Lk 1:37

Ps 70[71]:7

The Blessing of the Virgin

God is the author of all such benefits, but after him, praise is due first to the Virgin, who deserves to be blessed by all.[20] For this reason the angel said to her, 'Blessed are you among women',* as also Elizabeth said, 'Blessed are you among women'.* Eve, through pride and the sign of disobedience, brought down on herself a curse, and through her we are subject to the [same] curse. Pride deserves a curse, for God resists the proud but gives grace to the humble.* This is why it is written, 'Pride is the beginning of all sin. Whoever clings to it will be filled with curses.'* Mary, however, humbled herself and deserved a blessing. Let us consider, as best we may, the extent to which she humbled herself and how much she was blessed.

There is one sort of humility which comes from a command, another which comes from deliberation, another which comes from an example, another which comes from a resolution or vow, and another which comes from a curse. A command imposes an obligation, deliberation arouses free will, an example provokes emulation, a holy resolution or vow increases devotion, and a curse induces confusion. Humility which comes from deliberation is better than that which comes from a command. We are *commanded* not to rob others; we are *instructed* to abandon even what is ours. The former is more necessary, but the latter is the greater good. The former is more general [in its application]; the latter is more rigorous.

Humility which comes from an example, without a command and without deliberation, is clearly far removed from puffed-up pride and arrogant disdain.

Lk 1:28

Lk 1:42

1 P 5:5

Si 10:15

It is a mark of great humility, without any pressure or persuasion to esteem someone who is acting rightly more than oneself and to hold in contempt nothing worthy of imitation.

It often happens, however, that without command, deliberation, or example, the mind, by a hidden impulse, realizes that there is something good to be done and adopts it as a resolution or a vow. This is a wonderful [sort of] humility, for it is truly a great virtue to renounce our common liberty and submit ourselves to holy necessity.[21]

Sometimes, however, something which we realize is acceptable to God is found to be shameful among men and subject to a curse. Some, therefore, who are conquered by the fear of confusion, are often ashamed of their efforts in trying to reach perfection, and so long as they fear the tongues of men, they flee from the good things they so earnestly desire. Others, however, are so zealous for righteousness and holiness, and esteem them so highly, that they despise human curses and abuse. They count it glorious to suffer insults for the name of Christ* and esteem the reproach of Christ greater riches than the treasure of the Egyptians.* With this sort of humility, the less it fears the curses of men for the sake of God, the more abundant before God is the grace of blessing it deserves. Christ did not neglect this sort of humility, for in wishing to satisfy every [demand of] justice,* he was made a curse for us, as it is written, 'Cursed is he that hangs on a tree'.* But the way in which he was made a curse is shown us by [the Apostle], who says, 'He was rejected by men certainly, but chosen by God'.* And this too applies to him: 'They will curse, and you will bless'.*

Ac 5:41

Heb 11:26

Mt 3:15

Dt 21:23, Ga 3:13

1 P 2:4

Ps 108[109]:28

In the light of all we have said, let us consider the nature of the Virgin's humility. She dedicated her virginity [to God] not by a command of the Law [of Moses], but under the curse of that Law, for any woman who did not leave offspring in Israel was considered cursed. If God also said to those he blessed at the creation, 'Increase and multiply',* and gave them the grace of fertility as a blessing, surely she who has no part in fertility has no part in blessing? If fertility is a blessing, how can barrenness be other than a curse? And what is more barren, more infertile, more unfruitful than virginity? Nothing whatever—[provided we are talking about the time] *before* a virgin is made fertile! For fertile virginity is actually the most fruitful thing there is. The holiness of virginity is above the Law, since no law required it as a command; but when the Lord said, 'Whoever is able to receive this, let him receive it',* he *advised* it for those who wanted to achieve the perfection described in the Gospels.[22] The same is true of the Apostle: 'Concerning virgins', he says, 'I have no command of the Lord, but I do have advice.'*

No command of the Law, therefore, preceded this resolution of the Virgin; nor, as some would think, did any advice from the Law or example from the Law—although when I speak of an example,[23] I am thinking of women rather than men. In the case of Elijah and Jeremiah and Daniel, we consider that they did preserve the purity of their virginity, but among women, either before the Law or under the Law, I can think of no example of virginity preserved and dedicated to God.

The fact that the daughter of Jephthah obtained a delay of two months to bewail her virginity* may be interpreted in a number of ways, for the Scripture

Gn 1:28

Mt 19:12

1 Co 7:25

Jg 11:37

does not indicate her intention in doing this. But if the reason she bewailed her virginity was that she was sterile and without fruit and could not leave offspring in Israel, then this thought in her mind and profusion of tears are far removed from a resolution of holy virginity! Yet it seems that she had a more noble reason [than this]—and whatever it was is known to him who examines the heart*—since she said to her Father, 'My father, if you have opened your mouth to the Lord, do with me whatever you have promised, since he has granted you revenge and vengeance upon your enemies'.[24]*

How, then, could our Virgin really think that her virginity would be pleasing to God when [virginity itself] is as much the subject of a curse as it is nigh to barrenness? On the other hand, she could have read in Isaiah, 'Let not the eunuch say, "Behold I am a dry tree!" For the Lord says to the eunuchs, "In my house and within my walls I will give them a place and a name better than sons and daughters."'* Or she could have read, 'Behold a virgin shall conceive and bear a son, and they shall call his name Emmanuel'.* Since the honor of a name better than sons and daughters was promised to the eunuchs— that is, to the virgins—and since it was foretold[25] that the Saviour of the World would be born from a virgin, then by the suggestion of the same Spirit that inspired the prophet who said this, the Virgin (for whom was reserved the honor of being the virgin who would conceive God and give him birth) could have realized by divine inspiration that her virginity would be wholly pleasing and wholly dear to God. So whether she was instructed as to the merit of her virginity by the revelation of a prophet or whether it was through divine inspiration that

Pr 24:12

Cf. Jg 11:36

Is 56:3-5

Is 7:14

she became so thoroughly apprised of it within
herself, she fell in love with virginity, and the
virginity she embraced she offered to God in an
odor of sweetness and dedicated it [to him] and
despised the shame of the curse.

But [in her case], to that virginity which had
hitherto been barren was added fertility, and instead
of the curse she despised she found the grace of a
blessing. For other [women], the curse brought iniquity in conception, pain in childbirth, and, for
some, barrenness without fruit. She, however, conceived without sin, gave birth without pain, and
brought forth fruit from virginity. What kind of
fruit? A fruit in all ways unique, a fruit more precious than any fruit of marriage.

What is the fruit of marriage but the whole pos-
terity of Adam, this whole multitude of the children
of men? They are the offspring of the conjugal
union of our first parents and are born of fornica-

Jn 8:41   tion.* The entire fruit of the union of the flesh has
been condemned in advance, for it has sprung from
an evil tree and is contaminated by its corrupt roots.

Mt 7:17   An evil tree brings forth evil fruit.* What is this evil
tree, you ask? It is evil concupiscence, concupiscence
of the flesh, which drags with it all who are engen-
dered according to the law of the flesh, all who are
begotten by the transmission of sin. This is the
original evil in us, the seed-bed of evils, the leaven

1 Co 5:6, Ga 5:9 which has corrupted the whole lump,* the beginning
and end of our common condemnation.

It was fitting, however, that this original evil, so
calamitous and deadly, should be remedied by an
original good, something associated with man's first
condition, enduring after the first transgression and

the consequent law of natal corruption, and still to be found in those born now.[26]

God, in fact, tempered his sentence against sinful man in such a way that although nature was contaminated by its corruption,[27] it was on the one hand aware of the evil which it deserved but on the other was redolent[28] of the good which it [still] possessed. As a result of the sin of disobedience, therefore, corrupt procreation brought upon those who were born the law of disobedience — the corruption, that is, of concupiscence — but despite this, the [nature of our] earliest condition preserved in those who were born a certain integrity of incorruption. For every virgin born is accompanied by her virginity from the time she comes forth from the womb through all her growing years, and she retains the grace and flower of incorruption until the flesh, by failing to restrain the impulse of concupiscence, becomes corrupted and destroys the name of integrity and corrupts the flower of vernal virginity. Nevertheless, that which is lost in the union of man and woman when they mate is partly restored to a child at birth. But the virginity and integrity common to all who are born is lauded and praised as virtue most especially in those who preserve with the integrity of the flesh the chastity of their mind; and if we have virginity of the flesh without chastity of mind, then although this does not of itself deserve reproach or censure, it still does not warrant the commendation of true virtue.

The virginity of this blessed Lady, however, is praised as virtuous in a unique way, for she who deserved to be told, 'Blessed are you among women', obtained a unique grace of blessing. Blessed indeed!

First because she was exempt from the common curse, then because she was delivered from a just indictment, and finally — and this is most important — because she turned away the condemnation due [to humankind]. All other women, whether bearing or barren, are bound by the general curse, but [the Virgin], by grace, was excepted from this, for the share of blessing she received was such that it freed her alone from the general misfortune and set her forth as exempt. This is what we have called her exemption from the general curse.

It would have been possible for sinful man to plead that his sin was due to the woman, and he could have said, 'It is through you, accursed woman, you who deserve to be cursed, that I too am cursed! It is through you that I am cast out of Paradise, through you that I have lost all these goods, through you that I have found all these evils. Woe to you, for it is your fault that I must say, woe to me!' No woman could reply one single word to this. She could only be covered with confusion and confounded with consternation. This is why the whole female species could have been detested and deserve nothing but universal reproach. Such indeed was the case before the birth of the Virgin. But things now are very different! Women now have someone who can reply. In the blessed Virgin they have someone who can oppose this reproach, and it is this which we have called her deliverance from a just indictment. From this indictment the Virgin herself stands free, and by her merit she has delivered others. It was she who brought forth the Saviour of the world who destroyed death* and turned away the condemnation due to us, and it is to her, therefore, after God, that we owe everything:

2 Tm 1:10

that we are freed from the curse and blessed with all
manner of spiritual blessings in the heavens.* Thus,
as she is ever blessed before God, so too she should
be ever blessed by us.

BLESSED IS THE FRUIT OF YOUR WOMB

Every day we devoutly use this angelic salutation,
just as it was given to us, to greet the most blessed
Virgin, but we normally add to it [the phrase]: 'and
blessed is the fruit of your womb'. It was Elizabeth
who added this closing passage, for after she had
been greeted by the Virgin, she repeated, as it were,
the end of the angel's greeting and went on to add
[these further words]: 'Blessed are you among
women, and blessed is the fruit of your womb'.
This is the fruit of which Isaiah says, 'In that day the
shoot of the Lord will be magnificent and glorious,
and the fruit of the earth will be high'.* What is this
fruit but holy Israel, which is also itself the seed of
Abraham, the shoot of the Lord, the flower which
climbs from the root of Jesse, the fruit of life in
which we share? Blessed indeed in the seed, and
blessed in the shoot, blessed in the flower, blessed in
the gift, and blessed, finally, in the giving of thanks
and in the proclamation [of praise].

Is 4:2

Christ, the seed of Abraham, was descended from
the seed of David according to the flesh.* But if the
Virgin, who was pledged to Joseph of the house of
David, was herself of the seed of David, and if
Christ was born of woman,* from whom he was
born without seed—'of the seed of David', that is,
'without seed'[29]—why, then, do we not devoutly
believe that Christ was [wholly] descended from the
seed of David? [The reason is to be found in the
phrase] 'without seed'. Why does it say this? Because

Rm 1:3

Ga 4:4

Mt 1:18

the Virgin was found to be with child by the Holy
Spirit,* because she conceived in a marvellous way
and took nothing from the normal processes of re-
production.[30] She provided from herself the substance[31] of the flesh [of Christ], and in taking flesh
from her, he remained undefiled.

This, therefore, is the blessing of the seed: that he
was under no obligation to sin and that in his birth
no trace of iniquity was transferred or contracted.

Ph 2:7

He took the form of a servant,* but not that of a
slave, and he was innocent of sin in his birth. He
alone, therefore, he who acquits the guilty and
makes them free, [he alone] is free with a true, innate, and natural freedom.[32] To this blessing, which
is freedom from sin, there is added the blessing of
the shoot: the fullness of grace and of perfect
righteousness. He alone among men is found to be
perfect in all good since he is free from all evil. To

Jn 3:34
Mt 3:15

him was the Spirit given without measure* so that
he alone could fulfill all righteousness.* Compared
with this, all the righteousness of the saints is found
to be but a trifle, for none is holy as the Lord is

1 S 2:2

[holy].* Our own righteousness is barely adequate
even for ourselves, but his righteousness is sufficient
for all nations, as it is written, 'As the earth brings
forth her shoot, and the garden causes her seed to
sprout forth, so shall the Lord God make righteous-

Is 61:11

ness spring forth and praise before all nations.'*

This, then, is the shoot of righteousness, and
when it has grown with blessing, it is adorned with
the flower of glory. And what measure of glory? A
greater measure than we can conceive—or rather, in
a measure wholly beyond our comprehension. The
flower climbs up from the root of Jesse. How high
[does it climb]? Surely to the highest point of all, for

Jesus Christ is in the glory of God the Father.* His
magnificence is raised above the heavens,* so that
the shoot of the Lord may be magnificent and glorious, and the fruit of the earth be high.*

But what fruit is there for us in this fruit? The
fruit of blessing, surely, [which comes] from this
blessed fruit! From this seed, this shoot, this flower,
the fruit of blessing comes forth and reaches all the
way to us. First, as if in the seed, through the grace
of forgiveness; then, as though in the shoot, through
increasing righteousness; and finally in the flower,
through the hope and attainment of glory.

For being blessed by God and in God—so that
God, that is, may be glorified in him—he is also a
blessing for us, so that we too, being blessed by
him, may be glorified in him. Through the promise
made to Abraham, God gave him the blessing of all
nations, so that in the gift of blessing he should himself be a blessing for us and that for this gift he
should be ever blessed by us in the offering up of
thanks and in the proclamation of praise. May the
name of his majesty, therefore, be for ever
blessed and the whole earth be full
of his majesty. May it be so!
May it be so!*

Ph 2:11
Ps 8:2[1]

Is 4:2

Ps 71[72]:19

NOTES TO TRACTATE VII

1. Title as in PL 467–468. The tractate would seem to date from the days of Baldwin's abbacy. For an excellent account of the development of the theology of Mary in the Middle Ages (a development to which Bernard of Clairvaux made important contributions), see J. Pelikan, *The Christian Tradition, III: The Growth of Medieval Theology* (Chicago, 1978) 160–174.

2. In Latin (and French) the close relationship, both phonologically and etymologically, between *salus* 'salvation' and *salutatio* 'greeting, salutation' makes possible certain puns and word-plays which are not always apparent in English. There are a number of these in this tractate, but any attempt to render them literally produces a form of English which, though theoretically correct, is appallingly pedantic. *O salutatio salutifera*, for example, which occurs a little further on, could be rendered as 'O salutiferous salutation', but if anyone speaks like that, he has my sympathy.

3. *Angelus* means both an angel and a messenger.

4. Lit. 'Beware those who say to you "Hail"'.

5. Lit. 'condemned with a sentence of cursing'.

6. Thomas (37/122) has *gratia*; PL 469B reads *gratiae*.

7. A phrase borrowed from the liturgy. See Thomas 37/123, n. 1.

8. PL 469C has *Of the Triple Grace of God*, and another of the manuscripts used by Thomas has *Of the Triple Grace of Beauty*. See Thomas 37/124, n. 1.

9. Cf. Augustine, *De civitate Dei* XXII. 19. 2 (PL 41:781).

10. Lit. 'equality of comparable parts'.

11. Baldwin's terms—*pudor, pudicitia, verecundia*—are not easy to distinguish in translation. All three, for example, could be rendered by 'decency' or 'modesty'. The context, however, seems to suggest 'chastity' for *pudicitia* and 'modesty' for *verecundia*.

12. Si 26:19, which reads literally: 'A holy and chaste woman [has] grace upon grace'.

13. PL 472A (and certain of the manuscripts) provide these echoes of Baldwin's main text (there is another example at n. 17 below). MS Troyes 433 does not contain them, and Thomas prefers to omit them, remarking—rightly—that if they are section-headings, they are somewhat peculiarly placed (see Thomas 37/113). It is possible, however, that they are not section-headings, but simply asides from a preacher who was recapitulating his text and reminding his congregation of how far he had progressed in his exegesis.

14. This is an augustinian (and ultimately platonic) idea well known in the Middle Ages. 'We do not draw near to God in space (for he is everywhere and not contained in any space), nor do we draw apart from him in space. To draw near to him is to become like him; to withdraw from him is to become unlike him' (Augustine, *Enarratio in Ps.* 34.11.6; PL 36:337).

15. Thomas (37/138) reads *omnibus amabilior, omnibus honorabilior*; PL 472D has *omnibus pulchrior, omnibus amabilior*.

16. *Superspeciosa, supergratiosa, supergloriosa*. For these terms, Baldwin is almost certainly indebted to Anselm, *Oratio* 54; PL 158:960C.

17. See n. 13 above.

18. *Post Deum singulariter debemus, cui* has been omitted in PL 473A by hom.

19. The last part of this sentence has been omitted in PL 473A by hom.

20. Thomas (37/144) has *in omnibus*; PL 473C reads *ab omnibus*.

21. To appreciate Baldwin's point here it is necessary to recall Bernard's teaching on *libertas* and *necessitas*. We all have a body (whether we like it or not) and this body imposes certain demands upon us: it needs to be fed, for example, and cared for. This we may call 'natural necessity', and it is a necessary form of carnal love. We also possess free-will, and, if we may quote Gilson, 'a voluntary agent is able to accept such and such a thing or to refuse it, to say yes or no, and this in virtue of the sole fact that he is gifted with a will. It is this natural liberty, inherent in the very essence of volition, that is called "freedom from necessity"—*libertas a necessitate*' (*Mystical Theology of St Bernard,* 47). Baldwin takes this idea one stage further: this 'natural' or 'common liberty' may be renounced in favor of a total submission to the will of God, and in this case, by our own voluntary decision, we are no longer a free agent. The demands laid upon ourselves by ourselves bring us once again into the realm of constraint and *necessitas*, but in this case it is 'holy necessity' and not 'natural necessity.' And paradoxically, of course, it is this holy necessity which is true freedom.

22. Lit. 'No law made it a command, but evangelical perfection formed it as a *consilium*, the Lord saying, 'Whoever is able, etc.'' *Consilium* is 'advice' when it comes from another, and 'deliberation' (as we have rendered it above) when it takes place in oneself. This is the second form of humility—*humilitas sub consilio*—as it applies to the Virgin.

23. PL 474D, *quod de mulieribus*, should read *quod de exemplo dixi de mulieribus* as in Thomas's text (37/150).

24. Jg 11:36 with *vindicta* substituted for the Vulgate *victoria*.

25. *Praenutiatus* in Thomas (37/152) is simply a typographical error for *praenuntiatus*.

26. This is a fairly loose translation to bring out the sense.

27. Thomas (37/156) has *vitio suo corrupta*; PL 476A omits *suo*.

28. Thomas (37/156) has *redoleret*; PL 476A reads *recoleret*.

29. 'Of the seed of David' is a quotation from Jn 7:42. 'Without seed' (*sine semine*), as Thomas indicates (37/162, n. 1), is liturgical and occurs in the antiphon *O admirabile commercium* for vespers of the feast of the Purification.

30. Lit. 'accepting nothing *a gignente*'.

31. *Substantia* in Thomas (37/162) is a typographical error for *substantiam.*.

32. Lit. 'it is an innate and true freedom (*genuina libertas*) and a truly free condition of being free-born (*libera ingenuitas*) with which he alone is free'. PL 477C reads *gemina* for *genuina*.

TRACTATE VIII
ON THE WOUND OF LOVE
WHICH THE BRIDE INFLICTS UPON
THE BRIDEGROOM[1]

Sg 4:9

You have wounded my heart, my sister, my spouse, you have wounded my heart with one of your eyes and a single hair of your neck. *

T HERE ARE MANY WAYS in which God displays his charity towards us: now by deeds, now by words, now by blessings, now by promises, now by caresses and words of encouragement, now by certain mental representations [which are aroused by external phenomena].[2] By mental representations I mean the specific forms and dispositions of love—whether given or received, natural, social, or chaste—which are aroused in our mind when the latter is stimulated by the various external phenomena naturally suited to it. Thus, as a result of this stimulation and by being consciously aware of these forms of love, our mind might always be consciously aware of God, whom we should love with all our mind* and who should always be present in our memory.[3]

Mt 22:37

Natural love is that by which all living things, not only human beings, love those of their own nature. They feel within themselves the force of love and, by a sort of natural instinct, consent to the laws of love. There is also social love, and by this, as a result of their own choice, they live together socially when they agree to dwell together. And there is also chaste love, which strengthens and adorns marriage.[4]

The eagle, therefore, loves when she is concerned for her young,[5] and so too the hen loves when she gathers her chicks beneath her wings;* she stretches forth both her wings and her tenderness and is weakened by the greatness of her love. A father loves the sweet children born to him, and a mother cannot forget the offspring of her womb.* And as for brother and sister, when they each speak or hear the sweet name of their relationship, they awake loving affection in each other[6]. Friends are joined by a bond of friendship which cannot be broken, and bride and bridegroom lay aside their affection for their own homes and families to devote themselves to chaste embraces and the delights of love.

Yet more intense than all these is the love of Christ: more profound, more inward, more incisive, more penetrating, more compassionate, more sweet, more steadfast, more fervent. We can compare its power with every other love, but no comparison can surpass it, nor equal it, nor express to the full [its intensity]. Yet Christ is not ashamed to be compared to an eagle or a hen, and by this very fact he demonstrates his marvellous charity, his marvellous humility, and the wonderful sweetness of both of these [virtues]. He is a father when he says, 'From this time call me "my father", for you are the guide of my youth,'* and 'You will call me father and will not cease to walk after me'.* No mother is more tender than he[7] when he says, 'As a mother comforts her children, so shall I comfort you'.* He is a brother when he says, 'My sister is an enclosed

Lk 13:34

Is 49:15

Jr 3:4
Jr 3:19

Is 66:13

Sg 4:12
†Jn 20:17
††Sg 4:1
Sg 5:16

Is 62:5

Sg 4:9

Ps 88:11[89:10]

Ps 87:8[88:5]

Sg 5:7

garden'* and 'Go to my brothers'.† He is a friend when he says, 'You are wholly beautiful, my friend',†† and when it is said of him, 'Such is my beloved, and he is my friend'.* He is a bridegroom when he says, 'The bridegroom will rejoice over the bride, and your God will rejoice over you'.*

But when he says, 'You have wounded my heart, my sister, my spouse',* he is then both brother and bridegroom. When he calls her his sister, he points to the communion of nature and grace, and it is this which is the transaction of love: he assumed nature, and he communicated grace. When he calls her his bride, he points to the trust [implicit] in a betrothal and the sacrament[8] of an unbreakable union.

But why does it say of her whom he calls sister and bride that she has wounded the heart of her brother and bridegroom? Does it mean that love also has its wounds? It does indeed, but there are some wounds which offer healing and others which bring death. What wounds are more mortal than those sustained by the very author of death, wounded with the spear of envy and the sword of pain? Of him it is written, 'You have humbled the proud one like someone mortally wounded'.* But he is not the only one to be so wounded: through him many others have also been wounded and have died, and of them it is written, '[They are] like the dead who sleep in the sepulchers, whom you remember no more'.* But the wounds with which the bride is wounded — the wound of love and the wound of pain — are wounds which bring healing, and the wounds of the bridegroom — which are also wounds of love and pain — bring greater healing still. Of the wound of pain the bride says, 'They struck me and wounded me',* and of the wound of love she says,

'I am wounded by charity'.⁹ And if we may serve
the truth by introducing into so sacred and reverent
a matter the opinion of a distinguished poet,* then   Virgil
he too is a witness to the wound of love:

> *But the queen, long since suffering the sharp*
> *pains [of love],*
> *Nourishes a wound in her veins, and is*
> *consumed by an invisible flame.* ¹⁰

We are also told that the two old judges in Daniel
'were both wounded with the love of her'*—of   Dn 13:10
Susanna, that is—but this does not refer to holy love.
Holy love is much more effective in its capacity to
wound and much more powerful. Let us, then, consider the way in which the bridegroom announces
that his heart has been wounded by his sister and
spouse. He does not say it only once but repeats it a
second time: 'You have wounded my heart, my
sister, my spouse; you have wounded my heart.'*   Sg 4:9
It is surely because he loved us with so much chari-
ty, even when we were dead in our sins,* that he   Eph 2:4
wanted life for us and death for himself. This is why
he was wounded and hung upon the cross; this is
how the wounds of us sinners are healed; this is
how we have received salvation! His desire for our
salvation, therefore, and his desire to die for our salvation comprise two wounds: one of love and one of
pain, although both of them are really [wounds] of
love. For in both cases, the desire arises from a love
which preceded that of the bride, so that when she
had been loved first in this way, she could love him
who loved her and preserve herself unstained for him
in the perfect purity¹¹ of holy love and holy fear.

[Our text] then says that the heart of the bridegroom was wounded by a single eye and a single

hair of her neck, as if it were he who was lured into
love by their beauty, he who loved her [so much]
when she was ugly that he himself made her beautiful. But [in fact, the reference to] the beauty of these
things makes it clear that it was the bride who was
chosen by love. The whole loving intention [of the
bridegroom] was directed to the end that she whom
he loved so much before he made her beautiful
should be made beautiful, and thus, when he considers the ways in which he made her beautiful, he
says that his heart has been wounded by the enormity of his love. [In this way] the bride and bridegroom wound themselves with mutual wounds, but
whereas the bridegroom inflicts no wound unless he
is wounded [first], the bride wounds him when she
herself is not yet wounded.

But if, as he says, the bride is wholly beautiful,
why is the bridegroom only wounded by one of her
eyes and a single hair of her neck? Why not by the
whole of her beauty? He certainly loves all of her
and praises all of her—her cheeks and lips, breasts,
hips, and everything else—why, then, is he not
wounded by the beauty of her cheeks and lips and
all the other wonderful things? Why is he wounded
by the beauty of just one of her eyes and a single
hair of her neck, like someone snared by love? Is it
because [her eyes and hair] shine with a certain
unique grace of beauty and please him more than all
the rest? This is indeed the case, and because they
please him more than everything else, the whole [of
the bride] is pleasing to him. In what way, then, are
these [especially pleasing]? [It is because they repre-
sent] the purity of holy love and the purity of holy
fear: by one of her eyes we understand the former
and by a single hair of her neck, the latter.

In the [book of the] prophet Zechariah it says of
the vessel of wickedness (which is cupidity or the
love of the world) that 'this is their eye in all the
earth'.* This eye gazes at the earth and not at heaven;   Zc 5:6
at the world and not at God; at transitory things,
not those which are eternal; at visible things and not
those invisible. Nor can it do so since it is unclean
and darkened. But when the love of God is perfect
and undivided, it is an eye which is simple[12] and
pure. It is striking in its beauty and striking, too, in
the wonderful acuity with which it contemplates
not the things which can be seen but those which
are unseen. This is the countenance of Rachel who
is described [as having] a beautiful face and an attractive appearance.* It is the eye with which Mary   Gn 24:16
sees the better part, [the part] which she chose and
which will not be taken from her.* And although   Lk 10:42
this eye does not exist alone but is actually one of
two, it is in truth one, for since it is intent on one
thing alone, there is only one thing it loves and one
thing it cares about.

The bride also has another eye, but with this one
she does not now contemplate the beauty of the
bridegroom. Instead, she sinks deep into herself, unwillingly rather than willingly, and sees herself desti-
tute and miserable, open to a multitude of needs
and infirmities, not only from herself but from
others as if from herself. From these [arise] her pre-
occupation with the demands of everyday life, her
agitation of mind, anxiety of heart, and affliction of
spirit. This is why the mind is divided up among
dozens of different things and busy with a whole multitude of different matters, and this is why Martha is
worried and troubled over many things. Mary's
name was called only once because she had chosen

Ibid.

Lk 10:41

Gn 2:24

one thing once and for all, and that alone was necessary.* But since Martha was worried and troubled
with the concerns of the present and with providing
for the future, she was addressed twice as 'Martha,
Martha'.*[13] There are indeed many things which
must be considered, many things which must be
provided for, all sorts of needs for ourselves and our
fellows, and although it is impossible to fulfill every
demand laid upon us, we must at least attend to
those which, in all honesty, are right and proper.[14]
Thus, since this eye considers earthly things, how
can it avoid being sullied with the dust of earthly
thoughts? How can it be other than troubled?

It is not this eye, therefore, whose beauty wounds
the bridegroom, but that one eye which sees the
bridegroom alone and which abhors all other things
that it might be joined to him. For if a man leaves
his father and mother to be joined to his wife,* how
much more should the bride of Christ despise and
leave everything to be joined to her bridegroom?
But in what better way can she cleave to him than
by the eye? Where there is love, there too is the
eye.[15] It is the eye which usually guides us to love
and entices us into it, for it [is the eye which] can
see and be seen. It arouses love by its beauty and
declares it with secret signs. When I speak of its
beauty, [I mean] a faithful and true [beauty], not
one which is spurious and artificial. Someone who
colors her eyes with cosmetics feigns a beauty which
she does not have, and the eye of intention which is
colored[16] with a lie is colored in vain before the eyes
of God. He takes no pleasure in make-believe virtues, but truth he always loves, since he is himself
the Truth. The signs made with the eyes are also
sometimes false, as we read of certain people, 'They

have hated me without cause and make signs with
their eyes'.* But truly, God is not mocked!†

Ps 34:19[35:20]
†Ga 6:8

By means of these signs, the eye arouses love
when it turns towards the same person time and
time again, or when it stares fixedly, or when it can-
didly puts on a certain feigned expression.[17]

The bridegroom, however, loves the eye [of the
bride] when it is turned from him as well as when it
is continually turned towards him. Does it surprise
you that I said, 'when it is turned away from him'?
Listen to what he says to the bride: 'Turn away
your eyes from me, for they have made me flee
away.'* If one is in the rapture of contemplation[18]
and the unfathomable God is sought in an unfathomable way beyond the permitted bounds, then it
is good to turn away the eyes. Otherwise, it is he
who will hasten away and say, 'Turn away your
eyes'; it is he who will warn us with [the voice of]
Wisdom: 'Do not seek the things that are too high
for you, and do not search into things above your
ability.'*

Sg 6:4

Si 3:22

At other times, however, the bridegroom does
not love to see the eye [of the bride] turned away
from him; he loves instead to see it turned again
towards him. For it often happens that when someone is in distress and calls upon God, he lifts up his
eyes to God, but when he is freed from his troubles
and is relaxed and unconcerned, he looks elsewhere
and turns away his eyes from the Lord. But the
Lord immediately beats him with the rod of discipline,* and when he has been chastised, he looks
back [to God] and wants [God] to look upon him,
saying, 'Look upon me and have mercy on me'.* In
another psalm, therefore, [the following line] appears a number of times: 'And they cried to the Lord

Pr 22:15

Ps 24[25]:16

in their distress, and many times did he deliver them'.[19]

It is often the case, however, that the just are obviously not freed from the troubles which at present beset them. 'They were tortured', it says, 'and did not receive deliverance, so that they might find a better resurrection.'* They often despise worldly consolation so much that they do not want to be freed, although it is also true that since they are confident that God will provide something better for them, they often want it but do not hope for it. Or it may be that they were persecuted when they were faint-hearted and that after continual prayer they still fail to get what they prayed for. Then, little by little, their hope wavers and weakens as if he who could free them does not want to do so. This is why [the psalmist] says, 'My eyes are weakened because of wickedness',* and 'My eyes have failed while I hope in my God'.* Thus, when hope fails, the eye turns away; when hope is restored, the eye quickly returns.

All this, [however], should only be said of the hope of temporal consolation or liberation, which, for various reasons, makes headway one minute and falls back the next. But the hope of eternal salvation is not like this. Amid the greatest dangers and all sorts of temptations, it remains unmoved. Not to desire this salvation is forbidden; nor must we ever despair of it. This eye, therefore, is immovably fixed and never turns away [its gaze]. It remains for ever fastened on that from which it is never unfastened. This is why the Prophet [says], 'My eyes are ever on the Lord'.* Do not be concerned that it says 'eyes' in the plural here, whereas the heart of the bridegroom is wounded by one single eye. [The reference to]

Heb 11:35

Ps 87[88]:9
Ps 68:4[69:3]

Ps 24[25]:15

one eye is because there is one love wholly directed on one thing, but in one love there are many diverse affections, and these, by desiring and hoping in many different ways, direct it to that one end on which the eye is irrevocably fixed.

The eye adopts its feigned expression[20] when it is not opened fully but is closed, little by little,[21] with a covert and sort of furtive look, and conveys a secret understanding with no more than a hint.[22] Holy love can also give certain hints appropriate to it, but these are different from those of which it is written, 'The daughters of Sion are haughty and have walked with stretched-out necks, their eyes hinting [at improper things]'.* [The hints of holy love] are mysterious and aware of holy propriety, and with them the bride and bridegroom exchange meaning glances and intimations.[23] She wills or does not will [to respond] to his hints as he himself wills her to will or not to will. The bridegroom gives her a meaning glance when he suggests his will to her in a secret way; he gives her a sign when he grants her prayers and supplications. The bride gives him a meaning glance when she obeys God's commands imposed upon her. She gives him a sign when, by means of a secret intention, she sees in his secret good works—as if it were something just between the two of them—him by whom alone she longs to be seen. She gives him a sign when, in the humility of prayer, she gives him a secret and reverent hint of her desire.

Do not be surprised if we say that the eye 'feigns'* a certain expression in signifying this love which we are now discussing, when there is nothing feigned* in holy love. [The word] *fingere* does not always [refer to] imitating and falsifying, but sometimes to

Is 3:16

fingi

fictus

finxit
Lk 24:28
†*finxit*
*Ps 32:15[33:14]
†*finxit*
*Ps 93[94]:9
†*fingis*
*Ps 93[94]:20

constructing or forming or disguising, and it is in these ways—by constructing, that is, and forming and disguising—that we find and perceive that God 'feigns' things. Thus, it is written, 'Jesus appeared* to be going further,'* and 'He who has formed† the hearts of every one of them,'* and 'He who formed† the eye, does he not see?,'* and 'You who frame† labor in the commandment.'*24

OF ONE OF HER EYES AND ONE OF THE HAIRS OF HER NECK

'You have wounded my heart', he says, 'with one of your eyes and a single hair of your neck.' It is as if the bridegroom surveys the bride from all directions and sees that she pleases him on both sides, both in front and behind, and on both sides her unity is revealed: [at the front] by one of her eyes and [at the back] by a single hair of her head.

Listen now to how this single hair is arranged. From the top of the head, the hair falls in different directions: some of it falls to the front, some to the back of the head, and some to the ears and shoulders. And in the case of women who normally take care of their hair, they comb it, part it in the middle from the top of the head to the brow, and arrange it becomingly in two attractive waves. These they then draw back over the ears to the neck and shoulders and entwine them together there to form a single [plait of] hair. In this way, they make one hair from many hairs and bind it all up in a single knot.25 If this were not so, their hair would lie loose in disorder, unkempt and untidy, streaming here and streaming there and quite unbecoming. Such is the skill with which [women] who think on worldy things, who are concerned with pleasing those who look at them, groom and bedeck themselves.

So, too, the bride of Christ does not neglect to care for her hair. She wants to be pleasing in his eyes, and he does not find pleasure in just any sort of hair. On the contrary, it is written, 'God will break the heads of his enemies: the hairy crown of those that walk in their sins'.* And in Isaiah, 'The Lord will make bald the crown of the head of the daughters of Sion, and the Lord will strip them of their hair',* and a little further on, he threatens baldness in the place of curled hair.* And the Apostle [says], 'Not with braided hair'.*

But contrary to this, the holiness and sanctification of the Nazarites and the strength of Samson lies in their hair. Thus, the profound thoughts of holy resolutions and affections are divided into four parts from the highest point of the mind²⁶ (that is, from the knowledge of God) and are separated out by the comb of discernment.²⁷ The part which falls to the front pertains to things which are good and eternal; that which looks behind pertains to things which are bad and eternal; and the parts which are divided to the right and left pertain to things good and temporal and bad and temporal respectively. The bridegroom makes it clear that these hairs are pleasing to his eyes, for he says, 'Take away from my eyes the evil of your thoughts'.* And again it is written, 'The holy spirit of discipline will flee from the deceitful and will withdraw from thoughts that are without understanding'.* [But] he guarantees the safety of those whom he has chosen when he says, 'A hair of your head shall not perish'.* All the hairs of their head are numbered,* for the Most High takes care of them.*

In the case of the bride, however, all her hair is drawn back to her neck, and it is there that [we find] the yoke of obedience. It is bound together in a

Ps 67:22[68:21]

Is 3:17
Is 3:24
1 Tm 2:9

Is 1:16

Ws 1:5

Lk 21:18
Mt 10:30
Ws 5:16

single plait with the knot of fear, for we should always think to obey [God] in all things in the fear of God, as it is written, 'Whatever God has commanded, think on them always',* and 'Fear God and keep his commandments: this is the whole duty of mankind'.* The single plait at her neck, therefore, [represents] the unity and harmony of her thoughts under the yoke of obedience. It is gathered together into one by the fear of God and so bound together that it cannot be loosed. This is that holy fear which endures for ever and ever;* it is not that which charity casts out,* but that which preserves humility and strengthens charity. This fear gathers together whatever is scattered; it unites whatever is dispersed; it drives out whatever is evil; it nourishes whatever is good, and when it has nourished it, protects it. In a word, it makes the heart pure and clean and tries to guard it with every possible protection. The first form of protection [ensures] that nothing evil appears in one's actions. The second, that no evil word proceeds from one's mouth; the third, that nothing evil remains in the heart which would offend the eyes of the bridegroom. This is how the heart of the bridegroom is wounded, and this is how the bride is praised, for the woman that fears the Lord shall be praised.* Therefore, O Lord, grant that we may possess forever both the fear and love of your holy name.[28]
Amen.

Si 3:22

Qo 12:13

Ps 18:10[19:9]
1 Jn 4:18

Pr 31:30

1. Title as in PL 477–478. The tractate most probably dates from Baldwin's years at Ford.

2. The Latin simply reads *similitudinibus rerum* 'likenesses of things', but I would defend my explanatory rendering here on two grounds: firstly, Baldwin's own explanation of what he means; and secondly, I suspect that in using this phrase, Baldwin is echoing Augustine, *Confessiones* x.viii.14 (PL 32:785) where *similitudines rerum* refers to all the various mental representations or images stored in the great *thesaurus memoriae*, the treasury of memory.

3. These last two sentences are an explanatory rendering of a very tricky paragraph. A glance at the Latin text will show that a literal translation is of little use. As Thomas points out (38/17, n. 1), both Bernard (Div 10, 2; PL 183: 568A–C; SBO 6/1: 122) and William of St Thierry (Nat am xvii–xviii; PL 184:391B–C) have divisions of love which partly correspond to that of Baldwin (Bernard uses *amor socialis* and *amor generalis*; William has *amor socialis* and *amor naturalis; amor castus* occurs a number of times in Bernard), but there is no obvious relationship between their descriptions and that of our author.

4. *Conjugum* in Thomas (38/18) is simply a typographical error for *conjugium*.

5. *Amat igitur aquila desiderans super pullos suos.* This derives from one of the O.L. versions of Dt 32:11 (cf. Jerome, *Commentaria in Isaiam Prophetam* xviii [in Is 66:13–14]; PL 24:662A). The Vulgate has *volitans* for *desiderans*, and this is the reading which appears in PL 478D.

6. Thomas (38/18) reads *mutuos*; PL 478D has *mortuos*, which makes no sense at all.

7. Lit. '. . . more abundant than the bowels of maternal devotion'.

8. On the wide use of the term *sacramentum* in the twelfth century, see Tr. iii, n. 10

9. *Vulnerata caritate ego sum.* Thomas' suggestion that this quotation derives from a phrase (*caritate vulneratus*) in the cistercian liturgy of the Feast of St Bernard (see 38/23, n. 1) is incorrect. It is actually the O.L. version of Sg 2:5 and 5:8 (Vulg. *amore langueo*) and appears, for example, in Ambrose, *Expositio in Ps* 118, *sermo* 15.39; PL 15:1424A, and Bernard, Ep 42.11: PL 182:818B (SBO 7:109).

10. Virgil, *Aeneid*, iv, 1–2.

11. Thomas (38/24) reads *puritate*; PL 480A has *veritate*.

12. Baldwin is echoing Mt 6:22, and there is an explanation of what he means by an *oculus simplex* towards the end of Tr. vi.

13. These last two sentences are a fairly loose translation. See also Tr. x/ii, n. 3 for a similar exegesis of Lk 10:41.

14. This is a paraphrase of Baldwin's very concise Latin: *nec undecumque potest, sed unde licet, unde honestissime decet*.

15. *Ubi amor, ibi oculus.* It is possible, as Thomas suggests (40/144, n. 1), that Baldwin is here quoting Richard of St Victor, *Benjamin Minor* xiii (PL 196: 10A). On the other hand, the same expression is to be found elsewhere (e.g. in Adam of Perseigne, *Letter* ix; PL 211:596D [*Ep.* v in PL 211]; SCh 66:160; CF 21:135), and Thierry of Chartres tells us quite straightforwardly that it was a proverbial saying (see B. Hauréau, *Notices et extraits de quelques manuscrits latins de la Bibliothèque Nationale*

[Paris, 1890] 1:53). We cannot be sure, therefore, that Richard was Baldwin's source. See further, H. Walther, *Lateinische Sprichwörter und Sentenzen des Mittelalters* (Göttingen, 1967) 5:431, #32036.

16. Thomas (38/32) reads *coloratur*; PL 481B has *roboratur*.

17. *Aut sine fraude fingitur*. Baldwin explains what he means a little later on (see n. 22), and also offers some useful comments on the very real difficulty of translating *fingere* (see n. 24).

18. *Excessus contemplationis*. This is what *excessus* normally means in the spiritual writings of the twelfth century. It can, however, have a rather more general application. Cf. Tr. VI, n. 21.

19. This is a composite quotation: the first half is Ps 106: 6, 13, 19, 28, and the second half is Ps 105:43 (Vulgate).

20. Thomas (38/36) has *fingitur*; PL 482B has *figitur*.

21. PL 482C omits *paulatim*.

22. Baldwin seems to be describing some sort of slow wink; the sort of gesture, laden with illicit promise, which would be characteristic of a medieval Mae West.

23. *Quibus sponsa innuit et annuit sponso innuenti et annuenti*.

24. All the verbal forms cited here—*fingi, fictus, finxit, fingis*—derive from *fingere*, and *fingere* can mean to touch, handle, form, frame, feign, fashion, shape, mould, construct, alter, change, teach, train, invent, devise, dissemble, or disguise.

25. Thomas' text (38/40) reads *in uno modo* and is, for once, incorrect. We should read *in uno nodo* with PL 483A. In actual fact, after about 1120, it was usual for ladies of higher rank to wear their hair in two very long plaits, bound with ribbons, and reaching sometimes below the knees (see N. Bradfield, *Historical Costumes of England from the Eleventh to the Twentieth Century* [London, 1970[3]] 21; R. Corson, *Fashions in Hair* [London, 1965] 105–106). Many single women, however, preferred to wear their hair dressed in a plain knot or a single braid. Towards the end of the twelfth century, the long-hanging plaits began to go out of fashion, and the braids were often worn coiled around the head or in coils over the ears.

26. *Vertex mentis*. This is synonymous with *apex mentis, principale mentis*, etc., and designates the highest point of the soul. It always remains in contact with the divine world (the world of the Platonic Ideas) and is our immediate link with God. Hence Baldwin explains that the *vertex mentis* is *cognitio Dei*. For some further examples of its use in the twelfth century, see R. Javelet, 'Thomas Gallus et Richard de Saint-Victor, mystiques', in RTAM 29 (1962) 219–220.

27. *Discretio*. See further Tr. VI, nn. 9, 43, 45.

28. Thomas (38/45, n. 1) identifies this last sentence as part of the liturgy for the Feast of the Holy Name of Jesus.